# Education and Schooling

The French have a saying 'plus ça change, plus c'est la même chose'. The English colloquial equivalent 'same old same old' conveys a sense of the inevitable, a reminder that if we haven't learned the lessons of history we are doomed to repeat them. In over half a century, what have we learned about education, about schools as places for education, about learning and teaching and the relationship between them? What have we learned about policymaking and the policy process? Has the growing impact of globalisation informed or constrained radical change?

Written in an easily accessible style, and drawing on the author's personal experiences of working in education as teacher, researcher, government adviser and consultant with international agencies, each chapter of the book illuminates deeper-lying issues about the nature of schooling, learning, leadership, research and the impact of globalisation on the lives of schools, teachers, children and families. This first-hand account, spanning fifty years, addresses key questions through seven different lenses:

- policymaking: ideology, insiders, outsiders and dissenting voices;
- research and the myths of scientific rigour;
- international agencies and agents provocateurs;
- academics conferring and the power of place;
- new enlightenment and a university for children;
- being and becoming a teacher, and the end of idealism;
- going to school: plus ça change?

Each of the seven lenses offers a unique perspective of the education system, but all are drawn together to consider the greater implications for policy and practice in the UK and beyond. The book will be of value to teachers and school leaders, as well as to academics and students on education programmes.

**John MacBeath** is Professor Emeritus at the University of Cambridge, UK, Director of Leadership for Learning: the Cambridge Network and Project Director of the Centre for Commonwealth Education.

# Education and Schooling

## Myth, heresy and misconception

## John MacBeath

Routledge
Taylor & Francis Group

LONDON AND NEW YORK

First published 2014
by Routledge
2 Park Square, Milton Park, Abingdon, Oxon OX14 4RN

Simultaneously published in the USA and Canada
by Routledge
711 Third Avenue, New York, NY 10017

*Routledge is an imprint of the Taylor & Francis Group, an informa business*

© 2014 J. MacBeath

*British Library Cataloguing in Publication Data*
A catalogue record for this book is available from the British Library

*Library of Congress Cataloging in Publication Data*
MacBeath, John E. C.
  Education and schooling: myth, heresy and misconception/
John MacBeath.
  pages cm
  Includes bibliographical references.
  1. Educational accountability – England. 2. Education and state –
England. I. Title.
  LB2901.M225 2013
  379.1'58 – dc23
  2013015358

ISBN: 978-0-415-83914-3 (hbk)
ISBN: 978-0-415-83915-0 (pbk)
ISBN: 978-0-203-77460-1 (ebk)

Typeset in Galliard
by Florence Production Ltd, Stoodleigh, Devon, UK

Printed and bound in the United States of America by Edwards Brothers Malloy

For Sandra, Sharon and Andrea

# Contents

# Foreword

*Professor Maurice Galton*

My first meeting with John MacBeath was in the early 1980s in the dining room of Singapore's Novotel, opposite the old Institute of Education on the Burkit Timah road. Our brief encounter lasted less than five minutes and it was not until nearly a decade later that we crossed paths again, sharing a conference platform as keynote speakers at the headquarters of the National Union of Teachers (NUT). At the time his book on self-evaluation, *Schools Must Speak for Themselves*, the results of a study funded by the NUT, was the subject of considerable interest, while the Union had also supported my small-scale research on the benefits of reducing class sizes in primary schools.[1]

John's arrival at the Faculty of Education in Cambridge occurred shortly after my move from Leicester University's School of Education to Homerton College, leading to a series of four collaborative studies, again funded by the NUT, on the lives and work of teachers. These were subsequently published as a jointly authored volume with the title *Teachers under Pressure*.

Working with John has always been a pleasure, not withstanding his ability to confuse his fellow authors by sometimes adding revisions to the second draft of a chapter when everyone else is working on a third or fourth draft. All this is easily forgiven, for the quality of the prose he produces on trains, planes and in airline lounges – and perhaps even while watching his beloved Glasgow Rangers on TV – is truly remarkable. Above all he is a master of the quotable phrase, as illustrated by numerous chapter titles and paragraph headings throughout this book.

The experience of researching *Teachers under Pressure* helped to cement our friendship and whenever possible we try to arrange our visits abroad to coincide, so that we can not only work together but enjoy lively, and occasionally erudite, conversations stimulated by the occasional glass of red. He is, as the many references in this book demonstrate, an avid film buff, and the first question when we meet is likely to be, "What movies did you watch on the plane"?

Exploring the lives of teachers we saw much evidence of disillusion and weariness, coupled with a sense of worthlessness as governments of various hues introduced 'reform' after 'reform' consisting of ever increasing curriculum prescription and new forms of bureaucratic accountability. We were both puzzled by how it was that policymakers could happily sacrifice teachers' goodwill in pursuit of dogma and party advantage and at the same time expect the profession to enthusiastically implement their desired reforms. Part of our wonder arose from the initial actions of 'New Labour' under Tony Blair and the actions of his Secretary for State for Education, David Blunkett, who, in the face of a massive display of goodwill on the part of the teaching profession following the 1997 General Election, nevertheless chose to dissipate most of it by the naming and shaming of 'failing schools' (subsequently shown to be the wrong ones). This was compounded by the retention of a Chief Inspector as head of the Office for Standards in Education (OFSTED), whom one commentator[2] described as having been engaged during the previous government's time in office in a 'reign of terror'. Out of this experience came further collaboration, this time with John Bangs, a former assistant secretary at the NUT, where, for the price of a good lunch and generous consumption of wine, the policy 'movers and shakers' were persuaded to give us an insider's view of governments' educational initiatives and intended reforms. The conclusion of one interviewee, Mike Tomlinson, was that 'there is nothing rational about policymaking' – and he had only consumed sparkling water!

This book is, in many respects, John's personal testimony to the above conclusion. Interwoven with numerous anecdotes, characteristically often told against himself and ending in his own embarrassment (as with his first attempts to partake of a meal with a Japanese family, to fall foul of protocols in the United Arab Emirates, for his ideas to get lost in translation, or ignoring warnings that irony and humour do not always travel well), he charts during his time in academia the impact policymakers, international foundations, philanthropists, competing academics, researchers, and lone entrepreneurs have had on the development of schooling and the lives of teachers and their pupils.

Some of these accounts make depressing reading, as for example, his experience of belonging to the Labour Government's Task Force on Standards (1997–2001), which bore out the maxim that history is destined to repeat itself. John MacBeath's conclusion that academic advisors will only be listened to if the advice 'fell within the already conceived policy agenda' accords with my own experience as a member of the Interim Primary Committee, set up by Kenneth (now Lord) Baker at the beginnings of the National Curriculum, where we were summarily disbanded while our report was still at the drafting stage and told that since it was the property of the National Curriculum Council it would be entrusted to a council official to edit and complete.[3] Our error was to suggest that in striving for a 'broad and balanced' curriculum there was value in seeking to integrate parts of the English and mathematics programmes of study within topic work, when Mr Baker was a strong believer in a syllabus consisting of single subjects. In a similar manner Robin Alexander, as part of what was called the *Three Wise Men's Report*, found his drafts of sections advocating a balance between whole class teaching and other pedagogical strategies reworked to state unequivocally that the evidence pointed to the almost exclusive use of the former method.[4] More recently, as described in a chapter of this book, Professors Mary James and Andrew Pollard have found it necessary to resign from the committees that were set up by the present Secretary of State, Michael Gove, to recommend changes to the statutory primary and secondary curriculum, again because they found their advice based on research evidence either distorted or ignored.

John Bang's experience of dealing with the Department of Education over several decades leads him to conclude that there is no such thing as 'policy memory', so that in the words of the Spanish philosopher, Georges Santayana, 'those who cannot remember the past are condemned to repeat it'. Baker's insistence on subject-based programmes of study led, as the Interim Committee had predicted, to severe curriculum overload, which has been a dominant concern of the ongoing debate on primary schooling over four decades, leading to two reviews by Lord Dearing in the 1990s, Robin Alexander's extensive Primary Review[5] and Labour's attempt to pre-empt it by hurriedly appointing a rival committee under the chairmanship of 'its own expert', Jim Rose, described elsewhere as 'a safe pair of hands'. Now we have the present Government's deliberations chaired by Tim Oates, whose expertise appears to be in assessment rather than curriculum planning.

Against this dispiriting tale can be set considerable achievements, notably that of the '*Carpe Vitam* Project', which, starting in five sites in four countries, has eventually developed into a worldwide movement espousing the principles of Leadership for Learning (LfL), with its emphasis on consultation, partnership and distribution of power among all those with the capacity to effect students' learning, whether it be teachers parents, pupils, or ancillary staff. LfL has thus become a powerful antidote to the top–down 'instructional' forms of leadership where the School Principal's vision is the driving force for change and where power is delegated to specific individuals (the senior management team) rather than shared among the whole school community. Given the philosophical approach embedded in LfL, where terms such as *line manager* are anathema, it is predictable that both the school effectiveness and school improvement movements (what Robin Alexander once described as the 'Essex men and women' of educational research'[6]) should come under severe scrutiny in several parts of the book. This he attributes not only to the emphasis on performance outcomes in determining a school's success or failure, but in the reliance on quasi-statistical measures to determine the magnitude – or otherwise – of such outcomes.

John MacBeath advocates a more comprehensive and altogether more humanistic approach to schooling forged, in part, from his time as a student at a Glasgow High School – where he confesses to learning little academically but a great many life skills, such as dealing with authority in his frequent contretemps with the then Rector, who meted out frequent beatings in his effort to 'educate and civilise this MacBeath boy'. His account of his time at the High School resonated with my own early schooling at Saint Michael's in Inchicore, Dublin, under the supervision of the Christian Brothers. The only difference in my case was that there was 'no rule of six', and for failing to bring an addressed envelope for my report (my uncle, the only legible writer in the household, was away that week and I was too embarrassed to admit to this and so opted for forgetfulness as my excuse) I received two strokes for each day. By Friday, therefore it was five on each hand with two one-inch-thick strips of leather, joined together by metal rivets. These events remain as a vivid memory even after three decades and are a prime cause of the anger felt when politicians call for a return to 'traditional methods'.

John's advocacy of a more student-centred approach also emanates from his experience of the 'Schools in Exceptionally Challenging Circumstances' project, and from his earlier work on school evaluation and in letting schools speak for themselves rather than relying principally on the judgements of outside inspections. His work with the Quality Assurance Division of Hong Kong's Special Administrative Region Education Department is testimony to the fact that such internal evaluations, supported by critical friends, can be rigorous and can bring about substantial positive changes in schools. This approach leads to inevitable tensions when the author attempts to find common ground with the 'measurement men' of the school effectiveness movement, and confronts the baleful influence of the performativity agenda on high performing schools in the course of the Teaching and Learning Research Programme (TLRP) funded study, *Learning How to Learn* (LH2L). When, therefore, an education system such as that of Hong Kong's, despite its regular success in International League Tables, is nevertheless prepared to rethink its whole approach and incorporate many of the ideas advocated in the chapters of this book, then governments, such as our own, should surely sit up and take notice of these reforms.

The book is therefore not only a memoire of past glories and failures (happily more of the former than the latter) but a recipe for all our futures. It is written by a person of transparent honesty who always seems to be able to extract some nugget of wisdom even in the face of poverty and adversity, as when touring South African townships, visiting the relics of Auschwitz or eating the inedible in Uzbekistan. School principals and teachers will respond to his evident sympathy for and understanding of the dilemmas they face when seeking to remain true to their values while facing external pressures for greater account-ability and ever higher standards, irrespective of the environment in which they operate. However, most of all, I recommend this book to policymakers in the hope that even at this late stage they may be persuaded by its arguments that there is 'a better way'.

## Notes

1  Galton, M. and Hargreaves, L. (1996) 'Today I felt I was actually teaching: The effects of class size on pupil behaviour', *Education Review*, 10 (2) 26-33.
2  Brighouse, T. (1997) 'Leading and managing primary schools: The changing world of the Local Education Authority', in C. Cullingford [Ed.] *The Politics of Primary Education*, Buckingham, Open University.
3  See Galton, M. (1995) *Crisis in the Primary Classroom*, London, David Fulton.

4  Alexander, R. (1992) *Policy and Practice in Primary Education*, 2nd edition, London, Routledge.
5  Alexander, R. *et al.* (2009) *Children and Their World, Their Education: Final Report and Recommendations of the Cambridge Primary Review*, London & New York, Routledge.
6  The working class electorate in Essex were said to provide a core vote for the Conservative Governments under Margaret Thatcher. Essex men (and women) were the butt of many jokes to account for such behaviour at a time when the manufacturing industries on which their livelihoods depended were being demolished or sold off to foreign buyers for asset stripping. One such joke enquired about the difference between an Essex man and a supermarket trolley, the answer being that the trolley had a mind of its own. More saucy versions enquired how Essex girls protected themselves during sex, the answer being that they did so by performing the act in a bus shelter.

# Introduction
## Dancing on the demons

In Glasgow's Museum of Religion there is a small statue of the Goddess Shiva, below which are the words 'Dancing on the Demons of Ignorance'. These words had a powerful resonance with me because they might be said to capture the purpose of education. Yet, it has also been one of the cardinal sins of schooling through the ages to assume ignorance on the part of children and so to discount the wisdom, conception and misconception that small children bring with them into school and classroom. It is in the interface between who we 'are' and who our teachers would like us to be that dilemmas and paradoxes arise and heresies begin to stir. These are themes that run through this book and play out in each of the seven contexts and through each of the seven lenses through which education and schooling are viewed:

- The first lens: The vagaries and conceits of policy and policymaking.
- The second lens: Research, what it tells us and doesn't tell us.
- The third lens: International agencies and agents provocateurs.
- The fourth lens: The agencies who look after, and betray, our interests.
- The fifth lens: Conferences for conferring and brushing up on geography.
- The sixth lens: Being and becoming a teacher, or at least trying.
- The seventh lens: Going to school: for better or worse, but mainly worse.

My one and only visit to the Museum of Religion was to take an American guest on a tour of those places in one's home town which tend only to be visited on such hospitable occasions. The particular guest on that Saturday in June was Bruce Leslie, a close friend of forty years standing. I had often discussed with him writing a book about education, its singular empirical base being my own highly subjective, and inevitably biased, account of the educational world.

During four decades of friendship we had celebrated and lamented the vagaries of policy and practice. We had experienced a communal wintering of discontent as well as summers of hope, a resolute optimism in the prospect of a brighter educational future. Together we brought in the 1970s in the United States, full of risk and radical promise. We witnessed much that we valued falling apart in the 1980s, and welcomed the promise of education,

education and education in the late 1990s. And we despaired as the new millennium seemed only to take us backwards to a darker age.

In many ways, across those years the demons have grown more potent in their influence. For children and young people growing up in Britain in the third millennium it requires a resilience to navigate an increasingly hazardous social terrain. For parents, 'bringing up' children is less and less meaningful in an unequal competition with the power of the peer group, the persuasiveness of mass media and the insidious influence of the virtual world. For teachers, the classroom has become the arena in which those familial and social tensions play out. Only for the most favoured of school leaders, in the most propitious of social environments, is 'managing' a school a realistic proposition. Policy-makers find themselves increasingly constrained by global forces beyond their control and in face of international comparative tables that push them towards setting short term targets and quick fixes.

While schools today are infinitely more enlightened places than the ones I unhappily attended, the policies that encompass them still appear wilfully ignorant of the needs and aspirations of children and their teachers.

Someone once described the cannibalistic functions of education, devouring its own products, as a pupil being taught subjects at school only to return to classrooms to teach others those same subjects so that they might in turn go on to do the same with the next generation. That is the story of my own lifetime in education, captive since the age of five in schools, colleges and universities, condemned to relive the thesis, antithesis and synthesis of educational fashion; a function of policy and politics seemingly inured to the lessons of history.

This book is composed of twin themes. One is the different lenses through which we can see what education means to those who are touched by it, more or less lightly, for better or for worse. Like the multi-faceted eye of the fly, each lens contains a unique perspective on the education 'system' but, hopefully, all combine to produce a meaningful whole. The image is a particularly pertinent one as I failed my Zoology degree exam at Glasgow University due to an inability to identify the various elements and functions of the fly's eye. The power of the metaphor, however, remained long after almost everything I had 'learned' had been long forgotten.

The second theme, which is interlaced with the first, is the nature of coincidence. How events coincide to change the trajectory of one's life is the stuff of chaos theory, of Arthur Koestler's treatise on the *Roots of Coincidence*, of the film *Sliding Doors* in which Gwyneth Paltrow just makes it through the closing doors of the London underground, or (in the parallel narrative) fails to make it – the doors closing to leave her stranded on the platform facing a different unfolding of life history. Would my life have been very different had I not reluctantly agreed to open the door of my office on a busy day to James Priestley and Phil Maguire? If I had not on the spur of the moment phoned Tim Brighouse from Singapore and had the good luck to find him, unusually, at home? If I had not met David Hargreaves in a queue at Euston Station and travelled with him on the same train to Sheffield? Each event proved to significantly alter the course of my life – my pedagogy, my membership of Tony Blair's Government Task Force, my decision to go to Cambridge.

As a fourteen year old in Canada I eavesdropped as my father talked on the phone about leaving Toronto to take up a job at the Bible Training Institute in Glasgow, apparently, as I heard him say, a divine calling. It was a decision which, for a while, hung in the balance, and while God's will was fiercely opposed by myself, my future was irrevocably mapped out. The following five years, which I was to spend in a barely post-Dickensian high school for boys in Glasgow, set me firmly within a life in education, because I hoped to show that nothing could be ever be that bad and that I might, as a pupil (and one day a teacher perhaps) be able to change things.

Although my experience as a time traveller, a pupil in an alien world, was originally the first chapter in the chronology of things, the final published chronology is in reverse order – perhaps influenced by the Brad Pitt film *The Curious Case of Benjamin Button*, which starts with old age and runs progressively to childhood. My starting point is with government policy, perhaps the most significant of the sliding doors, casting its long shadow over the other six lenses.

The reader is, of course, entitled to start at any point and progress in any order, as each of the lenses is unique and tells its own story.

# Part I
# The first lens

# 1 Policymaking

## Ideology, insiders, outsiders and dissenting voices

The first of the seven lenses views educational practice through the vagaries and contradictions of policymaking, re-visiting from Conservative to Labour and Coalition governments the same intractable dilemma of schools and teachers simply not doing what they're told. Viewing things through a more jaundiced lens a critic might argue that it is, in fact, through teachers doing what they're told that genuine 'improvement' still remains such an elusive goal and why cheating by both pupils and their teachers has been progressively on the rise. Testimony to a Government Select Committee in 1998, and then again ten years later, raises the question as to whether anything has changed in the interim despite David Blunkett's claim that 'we had a crap teaching profession. We don't anymore'. This view through the first lens begins with a reflection on two decades of policy by the chair of the Government Select Committee, Barry Sheerman.

### If you can't measure it you can't manage it

Over the past twenty years we have seen Governments become increasingly concerned with identifying ways in which school standards can be raised. To achieve this we have seen a proliferation of measures from the introduction of a now daunting system of testing and assessment through to the strong reliance on the inspection of schools. Such mechanisms of accountability and school quality are found in many countries but it is England that stands out above most in terms of the intensity of its testing and assessment regime and the influence of its inspection services.

Who can now believe that the Department of Education was traditionally viewed as a marginal office? It is presently considered to be one of the most distinguished ministries for ambitious politicians. Power and responsibility once rested at a local authority level and testing, inspection and curriculum once resided in the hands of local education authorities. Perhaps it was a bright civil servant who had perused the 'One Minute Manager', asserting 'if you can't measure it you can't manage it', that changed all of this; published in 1984 it was perhaps the former Secretary of State Ken Baker who drew most influence from it.

The fundamental issue currently within education policy is to find the most accurate, valid and just way in which to measure schools' achievement. We have a schools system in which we test at 7, 11, 14, 16, 17 and 18. The Government is planning to introduce even more regular testing through single-level tests. Increasingly the tests and the associated school performance tables dominate the educational landscape. Accountability is necessary, but many of us fear that teaching to the test can prevent students from accessing a rich and varied curriculum and can distort effective teaching and learning.

So wrote Barry Sheerman MP, Chairman of the Children, Schools and Families Select Committee as a foreword to *Learning to Lead*[1], a research report describing schools that challenged the compliance culture and assumptions of students' ability and agency. Attending the conference and expanding on his written introduction he referred again to the nature of the educational terrain and the daunting obstacle course put in place by successive administrations.

Viewed through a long-distance lens the contours of the educational landscape have remained in many ways constant over the life of successive Coalition, Labour and Conservative governments. For teachers and children in the immediate foreground the experience is one of expectation and injunction, shifting on an almost daily basis beneath their feet.

While the architects of policy may attempt to bring rationale and coherence to the various agencies that preside over curriculum, assessment, inspection, teacher induction and professional development, their irrationality and incoherence is measured at the sharp end by the impact on the individual child and his or her teachers. Select Committees offer one of few opportunities for governments to address these issues and make the connections between policy prescription and professional practice. The Committee is a forum that allows genuine debate and continues to provide a rare opportunity for heretics outside the big policy tent to express their views. My direct experience of Select Committee hearings spanned a decade in which, despite the vagaries of government policies, it was clear that little – if anything – appeared to have changed over that period – plus ça change, plus c'est la même chose!

## Select words for a Select Committee

In 1998 a triad of university professors had given evidence to the Committee on the function and failings of OFSTED. For over an hour and a half panel members had engaged in open, lively, and often sympathetic, debate (Select Committee on Education and Employment, Minutes of Evidence, Examination of Witnesses, Questions 216 – 219, Wednesday 2 December, 1998). Peter Mortimore, at that time Director of the Institute of Education in London, had aired a particular grievance, claiming that a war had been declared on the Institute, 'attacked by an OFSTED team who were determined to pull our grades down':

*Peter Mortimore.* Having had one inspection and having top grades, then being subjected to the thought of a second inspection within two weeks of the first. We were told we were to have one, six months before we got the report for the first one. On the second one we did have untrained inspectors working with us feeling their way . . . with a number of dubious practices – and that is being fairly charitable about it. But there was certainly the sense of a war, that we were being attacked by an OFSTED team who were determined to pull our grades down. The stress and strain of that was quite horrific.

Frankly, in my judgment, OFSTED has lost the confidence of many in the system which it is supposed to serve. The conduct of school inspections varies too much and is too punitive. Reliability and validity (directly answering your question), are not there. It is the capacity of OFSTED to improve through inspection, actually to evaluate in a way that is objective and reliable, which is a problem. Schools serving disadvantaged areas are particularly subject to unfair judgment. . . . As well as that, if I can just add, Some of the pronouncements of the Chief Inspector on particular topics like class size, resources, research, failing teachers, as well as his attacks on individuals, has brought OFSTED into disrepute and taxpayers' money is being wasted.

The problem is that the strident tone and the mischievous implication that other people are not working for children in education is causing grave damage. Frankly, it is harming the improvement efforts of the nation and of the Government. I would fear that in this sort of situation, a head might feel pressured by that OFSTED information, that very partial information, to override their judgments which were built up over a much longer time.

*Professor MacBeath.* I was going to endorse that statement absolutely. From my experience of people who are excellent heads and who are running excellent schools, you would think they would have absolutely total confidence in their own judgment; nonetheless, at a time of OFSTED inspection they are under a tremendous amount of stress and doubt their own judgment because of the definitive way in which OFSTED produces its judgments rather than saying, 'This is a tentative judgment which we should look at. This is our view of a teacher. We want to know what is your own internal evidence, as a head, of the quality of that teacher and what is the teacher's own evaluation of the quality of that teacher?' Then you come to a judgment. But it is very worrying that head teachers actually feel their own judgment undermined because of the nature of the high stakes inspection.

*Professor Goldstein.* Too much of OFSTED up to now has been OFSTED evaluating itself, collecting its data and coming to conclusions on the basis of its own inspectors' judgments and doing the work itself. What is needed is some independent evaluation of its research and exposure of what OFSTED does and what its inspectors do in schools to independent judgment.

Professor MacBeath, how does this square with your own research on the quality of training inspectors? *Professor MacBeath.* Our research was really an evaluation of the training of OFSTED team members. The conclusion was that this had very much improved . . . The strongest criticism was that they were trained in classroom observation of teaching but they had no training whatsoever in how to evaluate learning. The strong message coming through was: 'We do not feel very confident to evaluate the quality of learning which we observe in schools.' This is a very serious problem because you can go in and you can look in a period of 15 minutes at what the teacher is doing and make some judgment, but ultimately if you want to know if you are raising standards and improving schools you have to look in a little more depth at the quality of learning. That was the team members' own evaluation of their training: that it had not given them expertise in that area.

A decade later (29 April 2009) the Select Committee returned to issues of inspection and self-evaluation. Barry Sheerman, in the chair, had a genuine and lasting interest in the collaborative model of internal and external evaluation and in alternative ways to measure school quality. He was keen to explore the impact of the performativity culture, the consequences of high stakes testing and comparative 'league tables'. The charge that it encouraged cheating (by teachers as well as pupils) was to be confirmed by numerous studies in both the US and the UK.

## Cheating, pizza parties and playing dirty

It is inevitable that the greater the pressure, the greater the competition, and the less intrinsically meaningful the purpose, the more it is likely to encourage conspiracy and collusion. A lengthy chapter could be devoted to the increasing incidence on both sides of the Atlantic of teachers' ploys to help their students, their schools or themselves look better in the face of what are sometimes intolerable and ill-conceived demands.

In the US the famous 'Texas miracle' under Governor George W. Bush was shown to be a deception of a high order. An analysis by Boston College's Walt Haney in 2000 showed a sharp decrease in test results despite heavy coaching for the test. An 800-page report in Atlanta in July 2011 documented the wide-scale alteration of student's test scores, coming to light when the state noticed an 'alarming number of erasure marks on students' answers. Teachers and principals were rubbing out students' answers and filling in the right ones', the report stated. At one school teachers held pizza parties to correct students' marks before handing them in. In Chicago, as Levitt and Dubner wrote in 2005, teachers' cheating on tests was now widespread, not because teachers were intrinsically untrustworthy, but because a high stakes environment destroys trust and collegiality.[2]

Similar stories with a similar underlying cause are told in England and Wales. Newspapers have carried stories of teachers changing pupils' work after tests and fabricating coursework in an attempt to drive up grades, with one pupil claiming that teachers entered the exam hall during a GCSE, prompting students to change their answers. Exam boards were accused of being complicit with two examiners being secretly filmed briefing teachers at paid-for seminars, during which they gave advice on exam questions and the exact wording pupils should use to obtain higher marks. Details of many stories can be found on the Internet[3].

In November 2012 the Office of Qualifications and Examinations (Ofqual) reported on unusual patterns of test scores indicating subversive ploys by teachers in England to allow marginal students to creep over the boundary between a C and a D. They concluded that there was 'so much weight on one grade in one subject as part of accountability and performance measures created perverse incentives for schools' (*Financial Times*, 2 November 2012). In an article in the *Illinois Times* the commentator, James Kroher, set these issues in a wider social and political context:

> How do we convince kids not to cheat when the most successful people in society cheat all the time? Today we learn how bankers pocket billions by rigging the interest rates they charge each other. Big Pharma fakes its drug trials. Admired athletes such as Lance Armstrong illegally use drugs to get to the top. And how many 'ordinary Joes' cheat on their taxes and their spouses? Before we dismiss an entire generation as morally flawed, maybe we should look at who taught them to play dirty in the first place.
> (*Illinois Times*, 13 September 2012)

## Living the legacy

An ungenerous observer might contend that 'playing dirty' is simply an inherent consequence of party political gamesmanship, an endemic feature of oppositional politics, of governments with a short tenure and inherent in the increasingly ideological tenor of government rhetoric.

Policy watchers have commented on a sea change in decision making that has occurred over the last two decades, manifested in the direct, and highly personal, intervention in curriculum, assessment and pedagogy by party politicians. The force of ideology is nowhere more powerfully expressed than in Secretary of State Michal Gove's personal crusade to shape the curriculum in the mould of his own childhood experience. What was obviously good enough for him in Aberdeen's Robert Gordon's College in the early 1980s was patently good enough for all children in 2013. Nor, in his view of the world, could it ever to be too soon to introduce children to the disciplines of Physics, Chemistry and Biology, as five year olds would soon be exposed to in this brave new surreal Govian universe. In 2012 Junior Minister Nick Gibb was to spend 45 minutes with incredulous Cambridge educators demonstrating for them how to do long division the proper way, as he had been taught at school.

The way for such a retro view of policy and practice had been paved by the previous Labour Government and by two conviction politicians par excellence, Tony Blair and David Blunkett.

## Gradgrind's Children?

The 'Dear John' letter, delivered in the early days of the 'New Labour' Government shines a powerful light on government ideology, and an irascible Secretary of State, whose conviction politics brooked no dissent. He was genuine in his outrage that three of his 'ambassadors' (Tim Brighouse, David Winkley and John MacBeath) should be present, let alone lend their names to a satirical drama production entitled 'Gradgrind's Children'.

Sanctuary Buildings
Great Smith Street,
SW1P 3BT
22nd May 1998

Dear John
**Gradgrind's Children**

I am writing on Friday afternoon having just seen a highly misleading flyer which bills your involvement with the above event on the 31st of May.

I assume the promotion is intended to be satirical. I'm afraid I don't find it amusing. If it is supposed to influence Government thinking, then it has not. It has simply made me angry – and I have to say disappointed that you should lend your name to such an event.

Yours Sincerely
David Blunkett

Such was Blunkett's conviction in the inherent rightness of New Labour policies that he was genuinely unable to grasp how there could be dissenting voices and particularly how someone he valued as highly as Tim Brighouse could lend himself to such blatant heresy. It might, with unintended irony, be described as Blunkett's 'blind spot' – that he simply did not understand the logic of dissent. With his singular view of the world, and without any substantive evidence to call on, he was able to tell a Government Select Committee in 2011, 'We had a crap teaching profession, we don't any more'.

He was a formidable presence in Great Smith Street, with junior civil servants in terror of the next salvo, or frontal assault from one his body of enforcers. Writing in *The Observer* in 1999, Nick Cohen describes one of that formidable group, Ryan, in colourful terms:

Ryan is both powerful and inconspicuous. Civil servants who cross him are fired or sent to the modern equivalent of an inner Mongolian basket weaving factory. David Blunkett's enforcer stands out among the 72 political appointees now in office 25 July 1999

('The Faceless Men Behind Mr Blunkett',
Nick Cohen, *The Observer*)

In one of the final meetings of the Government Task Force, Blunkett's almost apoplectic response to a group of teachers telling him 'how it is' out there, had to be restrained by Estelle Morris, who advised, 'David, just listen'. It was not a habit that came easily to him.

## Friends of Blair

The Task Force on Standards, the centrepiece of numerous advisory forums established by the Blair Government in 1997, is exemplary of a new venture in government sounding boards. As Brain Brivati was to write in the *Times Higher Educational Supplement* in March 1998:

> These Friends of Blair would replace the old framework of academic advisers to the former Conservative government. It would be the largest changeover of political networks for 20 years . . . If you think the role of academics as public intellectuals is a good thing and about the only meaningful contribution we can make, outside the classroom, to the renewal of our decimated public culture, then the forums exist to take part. Rich debates are developing and academics are leading many of the discussions. But, so far, Blair has had more of an impact on academics than they have had on the direction of his government.

These were to prove prescient words as it became increasingly evident to the elected 'friends' that their presence was more decorative than substantive. Blair and his small circle of real friends knew where they wanted to go and advice would be considered if it fell within the already preconceived policy agenda.

The Task Force on Standards was composed of ministers, advisers, head-teachers and teachers, local authority directors, academics and representatives of the business world. A fair number were known to me, among them the five Davids – David Bell, David Hargreaves, David Puttnam, David Winkley and David Blunkett himself. The group, 18 in total, could be divided in two ways. One division would be by those invited by Chris Woodhead and those chosen by Tim Brighouse. That I fell into the latter group is, as they say, a 'no brainer'. Woodhead had indeed exercised his right to put the black ball against my name, but had withdrawn it when Tim threatened to resign if I was not included.

The Task Force could also be divided by those whose voices counted and those whose views were politely, or sometimes impolitely, discounted. A league table, with myself and Heidi Mirza occupying the bottom rungs, would have featured in pole position: David (Lord) Puttnam, William Atkinson, David Hargreaves and, of course, Michael Barber, favourite son, seated conspiratorially to the right of David Blunkett, whose ear was constantly open to whispered asides.

My presence among this prestigious group came about as the result of a sliding door that had opened at an impulsive moment in Singapore when I decided to phone Tim Brighouse and found him, unusually, at home in Oxford. He had, months before, promised me a seat at that top policy table but my phone call had, apparently, renewed his resolve to confront Woodhead with his ultimatum. A few days later, phoning home from a Singapore disco at which my birthday and OBE were being celebrated, my wife gave me a number to phone at the Department – Sandy Adamson, who extended the formal invitation to join the Task Force.

Tim himself appreciated the nature of fading promise. The day after the election he had addressed a hundred head teachers, most of whom had been up until the early hours celebrating the Labour victory. Preceding the keynote that I was to deliver at nine o'clock, he informed them of plans to set up a task force in which he would be a key player. Whatever I said in the speech that followed was lost in the euphoric glow. As Tim later described it, in an interview for the book *Re-inventing Schools, Reforming Teaching*, Blunkett had said to him:

> 'I want you involved when the election is over'. I said in what way? So he said, 'what I'd really like you to do is give up your job and come and work for me' and he said 'we'll set up a Task Force and you will run it and we'll change everything.'

'Changing everything' would not have been uncharacteristic of Blunkett's millenarian view of the world and his own special powers. While Tim Brighouse was not prepared to give up his job as CEO in Birmingham, he did agree to chairing the Task Force. It was, however, to be some time before that appointment was to come to fruition, and not quite as anticipated, as 'changing everything' was set about from the outset by pragmatism and compromise. As Tim Brighouse himself tells it:

> They got swept up by a machine. I was real friends with these people and, well, it was like they had got on a boat in a fast moving stream and I stayed on the bank and, bit by bit, they got smaller and smaller in the distance and, you know, I kept waving from the bank.

Becoming swept up in the machine was to be a recurring theme. The compromise over the Task Force was hugely symbolic of how policy was to be shaped under what was then 'New' Labour. Tim recounts a series of telephone calls from David Blunkett:

> The Standards Task Force, I want you to chair it and I said, 'ok, that's fine', and then he rang me up two days after the election and said, 'I'm terribly sorry but you can't chair it, I have to chair it, you can advise on

it'. I said, 'ok'. Then he rang me up and he said, 'I don't want you to take this badly but we would like two vice-chairs and the other one needs to be Chris Woodhead', and I said, 'I think that's one request too far.'

In the event, Tim's generosity of spirit and commitment to the cause led him to accept the appointment, as joint chair with Her Majesty's Chief Inspector (HMCI). It was a marriage made in political expediency. Brighouse worked hard to consummate the relationship but could not bridge either the ideological distance or gulf in personal style. On the one hand, there was someone who was always open to another point of view, on the other, was someone for whom only one view counted – his own. In Judith Judd's words, 'Woodhead was a man who deals in certainties'. Comparing the two protagonists as representing the twin faces of government, she wrote: 'Teachers saw the former as their friend, the latter as their scourge. The two were meant to symbolise the twin policies of "pressure and support" which ministers have placed at the centre of their campaign to raise standards' (*Independent*, 18 March 1999).

## A ceremonial occasion

Sandy Adamson, at the time the senior civil servant in charge of administering the Task Force, presciently observed it as 'well meaning floating alongside, or abutting, a whole structure of policy making and delivering'. He asked rhetorically:

> These people you have invited, do you want them there because you genuinely want objective advice? But the points you [John MacBeath] and others, made fell largely on deaf ears because they had decided what they were going to do anyway. It quickly became a largely ceremonial occasion, reflected clearly in the attitudes of the participants, particularly those from the frontline.

It became quickly apparent from the outset that Blunkett and Barber were not looking for objective advice. They knew what they wanted to do, or perhaps more accurately what Blair and his kitchen cabinet wanted to do. Blunkett and Barber were the enforcers, although Barber, as the ideas man, became progressively more intimate with the Number 10 inner circle.

Several education secretaries suffered as a result of what insiders dubbed 'The Adonis Problem'. They felt that their role was not to make education policy but to promote the policies devised by Adonis and Blair. The most notable casualty was Estelle Morris, who, it was widely believed, resigned because she felt undermined by Adonis (*The Observer*, 27 October 2002). There were suspicions that Charles Clarke was told to keep quiet when he raised questions about the effectiveness of grammar schools. And Ruth Kelly found herself overruled when it came to some of the proposals in the 2005 White Paper (*Daily Mail*, 17 October 2005; *The Observer*, 23 October 2005).

'Changing everything', the Blunkett promise, was to prove illusory. Three days following the announcement that 'the status quo is no longer an option', a Department for Education and Employment (DfEE) press release announced that £54 million was to be spent on 'Tried and tested teaching methods such as phonics spelling and grammar'. In the same month performance tables were endorsed, and to the great chagrin of the Labour heartland, grammar schools were retained along with the Conservative legacy of HMCI Woodhead.

Writing in *The Guardian* in 1998 Clyde Chitty observed that New Labour was 'clearly basing its education policy on the principles of competition, choice and diversity', which had been the popular themes of all Conservative White Papers. Under the guise of 'modernising' the comprehensive principle, the government was 'effectively destroying it'.

## Put down to experience

One of my first interventions during the second meeting of the Task Force, and the first 'put down', was in response to the literacy hour being announced. This would be an hour at the beginning of the day when children were 'fresh', although, as I vainly pointed out, many children are not awake until ten, their brains still in dormant mode. The literacy hour would follow a prescribed formula, informed less by research than by bright ideas, as would become the nature of policymaking through the four years I was to spend in largely futile counsel.

I posed the question, rhetorically perhaps, that if, in visiting schools, I came across excellent thematic work with literacy and numeracy as integral to a broader more holistic approach to learning, would that not be acceptable? In posing my question I had in mind some of the outstanding primary schools I had visited, none more than Williamston Primary School in Livingston, Scotland. On my first visit to the school I entered not a school building, but an Amazon rainforest. As the front door swung open a large hirsute spider descended from the ceiling, and as I progressed up through a tunnel of trees and lush vegetation I was met by a host of other wildlife, finally emerging into a clearing with multicoloured butterflies, birds and birdsong. The whole of the school was a rainforest, created and managed by the pupils. I found them sitting under trees, in forest clearings and sometimes grouped around tables writing stories. They taught me something about ecology, about geography and about the technology that created the pulleys and weights that filled the 'sky' with birds and caused spiders to drop from the trees. They shared the poems they had written and the books they wrote that furnished the school library. Children could borrow books written by their peers and add their own book reviews. Returning to film the scene a month later the school was now a Victorian village.

Four hundred miles away from Williamston (geographically and symbolically) in Westminster, my intervention was met with an uncomfortable silence and a whispered aside from Barber to the man on his left. Blunkett replied that if it could be 'proved' that the school achieved higher standards by thematic methods such an approach might be sanctioned. My retort, 'why "higher" rather than equivalent?' did not receive a reply. Nor did I pursue this with a problematising of 'standards' or the nature of 'proof'. The business of the day moved swiftly on. MacBeath's card had been marked at this early juncture.

## An hour of literacy

The literacy hour was to be structured in four sequences, each of around 15 to 20 minutes, with a final 10 minutes reviewing learning that had taken place in relation to the objectives of the lesson. It took until 2006 for its limitations to be acknowledged and nearly a decade later I was vindicated. All too late. The *Renewed Framework for Teaching* (2006)[4] advocated much greater flexibility, 'with greater emphasis on how to teach these skills across other subjects and how to implement a range of approaches to structure learning within lessons'.

Having established my credentials as a troublesome priest from virtually day one, I was to cement that reputation by expressing disquiet over a succession of policy initiatives, few of which were to outlive the Labour Government. I did not greet with enthusiasm David Puttnam's proposal for Oscars for teachers. However, I was not alone. The idea was opposed as being divisive, too Hollywood and likely to be met with opposition from unions and teachers alike. Fast forward a few years and I would find myself presiding over one of the regional 'Plato' events held in Cambridge, shaking hands with the candidates and lauding Putnam's prescient vision. I had attended the very first and televised ceremony of the Platos and could not help but be moved by the celebration of teachers, all of whom, in the best of Academy traditions attributed their award to their colleagues, to children and to their parents.

With the benefit of an external eye, without portfolio or hidden agenda, Puttnam was able to perceive what others had failed to see and one of his first proposals was for grants to be given to schools to upgrade staffrooms. He was genuinely shocked by the staffrooms he visited and argued for a more dignified way to treat professional people, something that I was happy to sign up to. Of all those who offered their view David Puttnam was the most guileless, speaking from conviction not politics, exemplary in his honest and straightforward approach to any issue on the table.

If policy was meant to be openly discussed and advanced within this large assembly, it was eventually recognised that more sustained discussions could be engaged, and more accomplished, in smaller working groups. The most fruitful of these was charged to take forward perhaps the most promising of new Labour initiatives.

## Whatever happened to Beacon Schools?

Among the many bright ideas of the New Labour Government, Beacon Schools promised to change the face of education in England and Wales. It is a salutary tale of policies that rarely survive beyond the lifetime of a government, even without a change of political party. No matter how good an idea – and regardless of government money invested – it seems there are always better ideas just around the corner. Beacon schools lasted from 1998 before being absorbed by specialist schools in 2005 and finally being abandoned by the Coalition Government in 2010. The big idea was for outstanding schools, beacons of good practice, to be identified through a bidding process, selected by an expert panel, to share their expertise with less successful schools. This collegial process of school improvement rested on the sound principle that schools learn best from one another rather than from top–down intervention. An internal Task Force paper in 2000 referred to 'a pool of resource which could be tapped to try out some innovative ideas' and to exploit 'refreshing ideas locked up in individual schools'. This would provide returns to the system by unlocking the door to those secret gardens.

Under the heading *Approaches to Disseminating Good Practice*, twenty-four strategies were identified – for example, heads of beacon schools would work with heads of lower-performing schools. There would be shared visits and dialogue focused on the needs of non-Beacon schools, together with peer coaching; helping to develop business, parental and community links; and sharing knowledge across local education authorities. In light of what was to happen to Local Education Authorities (LEAs) both under Labour and its successor, it is significant that under the incoming Labour Government £1.1 billion had been given to LEAs to assist them in raising standards and playing an advisory role in the Beacon School strategy.

As a member of a small subgroup, chaired by David Hargreaves and including the occasional civil servant, I was to spend a number of long, and often frustrating, days sifting through hundreds of applications from schools, some running to thirty or more pages. The most important criterion we adopted to differentiate between the 'accept' and 'reject' piles was the priority they gave, and time invested, to work in support of other schools. Those that simply extolled their own virtues went directly into the growing 'reject' basket.

A succession of Beacon School conferences were held in various locations across the country. I was charged with helping to promote the programme, inspiring the selected heads with the vision of building capacity within and across their schools. Despite my own and others' initial concerns about elitism and a growing disenchantment with New Labour's evangelism, there was an embrace of the idea, with celebrations of successful and exemplary partnerships.

In many respects the transition to specialist schools and eventual abandonment of the programme were regressive steps, and inter-school networking has had to be re-invented in different guises over succeeding years. *How Schools Learn*, the paper I had presented to the Task Force, surprisingly well (or perhaps politely) received, had drawn on a large body of international evidence to demonstrate that collegial exchange with critical friendship support is the most powerful of strategies for building and sustaining capacity. As a final curtain was drawn over the financing, time and manpower for Beacon schools, the pool of expertise developed was quickly forgotten. Whatever had been learned, as is the way with adversarial politics, had been lost in the archives of yet another failed initiative.

A more cynical observer might conclude that good ideas were the province of ministers, not schools, and that, after all, top–down was best. They might even speculate that collegial exchange is too threatening and messy and that divide and conquer is a more apposite strategy for impatient governments. In their zeal for importing practice from other countries, the most useful lessons to be learned should be from jurisdictions where reciprocal networking and inter-school partnerships lie at the very heart of improvement strategies. In countries such as Singapore where collaboration is seen as crucial to systemic capacity building, there is always a balance to be struck between top–down and bottom–up, addressing the inherent tensions as an opportunity for system-wide learning.

In Singapore the *Teachers' Vision Statement: Singapore Teachers–Lead. Care. Inspire* was written by teachers for teachers, engaged in an envisioning exercise in which 2,000 teachers participated island-wide. Launched by Ms Ho Peng, Director General of Education, her speech celebrated 'the teaching fraternity' and the 'community of practitioners'. At the same time policymakers continued to keep a close watching eye on global competitiveness. Writing in 2012, Pak Tee points to some of the 'subterranean tensions' in marrying internal capacity with Singapore's place in international league tables.

The globalisation discourse essentially argues that the earth is now 'flat' and 'borderless', and that economies are now competing on a single international platform. The knowledge economy discourse argues that intellectual capital is the new competitive advantage and that 'talent' is the new strategic asset. Putting the concepts together, the globalised knowledge economy is one where global combatants, regardless of geographical locations, now manoeuvre strategically to outdo one another in an arena of 'hyper-competition' and with 'weapons' of knowledge rather than physical resources. In such a world, the continuous development of intellectual capital – human capital, infrastructural capital and relational capital – facilitated by deliberate government policies, becomes the strategy to gain the competitive edge. In particular, many economies attempt to develop themselves internally as learning societies and compete externally for talent to boost their capacities.

---

A footnote for the unwary Internet traveller, a Google search will take you to The Beacon City School District (also known as the Beacon City Schools), thirteen public school districts serving residents of Dutchess County, New York about 59 miles north of New York City, along the eastern bank of the Hudson River.

---

## Whatever to do with local authorities?

For the Conservative Government under Margaret Thatcher, local authorities were a cumbersome distraction from policies conceived and delivered straight from Number 10. Critics contended that the excesses of a few 'loony left' councils helped Mrs Thatcher to launch a party-political assault, as all the eliminated councils were controlled by the Labour party and/or favoured higher local government taxes and public spending, as well as being vocal centres of opposition to her Government. The weakening of local education authority influence would transpire by encouraging and rewarding schools that 'opted out' of local authority control to be funded directly by Government.

New Labour was to continue the Thatcher legacy. Open debate on the future of local authorities in the full Task Force forum was to generate more heat than light, with HMCI Woodhead leading the abolitionists and myself on the defence, and clearly the defensive, given what appeared to be yet another pre-determined agenda. The outcome (or perhaps palliative) was for a small sub-committee to be set up, chaired by David Hargreaves, with myself and HMCI Woodhead as combatants. David was not a neutral chair, at least in respect of his own position. As a radical reformer the status quo was never an option, and he obviously leaned towards abolition or root and branch reform.

The subgroup met, as far as I can recall, only once. As discussion or debate requires some level of agreement, the meeting took the form of simple assertion by Chris who, within the first fifteen minutes decided that there was no point in continuing as there could only be one point of view and one solution – his own. He stood up from his chair and declared he was leaving to do something more useful. At this point I did something for which David Hargreaves may still have not forgiven me. I challenged the departing HMCI to offer some evidence for his view. Woodhead resumed his seat and David Hargreaves gave me a despairing and reproachful look. The issue remained unresolved but Number 10 had already decided where it was going to go anyway.

The Woodhead exit was a portent of what was to come. His disillusion and detachment from Task Force proceedings had become more and more obvious. On the last full meeting his attempts at intervention were, at one point, cursorily dismissed by Estelle Morris in the chair with a simple admonition, 'Chris shut up'. In his own hagiography, Woodhead recounts a meeting of 'Mr Blunkett's Standards Task Force' at which 'a member said the term teachers should be replaced by "learning professionals". When none of those present – including the School Standards Minister, Estelle Morris, and Michael Barber, Mr Blunkett's senior adviser – seemed to agree, the time had come, I realised, to go. I concluded that he wanted me to go – and the sooner the better. He could then appoint someone who might cause less trouble' (*The Guardian*, 1 March 2001).

While the alleged incident was something I cannot recall, and it is an account to be treated with some scepticism, my reference to 'reflective practitioners' had been met with deep scorn and was parodied by Woodhead, asking whether the mechanic who fixed my car should ponder deeply on the issues or just follow the manual. I realised we would never be able to disagree sensibly enough. Sir Chris would exact his retribution on Estelle Morris later in dismissive reference to her intellect, and my comeuppance was to be nominated as one of the three men at the heart of the darkness in British education along with Ted Wragg and Robin Alexander. It was on a BA flight to London, on which the *Daily Mail* was being handed out, that I was met with my photograph and confronted with my new-found status as the arch enemy of standards. In subsequent phone calls with the two other members of the triad, Robin debated possible libel action while Ted treated at all as a joke. I took it as something of a compliment. For a year or more afterwards I was to be introduced at conferences as one of the men at the heart of the darkness, gaining me instant popularity.

## On reflection

It is impossible to forget the euphoria that greeted the election of the Labour Government in 1997 and the promise that schools and teaching would now be released from curricular prescription, from the iron grip of testing, and from policing by OFSTED and its deeply unpopular Chief Inspector. No incoming government, especially one on the Left, could afford to be seen as soft on standards or on teachers. It became clear virtually from day one of the newly established Task Force that there would be insiders and outsiders and that dissenting voices would fall on resolutely deaf ears. Although the year 1997 was not the birth of a deeply ideological approach to education, it was a significant milestone, preparing the ground for Govian dogma and deepening disillusion of genuine educators. Who can now believe that the Department of Education was traditionally viewed as a marginal office?

## Notes

1  Frost, D. and MacBeath, J. (2010) *Learning to Lead: The Story So Far*, Faculty of Education, Cambridge.
2  Haney, W. (2000) The myth of the Texas Miracle in Education, Education policy Analysis archives [on line- serial 8(41) http://epaa.asu.edu/epaa/v8n41/. Leavitt, S.D. and Dubner, S.J. (2005) *Freakonomics*, London, Allen Lane.
3  The following websites provide related stories: www.telegraph.co.uk/education/secondaryeducation/9259984/Headteacher-banned-from-handling-exams-after-re-writing-pupils-A-level-papers.html
www.google.fr/search?client=safari&rls=en&q=The+secret+filming+that+exposed+exam+boards,+07+Dec+2011&ie=UTF-8&oe=UTF-8&redir_esc=&ei=i_KEUbWx M4fBhAe1-4C4Cw
www.google.fr/search?client=safari&rls=en&q=Headteacher+in+exam+cheat,+11 +May+2012&ie=UTF-8&oe=UTF-8&redir_esc=&ei=g_GEUZyZFIGjhgfzt4 HgBQ
www.telegraph.co.uk/education/secondaryeducation/8944190/Exam-boards-Telegraph-investigation-reveals-exam-board-boasting-about-ease-of-syllabus.html
www.telegraph.co.uk/education/educationnews/9229882/Ofqual-exam-seminars-to-be-axed-after-Telegraph-probe.html
www.telegraph.co.uk/education/secondaryeducation/8943300/Exam-boards-examiners-suspended-in-corrupt-practices-row.html
4  Department for Education and Skills (2006) *Renewed Framework for Teaching*, London, DfES.

# 2 Policy perspectives and priorities
## Hearing voices

Scotland, due in part to its size, in part due to the central authority of the Scottish Office and the much vaunted 'vertical partnership' with local authorities and schools, has been able to change practice at a stroke of the policymaker's pen. The creation of school boards, an appraisal system and the associated training programmes exemplify how top–down mandate plays out system-wide. Whose voices count in policy and in school improvement? What has been the impact on policy and practice of honouring teacher voice, and children's perspectives on teaching and learning? The creation of self-evaluation, with the voices of children and young people centre stage, was to have a profound impact not only in Scotland, but also travelling to England, Germany and Hong Kong. The story begins in a motorway service station.

### The third toilet on the left

Policymaking can take strange forms and occur in unlikely places. The story of the venue for our meeting with Her Majesty's Senior Chief Inspector, Walter Beveridge, in 1989 has been much embroidered in the retelling. The apocryphal tale locates the rendezvous as the third toilet on the left at the Harthill Service Station, halfway between Edinburgh and Glasgow. Although, in fact, the meeting took place in that motorway café, it did have something of a cloak and dagger air about it. A bargain was to be struck to provide a training programme for School Board members over the following two years, a highly ambitious project given the number of schools involved across Scotland, the catholic composition of boards and the ambivalent response to their laboured conception.

The creation of school boards in Scotland (the School Boards Act 1988) was designed a) to avoid the perceived perils of governing bodies as current in England; b) to be careful not to undermine local education authorities to whom boards would be accountable; and c) to function more as a bridge to the community. Boards, an advisory body, would be voluntary and composed of parent and teacher representatives, pupils (in secondary schools) plus local community businesses and, typically, 'the Church'. Board members were to hold office for four years, with half the parent places coming up for election every two years.

On 19 August 1994 'Quintilian' of the *Times Educational Supplement* (TES) commented, tongue firmly in cheek, on the success of this Government initiative.

> As school board members drag themselves back from the long hot summer, shake the sand from their brains and compare suntans, they find themselves invited to consider *Making School Boards Better*. Surely by definition that is an impossibility! However, this is not one of those slightly ridiculous requests from the Government, like the exhortation in the Parent Charter for parents to ensure that their offspring behave well in school. *Making School Boards Better* is the sequel to the much-praised *Making School Boards Work*,[1] and is another production by John MacBeath and the Quality in Education (QIE) Centre at Strathlcyde University. As the introduction explains, the earlier book proved such a blockbuster that the QIE was invited to set up a series of seminars to enable school board members to discuss with each other exactly how school boards work.

The series of seminars that Quintilian alluded to was a revisiting of the workshops held for school board members half a decade before. The clandestine circumstances in which we had been entrusted with the training of board members was a unique insight into the ways big policy decisions were made, at least in those headier days. Design of the training programme was entrusted to a triad of College of Education lecturers (Bill Thomson, Jim O'Brien and myself) with the mandatory accompaniment of a representative from private enterprise, in this case, one Conrad Brunstrom. A most amiable colleague, his signal contribution at salary of £1000 a day, at that time treble what we were earning, was to suggest that overhead transparencies be numbered backwards so that the audience would know we were coming to the end of the presentation.

The embrace of private enterprise as bringing an expertise lacking in the education establishment was a Thatcherite legacy, lucrative contracts being given to Price Waterhouse, McCann Erikson, Accenture and other private providers. Scottish decision makers were, for a short period, seduced by the myth of private enterprise, until it became obvious, through School Board and other consultancies, that the academics were spending a great deal of their time advising and training their colleagues from industry. In the fullness of time Conrad was politely shown the door.

The output of training materials was prodigious and extravagant, a literal trunk load of materials unveiled to our training triad by an excited Walter Beveridge in the bar of the Macdonald Hotel outside Glasgow.

## Papal purple

The plethora of materials for School Board Training came in a range of delicate pastel shades, exhausting the entire repertoire of available colours. Immense care was taken to avoid green or blue as these were not simply colours but religious symbols with deep divisive significance in the West of Scotland, where allegiance is either to Celtic Football Club, wearing of the Irish green, or to their Rangers FC counterparts, 'true blues', flying the Union Jack over Ibrox Stadium. Jim O'Brien recounts a dinner conversation with the manager of the printing firm responsible for steering this delicate and contentious line in the choice of hues. As the story goes, the company director turned an ashen shade when Jim informed him that the studiedly neutral colour chosen for the glossy ring binders was officially described as 'papal purple'. He promised never to disclose this alarming fact. Until now.

The trunk load of materials unveiled by Walter contained twelve modules and fifteen units bearing titles such as 'Managing Meetings', 'Communicating with Parents', 'Understanding Curriculum' and 'Children with Special Educational Needs'. The modules came in the form of large ring binders while the units comprised a pack of tear-off worksheets, designed to engage board members in interactive tasks prior to the serious, and often tedious, business of the evening. Each board would nominate a training officer who would attend these three-day workshops, equipped with the wherewithal and expertise to conduct a short training event prior to the evening's school board business. Appointed as a training officer for the board of the primary school attended by our two daughters, I was pleasantly surprised by the enthusiastic engagement of the local minister, bank manager, parent, teachers and headteacher with the interactive approach to the issues. The most popular of the modules proved to be 'Interviewing Skills', as one of the few areas of responsibility for board members was to take part in the appointment of senior staff.

## Extra potatoes

It was the best of times. The venues for the training events were chosen with loving care, although the well-researched boutique hotel, Murrayshall Hotel in Perth, would prove to be a disappointment to hungry headteachers, lamenting the absence of the traditional Scottish breakfast as they picked their way through dainty portions of nouvelle cuisine. They were, sadly, unimpressed by the head chef's forays into the herb garden in the early hours to select the freshest of ingredients, decorating the single poached egg with a flourish of tarragon.

Craigendarroch in the highlands, close to Balmoral and the favourite watering hole of Princess Diana, served more substantial fare, but one had to wait patiently for the orchestrated removal of the silver domes by reverential dinner-suited waiters. A worried phone call from the Scottish Office advised us to go a little easier on the wine and to resubmit the previous wine bill in the guise of extra potatoes. On day four of the two-week training event we waved goodbye to our Scottish Office minder, John Smith, who reluctantly took the bus to Aberdeen, from there to catch the train back to his dreary office in Edinburgh. As we sat down to the evening repast and the statutory removal of the silver domes, John appeared sheepishly at the door. He had only got as far as Aberdeen before the magnetic pull of extra potatoes drew him back.

Among the large body of trainers, from Scottish universities and colleges of education, evaluations were closely scrutinised to see which tutorial pairs had gained straight fours, the ultimate accolade. A scurrilous anecdote from fellow trainer, Jim O'Brien, describes the propensity of one of our colleagues to carry an eraser so as to moderate participants' evaluations, such was the self-imposed high-stakes nature of the exercise. Around once a week my plane landing in Glasgow takes me over the Normandy Hotel and I recall a distraught Gaye Mainwaring in need of consolation after our double act had failed not only to receive straight fours but, from some ungrateful attendee, a '1', producing a deleterious effect on our mean rating. Perhaps, I suggested, the ungrateful attendee hadn't understood the four-point scale and really did intend a four.

In policy-land all good things come to an end and school boards were abolished by the Scottish School Act 2006, which saw them replaced by a two-tier system of Parent Forums and Parent Councils. Having established a framework, protocols, venues and a hugely successful modus operandi, when the need for training in Staff Development and Appraisal came along we were already off the starting blocks. While school boards had not been universally embraced with enthusiasm, the introduction of appraisal was an even greater anathema. For many, appraisal smacked too much of big brother 'snooper-vision', attended by sanctions and a performativity agenda. As it required some fancy footwork to sell appraisal to teachers and, particularly, to their union gatekeepers, a revised nomenclature was a first step – Staff Development and Review – followed by a teacher-friendly 'training' programme, which fell heir to tried-and-tested hotel fare and a cadre of battle-hardened 'trainers'. It was the second best of times.

## A f****** daffodil

My first meeting with the redoubtable Senior Chief Inspector, Walter Beveridge, had been particularly memorable. He greeted me with these words, 'So you are the daffodil man!'. It was a reference to an incident recounted in our study *Home from School*, in which a teacher had written in the politest terms to a parent to suggest that she do something about her son's B.O., which was causing his classmates to give him a wide berth. The mother had sent her reply on a used City Bakeries bag containing these immortal words, 'I send him to school to be teached, no to smell like a fuckin daffodil'. It was a story Walter had dined out on and often included to liven up some of his inspectorial speeches.

## Ethos indicators

As the story goes, Michael Forsyth, Scottish Minister and Thatcherite, darling of the Right, had excitedly phoned from the House of Commons asking Mr McGlynn HMI to get in touch with the author of *Home from School*. On a day which, unusually, found me at my desk, I was asked to take a call from one Archie McGlynn, at that time Director of Research at Scottish Office. He wished to meet me forthwith, if not sooner, to discuss a publication that would pull out the key policy implications from our study of parental relations with school. It was a pertinent moment as parental voice and choice were high on the Thatcher Government agenda.

Archie brought with him his senior researcher and policy adviser Judith Duncan, her only contribution to the conversation being to remonstrate with her boss over the sum offered me to write a policy paper, to be entitled *Home from School: Its current relevance*. Archie's response to the effect that he could do what he damned well liked was to be my introduction to the maverick McGlynn who would prove to be an exemplary rule breaker, a generous funder and close ally.

It was, for HMI McGlynn, a short step from honouring the 'voice' of parents and pupils, to conceiving of a quality assurance system that would be built around the expectations and satisfaction of these key 'consumers', or better still, key 'actors'. To test the hypothesis I was charged with identifying five schools, primary, secondary and special, in which we would meet with groups of children, teachers, parents and school senior managers and record what for them would be key 'indicators' of school quality and effectiveness.

The results were surprising and profound. A group of the most revered academics or seasoned inspectors could not have come up with a more telling, more incisive list of discriminators. While these four distinct 'stakeholder' groups looked for different things from their positions as insiders and outsiders, full and part-time players, there was a common core of items that defined what a good school would look like and how it could be measured.

Archie was delighted with the outcome, which had surpassed even his expectations. But policy could not be built on findings from five selected schools. I was charged with finding ten schools and repeating the exercise. The outcomes were the same. But policy could not be built on findings from ten selected schools and I was then charged with carrying out the study with twenty-three schools. There was no further validation needed. In 1992 the policy document *Using Ethos Indicators in Secondary School Self Evaluation; Taking account of the views of pupils, parents* (followed by the primary and special school versions) was launched with a foreword by HM Chief Inspector A.S. McGlynn:

> At a time when the development of home–school relationships is receiving increased emphasis and attention, it is important that the perceptions of pupils, teachers and parents are taken account of in school inspection and self-evaluation. The purpose of this document is to encourage schools to engage in this process themselves, and to offer a set of guidelines on how to set about it. The experiences of 23 pilot schools are documented in order to offer a range of approaches and suggest some practical ideas.

The suggestion was that schools embark on the process for themselves rather than lifting a set of ready-made indicators off the shelf. To encourage such an enterprise, I suggested we make a series of videos demonstrating how the process worked, how schools could go about it and what the potential rewards could be to school life, to teachers and to pupils' satisfaction. At the launch of the first of a series of VHS modules we chose an extract in which an eleven-year-old boy was leading a discussion with his peers on what makes a good school, and interrogating by what criteria his peers would judge its success and shortfalls. There were two responses from the assembled audience – one, that this was an exceptional youth bound for stardom and, two, that such things are only feasible in a privileged school such as this. We had, in fact, chosen one of the most disadvantaged schools in Scotland in anticipation of such an objection.

The most powerful and lasting contribution of the ethos indicators initiative was in exemplifying the power of student voice, the 'treasure within', too ritually silenced but when given scope for expression often startling in the level of children's insights. Although very often paid lip service to, 'voice' has been recast in more potent forms, from decoration to authentic decision making and leadership. Six-year-old children's depictions of leadership in their schools were surprisingly insightful.

When referencing student voice it is common for academic articles to refer to Jean Rudduck, 90 per cent of the time her name misspelt. 'Voice', as playing an integral role in school self-evaluation and national policy is of a different order and gives it a more robust and valued place. As developments of indicators in Scotland, and later in England and Wales, showed, what young people have to say about their learning experience, and what they expect of their teachers, lies at the very epicentre of self-evaluation. Gaining access to inner thoughts and true feelings is fraught with difficulty in the pressing priorities of school routine, and is very typically submerged into the underlife of the classroom. Creating opportunities for voice to be heard gives us new insights into what it means to be a pupil, what it means to keep alive the natural inborn drive to learn, to be alert to how learning travels between home and school, self and peer group, and what schools do to both constrain or enhance that inner drive.

In Scotland, ethos indicators were eventually subsumed under the policy *How Good is Our School?*, which remains as the framework for school self-evaluation in Scotland and elsewhere in the world, in Germany translated as *Wie gut ist unsere Schule?*

## We want one too

The example of a bottom-up approach to the development of indictors caught the imagination of the NUT in England and Wales, and specifically John Bangs, Head of Equal Opportunities at the NUT. We were invited to replicate the development process in a dozen schools in England and Wales.

A typical day would be spent initially with the headteacher, followed by a sequence of focus-group brainstorming sessions, with pupils of different age levels, with teachers, parents and support staff. The indicators from each group would then be reduced to a viable number without losing the originality and even idiosyncrasy of expression, progressively combined with those emanating from other groups, so as to provide a set of no more than twenty key items. These were congenial and often inspiring occasions. Children valued being listened to and teachers enjoyed having their views honoured. Parents brought another dimension to the indicator suite, viewing schools and classrooms from an external perspective but making the vital connections with home and community, which can often be missed by teachers. The most memorable of these consultations with schools took place in Merthyr Tydfill in Wales, where our meeting with parents was lubricated by generous helpings of wine, only to be outdone an hour and half later by the governing body who insisted on even more copious libations. So inspired were the proceedings and the eventual outcomes that my colleague, Jim Rand, and I were invited to join parents and governors in a local pub that, in the event, did not close its doors until well after midnight, by which time discussions on indicators had become ever more frank and erudite. The following day, to be devoted to researching the voices of teachers and students, passed in something of a haze.

The NUT publication *Schools Speak for Themselves* was to become NUT policy and, perhaps surprisingly to some, to be warmly endorsed by union members, the antidote to government-inspired performance indicators. Being asked to give a presentation to the 2000 or 3000 assembled union members at their annual conference in Brighton was a daunting prospect, given the militant tendency among their number. Nor did I greet with anticipation the announcement that John MacBeath would be available to sign books in the foyer. At the break I crept down to the foyer, sliding behind columns like a cartoon cat so as to spy out the land and not to be seen in embarrassed isolation. To my relief a queue had formed and I engaged in my very first (last and only) book signing.

## A derisional discourse

The notion of pupil voice and self-evaluation was to be much less warmly received by the Conservative Government Minister Eric Forth. I had not been prepared for the derision that awaited me at the Tory Party conference, lulled into a false sense of credibility by Minister-in-waiting Estelle Morris at the Labour Party conference the previous week. She had warmly endorsed the self-evaluation approach and promised that the next Labour government would give serious attention to these ideas. A rude shock awaited a week later.

I had barely finished my talk to the assembled Tory heartland than Junior Minister Eric Forth rose to his feet, ceremoniously tore up his prepared speech, apologised to his minder, and turned to address the clearly unhinged professor who apparently believed that children had anything useful to contribute in evaluating teaching, learning or schools in general. Nor, for that matter did teachers, who simply taught subjects, and obviously had little to offer by way of evaluation of their schools, this being the province of inspectors and wise policymakers. Following his outpouring of scorn on the deluded 'professor', he invited questions from the floor. I could not have anticipated the spleen that was to follow from the Tory faithful. I understood what it must have felt like to be tied to the stocks in the town square and assailed with rotten fruit. Among the many accusations of heresy was the charge from one outraged delegate, 'It's people like you who have done damage to our system, talking down our teachers.' I replied, 'Sir, you have eye contact with me but I assume your remarks are addressed to the Minister.' It was a sharp reminder of attribution theory. Eric Forth good guy, MacBeath bad guy. Negative utterances, then must come from the latter! Doug Macavoy, NUT President, rose splendidly to the occasion, wondering why this Junior Minister should be so unaware of his own Government's employment of this heretic as a consultant.

## Voices travel

Switzerland might not seem to be the most likely venue for replicating the process but, as we were to find in England, and later in Italy, Slovenia and Poland, it only takes one committed enthusiast to begin to change a system. In the Canton of Ticino, Emmanuele Berger, was able to convince the powers that be that this Italian-speaking Canton could offer an exemplary model for the Swiss federation of schools speaking for themselves.

There are few places more beautiful than Locarno on the northern tip of Lago Maggiore and few hotels more elegant than the Hotel Reber, sitting on the lakeside and commanding a panorama from the balcony of what was to be my bedroom for three successive Septembers. Brought together by Emmanuele, a quartet of formidable Swiss enthusiasts worked together to shape school self-evaluation, developing indicators from the perspectives and priorities of students, teachers and parents. The presence of Norberto Bottani in these workshops, a key player in the Organisation for Economic Co-operation and Development (OECD)'s development of indicators, helped to endorse and add gravitas to the process, Norberto himself being Swiss, from the neighbouring city of Lugano.

For three years the exemplary approach to school evaluation, resting on stakeholders' voices, enjoyed ground-breaking success. As virtually everywhere else, however, the relentless march of standardization and the accountability machine overtook the messy bottom–up approach to evaluation and my late autumn visits to the wonderful Hotel Reber were no more. Perhaps it was symbolic and a sign of the times that the hotel would close and its site converted to the much more lucrative use of luxury flats.

## Bien-être et mal-être a l'ecole

Pupil voice and bien-être (or wellbeing), I was told by a French Chief Inspector, was not something that figured large, if at all, in French schools. But it had not escaped researchers' attention, and in November 2012 a very long and very French day (nine until six thirty) was given over to around twenty successive treatises on the subject from 'scientific experts', as the French like to call their academics. 'Workshops' or 'ateliers' are a dangerously misleading descriptor for extended monologues.

The International Conference on Educational Evaluation and Monitoring (ICEME) is a curious alliance of French and Chinese policymakers, educators and inspectorate who meet bi-annually to exchange ideas on school monitoring and evaluation. It was an occasion to renew acquaintance with Alain Michel, one time adviser to Prime Minister Lionel Jospin, maverick and raconteur extraodinaire. His immersion in the English language, he explained over lunch, was owed to his early reading matter, Shakespeare and nineteenth-century novels, giving him his arcane linguistic turn of phrase, a source of some merriment to his English listeners – 'Forbear with me for thrice I have tried in vain to explain'.

The lavish dinner and unlimited wine on one of the grander bateaux-mouches on the Seine was brought to an undignified end as the *Princesse Palace* collided with one of the pillars on the Pont Neuf. It brought to premature conclusion the discussion of European quality assurance systems between Graham Donaldson (former Chief Inspector in Scotland) and his Belgian counterparts. Graham was sceptical when I pointed out that life jackets were being hastily assembled at the rear of the vessel, but half an hour later eighty or so Chinese and European diners, attired in orange life jackets were being helped by the police and sapeurs-pompiers onto police barges.

## The perils of gin at lunchtime

A footnote to my close encounters with policymakers in Scotland took place on a not-so-quiet afternoon on our small private estate outside Glasgow, imminently to be divided in two by the M77 motorway. A report in the Herald on 8 January 1995 described the occasion:

> A defiant Alan Stewart said he was determined to fight on as the constituency MP for Eastwood. He had resigned his Ministerial post 'after a weekend fracas with anti-motorway protestors' during which 'he picked up a pickaxe'. He said he had simply been exercising his right to walk legally and peacefully in his constituency. He firmly denied any allegations that he had been drinking heavily at a family party before the incident took place. He is quoted as saying 'It was a normal family Sunday lunch – a gin and tonic and a glass of wine'.

## On reflection

It was the best of times. There was excitement in the ether and a promise of better things. In Scotland a thousand flowers bloomed. New government policies were accompanied by ambitious and expensive development programmes and the voices of children and young people were celebrated in school self-evaluation policy. Ground-breaking initiatives brought to the surface the treasure within and schools discovered that children and young people had something valuable to say about what good schools looked like and how they could improve. For a brief period voices travelled across national borders until the relentless march of standardization and the accountability machine gradually overtook 'the messy bottom–up approach to evaluation'. 'Voice' is however, not to be so easily silenced and attempts to do so will ultimately prove to be self-defeating as bien-être, or wellbeing, is reciprocally related to self expression and to achievement.

## Note

1   MacBeath, J., McCaig, E. and Thomson B. (1992) *Making School Boards Work*, University of Strathclyde. MacBeath, J. E. C. (1994) *Making School Boards Better*, University of Strathclyde.

# Part II

# The second lens

# 3 Research and the myths of scientific rigour

Research, we are led to believe, offers us the most robust and objective lens through which to view school practice, policy and their interrelationship. However strong its methodological warrant and claims to validity, there is always the option to either dispute or disregard its findings. Cherry picking outcomes that have a more intuitive appeal is not only a very human response to findings, but also endemic in political decision making. Does research, even when commissioned by the government itself, have any impact on policy? How much of key decision making in government is based on policymakers' own personal experience (or that of their children)? How much derives simply from their own values or prejudices? The Primary Review, the advisory panel on the curriculum, and the government-sponsored research on schools in exceptionally challenging circumstances all provide unambiguous answers to these questions. If governments can change schools, it proves not to be by giving credence to the nuanced, complex and contested findings of academics.

## Policy, prejudice and the persuasion of personal experience

Policymakers and researchers have not always been best of friends. While governments have continued to sponsor educational research that does not mean they have to give it any credence. And very frequently they don't. Research in education has none of the glamour of its counterparts in medicine, science, or exploration of space. It cannot claim to save lives, to identify the very origins of life itself or to pave a way for inter-planetary travel. Yet the myth of purity and rigour in scientific research has been exposed. In a *Sunday Times* article (12 August 2012) on science's 'dirty secret' it cited the three big sins – the first plagiarism, the second falsification, and the third fabrication. While these sins are not unknown to educational researchers, those who claim it to be a 'science' cannot also promise an instant cure or monetary profit. There are a very few findings that are not open to counter-argument or controversy. So, while politicians and policymakers may be ready to embrace research findings in other fields in which they can claim little personal knowledge, education is something they know about at first hand, having themselves spent ten to fifteen years in school. Researchers' insights into pedagogy, curriculum and assessment are often then simply dismissed in favour of a minister's personal experience or particular prejudice.

Two recent cases – Robin Alexander's Primary Review and the Expert Panel on the Curriculum appointed by Michael Gove – are an exemplary starting point for testing the perceived validity and impact of research on policy.

## Re-viewing the review

In its final report in 2010 the Cambridge Primary Review (CPR) evidence base included detailed submissions from major educational organisations, 250 focus-group sessions up and down the country, a re-assessment of national and international data on standards, twenty-eight specially commissioned surveys of published research from sixty-six leading academics in twenty-one universities, many of them dealing with events, initiatives and processes of the past thirteen years, and incorporation of over 4000 published sources. The Review was manifestly not to the liking of the Labour Government, and Ed Balls was to write dismissively to Robin Alexander, the Government preferring to conduct its own review. Jim Rose was hastily commissioned to cover the same ground as the Primary Review but with considerably less evidence and rigour, by virtue of the political constraints imposed on it.

How capacious yet capricious is the dustbin of history. Just over a year ago, the 600-page final report of the Cambridge Primary Review, product of the most comprehensive inquiry into English primary education for half a century, was dismissed by Labour, misrepresented and unread. For many, this underscored the report's significance. Meanwhile, the 'independent' Rose curriculum framework was imposed on England's primary schools. According to Mick Waters, then Head of Curriculum at the Qualifications and Curriculum Development Agency (QCDA), this, too, was a pre-emptive strike against the inconvenient truths emerging from Cambridge (*The Guardian*, 15 March 2011).

In Robin Alexander's own words:

> The Rose Review is a tidying-up operation rather than the promised 'root and branch' reform. Its off-the-shelf aims for primary education, like its references to the Cambridge Review's own proposals are cosmetic. Its seductive promises of professional freedom are nullified by continuing central control.
>
> (*Children, Their World, Their Education*, p513)

Writing in *The Guardian* in 2010, Robin Alexander pointed out the extent to which the compliance culture had impacted on schools and teachers' professional lives. The report questions the way governments, since the 1990s, have chosen to tackle the essential task of raising primary school standards, using high-stakes tests, league tables, prescriptive national teaching strategies and procedures for inspection, initial teacher training, continuous professional development and school improvement, which require strict compliance with official accounts of what primary education is about and how it should be undertaken. Perhaps the most frequent and disturbing comment voiced by teachers at our dissemination events has been this: "We're impressed by the Cambridge Review's evidence. We like the ideas. We want to take them forward. But we daren't do so without permission from our Ofsted inspectors and local authority school improvement partners." (*The Guardian*, 27 April 2010).

In my own contribution to the edited volume *Children, Their World, Their Education: Final report and recommendations of the Cambridge Primary Review*, published by Routledge in 2010, I referred to interviews with headteachers who professed to being 'fed up with interference, mindless paper work, lurches in policy, and daily announcements of gimmicky initiatives'. I quoted David Milliband:

> Accountability drives everything. Without accountability there is no legitimacy; without legitimacy there is no support; without support there are nor resources; and without resources there are nor services. It is within this political imperative that school leaders and inspection teams have to negotiate, exploring where trust and support reside, what those words mean and how they are tested.
>
> (p441)

## And now for something completely similar

In 2011 Michael Gove, Secretary of State for Education, commissioned four leading academics in the field of curriculum and assessment, Professors Mary James, Andrew Pollard and Dylan Wiliam, and Tim Oates of Cambridge Assessment, to advise on policy in those areas. They were described as an 'expert panel'. As it transpired after a year of intensive work, they were either not 'expert' enough, or perhaps too expert for Mr Gove's liking. Following her appointment in late 2010 Mary James' twelve point letter to Nick Gibb in September 2010 had made it clear, in her own words, 'where I am coming from', citing forty years as a teacher, educational researcher and academic. Her position, prior to appointment was made abundantly clear:

> There should be no attempt to recreate the detailed attainment targets and statements of attainment that were intended as assessment criteria but have come to define the curriculum itself. The high stakes attached to test outcomes have led many teachers to teach to the assessment criteria rather than the substance of the programmes of study, thus sacrificing deep learning and understanding of content and skill. There are good ways of ensuring valid assessment, within schools and by awarding bodies, which do not depend on the mechanistic tick box approach that atomistic criteria encourage.
>
> The NC framework should not prescribe how the content is taught, either in terms of curriculum organisation e.g. separate subject lessons, or

integrated courses, or in terms of pedagogic approaches. These decisions should be based on the professional judgement of teachers, schools and governors, taking account of their particular contexts and informed by good evidence.

However, evidence of effective practices, informed by sound research, needs to be available and accessible to schools and teachers in order to make such choices and to encourage innovation. An evidence information service needs to be created although this should be the responsibility of the profession, probably in partnership with universities and funders, but independent of Government.

(Cambridge headed letter to Nick Gibb, September 2010)

Just over a year later Mary James and Andrew Polllard wrote to Michael Gove, referring to the Mary James letter and tendering their resignation in the following words:

We do so because we are concerned with the direction which the Department now appears to be taking. Some of the directions fly in the face of evidence from the UK and internationally and, in our judgement, cannot be justified educationally. We do not therefore believe that the review, if it continues on the course which now appears to be set, will provide the quality of education which pupils, parents, employers and national stakeholders have a right to expect.

(10 October 2011)

In a reply to Tim Oates, Director of Research and Assessment at Cambridge Assessment, thanking him and colleagues for their 'tremendous' work, Gove outlines just how much he has taken account of his expert panel's advice: 'In Mathematics pupils will know number bonds to 20 by Year 2 and times tables up to 12 x 12 by the end of Year 4. Long multiplication and division will be given, emphasising using fractions, decimals and negative numbers.' These were, of course the staple in the good old days predating decimalisation (hence the emphasis on the 12 times table) and computerisation, making the skill of long division somewhat arcane. On 12 June 2012 Andrew Pollard posted a blog containing this reflection.

Why Mary James, Dylan Wiliam and I were appointed to the Expert Panel remains something of a mystery, for we were hardly likely to accede to this crude design for curricular reform. For my own part, I would not deny that subject knowledge is important nor demur from sustained efforts to consider how it should be most appropriately represented in a programme of study. And of course, the idea sounds wonderful – yes, let's sort out, once and for all, when spelling of particular words will be mastered, and the use of apostrophes, and the subjunctive, and so on. So this approach is likely to be very attractive to the public.

But the approach is fatally flawed without parallel consideration of the needs of learners. Primary teachers consider the overall experiences of each child, and try to provide a broad and balanced curriculum as is required by law. The skill and expertise of the teacher lies in building on each pupil's existing understanding and capabilities, and in matching tasks to extend attainment. To do these things, they need scope to exercise professional judgement.

However, on the basis of the new National Curriculum proposals, they are to be faced by extremely detailed year-on-year specifications in mathematics, science and most of English. This is to be complemented by punitive inspection arrangements and tough new tests at 11.

A Department for Education (DfE) web page entitled *Popular Questions,* justifying the choice of curriculum subjects, poses this child-friendly question – Why do we have to do subjects like foreign languages or algebra at school? Any bright eleven year old who had posed such a question would have been less than satisfied with the answer.

> Schools aim to ensure that pupils are literate, numerate and at ease with new technologies, providing their pupils with the essential skills they need in preparation for the opportunities, responsibilities and experiences of later life.

## Exceptional challenges

The story told of research and policy finds parallels with a Government-sponsored study, the outcomes of which were to be published in two books appearing around the same time in 2007. One, *Schools in Exceptionally Challenging Circumstances,* was an 'insider' account while the other, *Schools on the Edge,* was written by the Cambridge research team. The two accounts of the project were in many respects coincident, in part because the Harris/Department for Education and Skills (DfES) version had simply lifted long passages from our own report (without attribution) but not those passages that were critical of the processes and findings of the study. The independent researchers' account was considerably more critical and objective. The study, one of the key initiatives to come from the Standards and Effectiveness Unit, was politically high stakes. The 'big idea' was to introduce an innovative school improvement project to a small selection of urban schools in the most disadvantaged communities, building on current knowledge of school improvement, to demonstrate how these key elements would work together to improve schools, even in the most unpropitious of circumstances.

Evaluation of the programme was put out to tender. I was invited to apply and, serendipitously, on the day of receiving the tender I ran into my colleague John Gray, ruminating on a street corner outside the John Lewis department store. He too had been invited to tender and, a few weeks later, in the course of the interview at the Department, his statistical nous and expertise in multi-level modeling was undoubtedly a critical factor in winning the contract as, ultimately, raised standards would be the touchstone of the project's success.

Our task, a team comprised of David Frost, Sue Swaffield, Susan Steward, Jane Cullen and the two Johns, was to evaluate the impact of this high-profile, high-stakes and hugely expensive initiative on eight schools, to be known as the 'Octet'. All eight schools were characterised by some or all of the indicators of economic and social disenfranchisement. Some were located in areas where there was formerly a strong manufacturing and heavy industry base, in which there had been at one time a secure future for young people, particularly young men. Over the last twenty to thirty years, cities such as Halifax and Sunderland had struggled to attract equal levels of light industry and service-based employment, and where such work existed, it was often casual. Maritime communities such as Grimsby, Folkestone and even Liverpool had also tried to attract alternative employment as traditional industries were in steep decline. Communities in parts of all these cities were marked by insularity and disillusionment as their work-based identity has been progressively eroded. Birmingham and London, which registered highest on indices of deprivation and showed complex historical patterns of decline, were also home to highly transient populations, including people drawn to the casual work and the twilight economics of major urban centres. Among their numbers were asylum seekers and refugees in temporary accommodation, and others leaving troubled domestic and social situations behind. 'Family life' rarely fits the image that such a phrase might conjure up. In some areas, the character of the local population can shift rapidly and continuously in terms of its mix of background, ethnicities and cultures. For schools this has meant a constant process of catch-up in order to offer the appropriate services to parents and students.

## Radical solutions to perennial problems

The *Schools Facing Exceptionally Challenging Circumstances* (SFECC) project was to be a 'cutting edge' strategy, encouraging schools to develop radical solutions to the problems of educating the next generation. The 2001 Green Paper *Building on Success* had contained the seeds of the project:

> **4.59** ... for a small number of schools in exceptionally challenging circumstances which, for example, are sited in extremely disadvantaged communities, have very high pupil mobility or a large number of asylum seekers, we intend to develop an option which is more radical still. Starting this year we intend as a pilot to offer substantial additional support and funding to about eight or 10 well managed schools in these particularly difficult circumstances.

> **4.60** The pilot will include a strong emphasis on much smaller classes and more flexible approaches to the use of time. We want teachers who choose to work in these extremely challenging circumstances to have additional support and pupils to benefit from an extended learning day and weekend and holiday learning.

> (DfEE 2001:57/58)

In the event, eight of the lowest performing schools in the country were identified. All would have strong headteachers who could be enlisted, together with financial sweeteners, to turn their schools around and 'raise standards'. There would be direct funding to each school of £150,000–£200,000 a year; funding to develop innovative uses of ICT, such as video conferencing and interactive whiteboards, together with a common website; a bespoke reading programme to improve literacy in Key Stage 3; training in the strategic use of data, especially to track pupil progress, but also in the use of CATs data to broaden teaching strategies; training and development of a School Improvement Group (SIG) in each school; and training for the middle managers. The eight headteachers would benefit from continued support and advice from the Department in the form of regular seminars, residential weekends, and ad hoc exchanges among headteachers through their own internal network and visits to one another's schools.

Each member of the Cambridge team was attached to one or more of the 'Octet'. My adopted school was Phoenix High School in Hammersmith and Fulham. My relationship with the other seven schools – Havelock in Grimsby, Pennywell in Sunderland, St Alban's in Birmingham, Whitefield School in London, The Channel School in Folkestone and The Ridings in Halifax – was mainly second hand, although I met all their heads at the various meetings and weekend workshops. The Ridings, in the final analysis, one of the least successful schools in the Octet, suffered from too much media exposure, too frequent intervention and destabilisation, eventually to be closed soon after the project ended.

## Out of the ashes

In Phoenix I was able to hit the ground running as its head, William Atkinson, was well known to me through the Standards Task Force and we had already developed an easy mutual relationship. It allowed him to speak candidly and at times 'off the record', providing insights into the Octet and its personnel, which would, in other circumstances, have been beyond the protocols and niceties of the researcher. In an early description of the local context I had written the following:

> Many of the young people who come to Phoenix High School arrive by bus and walk up from Uxbridge Road, passing Queens Park Rangers Football Club and heavily armoured shops, many of the students taking the short cut through the White City Estate which sits cheek by jowl with the school. The exterior the estate presents to the world is of a tidy well kept gardens, with little external evidence of the problems that lie behind these relatively pleasant facades. Pupils describe the prevalence of drugs and are able to pinpoint where the dealers live. Some of the violence is territorial, gang fights often initiated by 'intruders' from other boroughs. Pupils' accounts of drug dealing, violence and gang warfare which take

over the streets at night, are confirmed by teachers and community and social workers, some of whom live locally and have a close knowledge of the community.

The area is a volatile one due to the constant turnover of the population. As parts of the community are visibly improved others go down. It is described by a community worker as 'a zero sum game', a balancing act in which each step forward is attenuated by a step or two backwards. There is a dynamic at work in a community which is not a 'community' at all but a collection of neighbourhood pockets which never remain static as people move in and others leave. There are refugees from war zones, many are in short-stay accommodation to be re-housed; others are in care; some have been excluded from other schools and a number, awaiting outcomes of custody judgements, live in extended families. Many move on to go abroad or to other parts of the British Isles. In 2003 [when the project began] 104 pupils were refugees, primarily from Somalia, and 113 pupils were from traveling families.

Phoenix, at the time, one of the lowest achieving schools in the country and subject to HMI special measures, was to be the most successful of the Octet, at least in terms of raised attainment. This was primarily owed to William Atkinson remaining faithful to the school and its community, rather than moving on to greener and less challenging pastures. In July 2012, *The Times* newspaper was to describe him as 'one of the most successful heads in the country', the accolade simply one of many newspaper and television homages to the headteacher credited with raising Phoenix School out of the ashes. Played by Lenny Henry in the television series 'The Headmaster', William has achieved almost mythic status. That he was, in many respects, the least engaged of the eight heads in the project is not to infer any causal relationship, but William is an exceptionally ebullient and charismatic individual who knows his own mind and knows where he wants to take his school. He was, perhaps of all the headteachers, least in need of support or direction. While intolerant of fools he combines this with a wonderful sensitivity, a good listener when he trusts the source and the relationship in which it is embedded. His humanity was demonstrated in his tearful announcement at morning assembly that one of their number had been stabbed to death while on an errand for his housebound mother.

## Promise unfulfilled

The radical intent of the initial Octet design was never realised. Redefining the school year into four or five terms to give students extended schooling, and in particular reducing the long summer break, never came to pass. Nor did the suspension of the National Curriculum or substantial reductions in class size come to fruition. The technology could not support proposed innovative uses of ICT in classroom pedagogy with a video link across the eight schools and a common website and streamlining the use of data in the eight schools. During the early stages the project quickly settled into a more conventional package of support.

It was not simply that the DfES got cold feet, although as one senior member of the DfES explained, in spending public money the Civil Service is naturally 'risk averse', not prepared for the major shift to a radically different kind of school or school year. The possibility of profound structural change was ruled out even before the project began. The concept of action research with agency lying with the schools was lost as the DfES took more and more central control of the project. None of the eight LEAs were directly involved at all in the project and so the model became one of centralised control, with a direct relationship between each school and the DfES ('London Calling' as one headteacher put it). A system of monitoring through termly visits by HMI, and half-termly requirements to provide the DfES with attainment data, constrained any attempts at recasting schools in a new mould. It was unrealistic to believe that eight schools could drive forward a coherent programme of radical change from the beginning. There were no strategies that moved outside the school, for example, working with outside local agencies, and no link up with any community regeneration.

Originally SFECC was planned to last for five years, a time span that would have allowed for developments in learning and teaching to have maximum effect on students who were in Year 7 at the beginning of the project, and which would have provided a longitudinal view of the cumulative change on the school. It also would have been a realistic time span to bring about systemic or structural change. However, in the event the project only lasted three years and was only fully active for two of those.

## Can governments change schools?

Direct intervention in the running of schools was a legacy to the Labour Government from its Conservative predecessors, no one more aggressive in micromanagement than Lady Thatcher. There are important lessons to be learned from Government initiatives that promise radical reform with one hand while with the other tying schools to short-term expedient measures. Among the fifteen conclusions and recommendations at the premature end to the SFECC initiative we wrote:

> Being required to compete in a high-stakes competitive environment means that disadvantaged schools are unlikely to risk the stigma of failure and will always be constrained to play it safe. The survival and transformation of schools in such areas demands radical rethinking at policy level not simply at individual school level.
>
> Change takes time. But change takes longer where there is a legacy of diminished social capital. Impatience for short-term results can inhibit longer term capacity-building. Initiatives in disadvantaged communities

should not be premised on what is possible in successful and relatively stable school contexts. It is easy to underestimate the complex nature of disadvantaged communities and how they interface with conventional school structures. The obstacles to school improvement are plural rather than singular, interlocking rather than specific and often stubbornly change resistant. The direction of school change in challenging circumstances has been likened by an Octet headteacher to turning a supertanker, both in the length of time it takes and the delay between operating the levers of change and any perceptible shift in trajectory. The time span of the SFECC project has demanded visible evidence of improvement within the space of two to three years, inevitably resulting in what is termed 'hard' evidence having to be demonstrated in raised attainment scores.

> Nothing else is a priority; we have to get these 5 A*–Cs . . . until we can wave that bit of paper, they will never be off our backs . . . I have said to them [the DfES] you need to wait . . . change and improvement takes time (Octet headteacher).

Ill-informed inclusion policies impact disproportionately on disadvantaged schools. 'Special needs' is open to variety of interpretations and provision is often ad hoc and inappropriate. This is compounded by these schools accepting students that other schools don't or won't accept and a failure in provision of more suitable local alternatives. The creation of a market and parental choice has effected a major shift in public attitudes. Much of that has, however, been to the detriment of schools facing challenging circumstances, especially when spotlighted as being in serious weaknesses or special measures.

## A false premise?

The premise on which the project rested was derived from effectiveness and improvement studies which, when applied to schools in exceptionally challenging circumstances, receive a stern test. None of the initiatives were able to effect the depth of penetration on students' learning needed to revitalise and energise disaffected and alienated young people. None were able to factor into the equation the lack of social capital and its often devastating impact on children and families, whose lives are lived out in private, hidden from the school – 'out of hours':

Anoukas' story

Playing too close and too inquisitively with D-I-Y electrical wiring, Anouka was subject to an intense electric shock and severe burns to her right arm. Her mother, in panic, knocked on a neighbour's door and then on another door to see if she could borrow some cream or bandages to put on the child's burn, or perhaps an aspirin to stop the pain. Neither neighbour was willing to open a front door at that time of night. As Mrs Okede's phone had been cut off she was unable to call her estranged husband, now living at the other end of the city. She decided she would take Anouka to the casualty department of the nearest hospital. With Anouka in her arms she walked the quarter mile to the bus stop where she knew there would be late running buses. She was lucky as one came within fifteen minutes and took her quite close to the hospital. The receptionist there was sympathetic to the child's clear distress but advised Mrs Okede that this was the wrong hospital and gave directions to another hospital two miles away. Two bus rides and an hour later mother and child arrived at the casualty department of the second hospital where they waited patiently in an overcrowded room for Anouka to be seen.

(MacBeath *et al.*, 2008. *Schools on the Edge*, p24)

## Revisiting challenging circumstances

If governments can change schools they will not do so by forever changing the curriculum, as the 'curriculum' is not at the root of the problem for neighbourhoods such as Anouka's. Nor is it the solution to the disaffection and alienation of young people, the roots of which are not in the arcane problems they are expected to engage with on 'Groundhog day' (as one teacher in Phoenix School put it), a reference to the Bill Murray movie in which the main characters relive the same day over and over. 'Remember we were doing this yesterday?' is met with a blank look as too much of consequence has intervened between the classroom of yesterday and the reality of today.

There can be few places that merit the term 'challenging circumstances' than in those countries which have, for the last half decade, been part of the Cambridge Commonwealth Education Centre. In these countries the distance between classroom and the local community may be measured both culturally and physically. The ten mile round trip to school, by foot, often through inhospitable, and even dangerous places is, for many children, still a daily reality. Even more threatening are the cities to which children are drawn but then find themselves isolated, homeless and vulnerable, subject to exploitation by a range of urban predators buying sexual favours, with illegal drugs, and AIDS, to be factored into the equation.

To be young in Africa has come to mean being disadvantaged, vulnerable and marginal. Schools, cast in a colonial mould with their inflexible starting times, arcane conventions and esoteric curricula sit in uneasy juxtaposition with the life and values of their communities. In Ghana, where Sue Swaffield and I have been privileged to work over the last four years, coming to understand the paradoxes of life in families and communities and life lived out in the classroom.

Teachers posted to rural communities struggle to cope with the lack of electricity, drinking water and basic amenities. The 'classroom' is often the shelter of tree, one teacher and perhaps a hundred or more children. It is against this backdrop that 15 professional development leaders from across Ghana were invited by George Oduro from the University of Cape Coast, to collaborate with us on a LfL programme, in which a critical approach to learning would be centre stage and leadership with a central focus on learning. Following workshops in Ghana and in Cambridge this inspired group of change agents led professional development around the country, initially with 125 selected headteachers whom they, and we, have continued to work with over a three year period. The premise was that quick wins were more likely to be demonstrated if a powerful cadre of headteachers, selectively chosen, were to be leading-edge ambassadors among their colleagues.

There was no simple blueprint for change, but a conviction that with right people the initial investment would generate its own returns, met over time by a top down policy endorsement persuasive enough to be endorsed by government as a big idea. Leadership for Learning resonated persuasively with these headteachers as if a hidden aspiration had been resurrected and had new life breathed into it.

In the event, the tangible evidence of change has so gained the respect of the Ministry and Ghana Education Service that policy makers have been willing to invest in the continuing development of the programme and to extend it country wide enshrining Leadership for Learning principles in the Headteacher's Handbook – the school improvers' bible.

The transition from officer administrator to leader of learning has been a significant change for the heads whose authority had previously been located in their office, symbolically, in a distance from the classroom. The head's focus was typically, not 'downward' to teacher and pupils but 'upward' to their local circuit supervisors, and to district, regional and Ministerial authorities. As one head said 'Before you just sat in the office and thought everyone must come to you', but she had come to realise that the distance between the authority of the head and the teacher reinforced in turn the distance between teacher and pupil.

The role of the Cambridge team in leading the development work has receded with remarkable speed as the LfL programme is taken forward by a combination of key Ghanaian players, who together fashion and lead a national programme. Far from yet another short life 'aid' programme, the aims of capacity building, sustainability and local ownership are being progressively realised.

## On reflection

How capacious yet capricious is the dustbin of history? In that receptacle are ambitious programmes such as SFECC, abandoned mid term because of a failure to show that it is schools not neighbourhoods, social class or poverty that make the difference. The failure to address the unmoveable obstacles of curriculum and assessment was to be replayed a decade later as the 'expert group' commissioned to review the curriculum proved to be less expert than a Secretary of State who had himself been to school. How different the response from policy makers in Ghana, where the insights of researchers and the breakthroughs by committed practitioners are celebrated and embedded in policy.

# 4 Telling stories
## From dutiful compliance to defiant risk taking

In Scotland there has, traditionally, been a happier entente between researchers and policymakers than in England. The 2009 study on recruitment and retention of headteachers was, however, to cast a different light on that association and open to question the relationship between the piper's payment and the tune. Four other policy-related studies, with the NUT, the Economic and Social Research Council (ESRC) and two further studies with the Scottish Office, identify a common dilemma for researchers and policymakers – how can research serve differing audiences and purposes and be made accessible to differing political and public stakeholders while maintaining its honesty and integrity?

### You can't scare me, I've got children: a Scottish tale

While my experience of research in Scotland had been a happier one than in similar ventures 'south of the border', with never, or rarely, a request to take a less uncompromising stance, the 2009–10 study of *Recruitment and Retention of Headteachers*[1] proved to be an exception. At successive meetings at Victoria Quay, home to the Scottish Office, suggestions were offered by the government side as to how to omit or moderate some of the more extreme quotes from interviewees. The public release of the report was to be subject to a little political chicanery, which I matched with some of my own.

The final report was embargoed until Thursday midnight so that it would not appear in *The Times Educational Supplement* on the Friday, the day of the minister's speech, intended to grab the headlines and the TES front page. In the event, the minister was consigned to an inside page as our study took both front and inside pages. I had phoned Neil Munro, the editor, with the story, letting him know of its embargo, but as the paper would not appear until Friday morning I calculated that this would not be an infringement of the contract. This was not, however, as the Scottish Office saw it and we were immediately threatened with a withholding of the final payment for the research – a substantial sum. This was enough to terrify my co-director Peter Gronn. I was unmoved by the scaremongering and ultimately we were paid and the minister resigned. I made no causal connection between my treachery and her demise. It took more than two years, however, for Peter to forgive me.

It was hardly surprising that the Scottish Office did not like the report. The story it told was of an oppressive policy climate which made recruitment to headship highly problematic given the demands and, often, unrelieved stress of the role. Feelings of being 'done to', 'put upon' and 'hemmed in', without the latitude to make decisions and to 'have responsibility without control' was a primary source of stress. Some headteachers spoke of a reluctance to speak openly with their local authorities for fear of reprisal, while for more than half of those interviewed, their experience of inspection was described as 'adversarial', 'undermining' or 'stigmatising'. This upward accountability was described as in tension with the immediate and 'downward accountability' to pupils and staff. For headteachers new to their post, walking the tightrope of 'complex and multiple accountabilities' (to staff, to teacher unions, the School Board/Parent Council, the local authority, Her Majesty's Inspectorate of Education (HMIE), the Scottish Government and parents), while continually 'watching your back', was described in interview as a new and 'scary' experience.

In very disadvantaged neighbourhoods, heads spoke of the 'heartbreak' of children's lives where the term 'family' was a misnomer and where instability was the only constant. Citing a catalogue of mental health problems, substance, alcohol and drug abuse, parents in prison, children with Foetal Alcohol Syndrome, and 'real poverty, real poverty', one headteacher spoke of a missing generation, what she referred to locally as the 'widespread granny syndrome', 'a huge number of sole parent families', a lot of grans running the family because mum is, 'quote, a waste of space, don't talk to her, don't speak to my daughter, she's better off out of this life'.

The study identified five leadership strategies into which each of the forty-three Scottish heads could be placed. These categories may well have applicability in other national contexts:

- Dutiful compliance
- Cautious pragmatism
- Quiet self-confidence
- Bullish self-assertion
- Defiant risk-taking

The *dutifully compliant* mortgaged their energy and time to their role demands, with the tendency not to experience autonomy nor to exercise much personal latitude in decision-making. This often came at a heavy price in terms of bureaucracy, paperwork and heavy workloads. Recognising that such an open-ended commitment could be detrimental to both private life and wellbeing, and learning how to prioritise, characterised the *cautiously pragmatic*. Where headteachers had a sense of being on top of their work it allowed them to go about their business with a *quiet self-confidence* and a sense of mastery, modelling what it means to have taken active steps to try to deploy time and energy to their advantage, on terms which are theirs, while not overtly pushing against the tide. The ability to thrive on challenges with high levels of self-confidence and self-assurance was a hallmark of the *bullishly self-assertive*, refusing to be dictated to or to be cowed by authority. Even more assertive were the *defiant risk-takers*, highly experienced headteachers, sailing close to the wind, self-confessed risk-takers and rule-breakers. They were inclined to go their own way in full knowledge of the risks and consequences of what they could get away with. As one woman head put it, 'You can't scare me, I've got children.'

A summary report in *The Scotsman* newspaper captured the intensive nature of the headteacher's job:

> Guess whose is the first car in the morning in the school car park and the last to depart at night? Who eats their lunch on the run – if they eat at all? How many working professionals have a job description ranging from changing light bulbs through to preparing strategic plans? How many people work with a range of children from neighourhoods of grinding poverty and generous wealth? How many have to endure being verbally (and sometimes physically) abused by parents? But who else experiences the joy of watching children flourish and seeing staff growing in confidence.

> Despite the many rewards of headship, for even the most resilient of school leaders, there were times when the 'horrible days' took their toll – dealing with complaints against staff members, allegations of abuse, litigation, interventions by police or social work, the attendant form filling, witness statements and attendance at court. The all-consuming nature of the job is revealed in comments such as: 'It's like day and night. I couldn't switch off', 'I eat, sleep and breathe it. It's just in my blood'. (Heads need Hearts to Survive in Scottish Schools, *The Scotsman*, 8 November 2009).

## A life in teaching?

The script could easily have been written by the English teachers whom Maurice Galton and I interviewed over the course of four studies of teachers' lives between 2006 and 2009. Sponsored not by government but by the NUT, the only need to temper the account would have been to portray the NUT in a bad light. As this issue never arose, that moral dilemma did not have to be confronted. It was not until the fourth of our studies that we were to come under heavy fire – in this case from our Cambridge colleagues.

The first of the reports, *A Life in Teaching?*, documented the lives of primary teachers, the recurring themes – stress and ill health, pressure and deskilling, loss of control and professional initiative – attributed to ill-conceived targets and competitive league tables.

> I felt my confidence suddenly going. I felt de-skilled, as if everything we had been doing all these years, in a way it was almost like the government saying, 'You haven't been doing it well enough. This is how it should be done now. This is what we're prescribing. This is what we want you to

deliver'. That was a hindrance because my confidence was suddenly plummeting again and that had to be built up.

(Primary Teacher)

Like their primary counterparts, secondary teachers reported being 'swamped' by too many national initiatives, an overloaded and prescriptive curriculum and lack of time for collegial discussion and reflection and constant pressure to meet attainment targets.

> So much time is consumed with trivial things that little time is left for professional development. No adequate time for the real reflection. We can't talk with colleagues at leisure. There isn't that time. There isn't that professional space. But that's where you learn best, from each other, and when I think I am being disenfranchised from that I wonder about my role but people just say, well you have to just get on with it.

(Secondary Teacher)

Topping the list of concerns was deteriorating discipline. For many teachers it had become a running sore, one they felt unable to address without adequate sanctions or support from a parent body, itself often unable to deal with young people beyond their control.

The only 'political' fallout was after the fourth of our studies, in this case with our Cambridge special needs colleagues. Martin Rouse, at the time a senior lecturer in the Faculty, accused us of undoing thirty years of his work, although less than a year later he was appointed to a Chair in Aberdeen University. Inclusion, as we learned, is a topic hugely fraught with ideology and wish fulfillment.

## Inclusion without education

The fourth of our studies for the NUT, the source of internecine tensions, was entitled *The Costs of Inclusion*, a critique of the ill-considered policies by which 'inclusion' was interpreted as 'including' children with special needs in mainstream classrooms. The critique was not of our making but emerged from a veritable flood of grievances, not only from unhappy families, but from teachers and headteachers who we interviewed. Teachers, highly committed and keen to do their best for a large number of children with special needs, said that is had 'taken its toll on staff' and some had simply left, unable to deal with the pressures of curriculum and testing on the one hand and the demands of 'difficult' children on the other. The open plan design of primary schools also meant that disruption extended more widely than just one class. In our report, we quoted the National Autistic Society (NAS) 2002 survey *Inclusion and Autism: is it working?*, which found that children with autism and Asperger's syndrome were on average twenty times more likely to be excluded from school than their peers. One in five (21 per cent) were excluded at least once, compared with an estimated 1.2 per cent of the total pupil population. The situation was worse still for more able children with autism. A total of 29 per cent of these children had been excluded from school at one time or another. Speaking for her staff, a primary headteacher described teachers 'as their own worst enemy' because of 'always putting the child before themselves'. Another teacher spoke of the guilt she felt at letting children down.

> I think, it's a funny thing to say, I think they [SEN children] add guilt to my job. I go home sometimes and feel I haven't done a good job because I haven't given them enough time and I think it's because the progress they make is so slow that you can think that you're failing.

A very experienced primary school teacher, who constantly strived to frame the issues in positive terms, spoke emotionally about the sense of guilt and failure:

> We were doing something in Maths last week and they still hadn't got it and I felt a failure in myself. I got so emotional and I said to my TA [Teaching Assistant] because I was close to tears 'I've got to go out of the classroom'. I felt it was something I was failing in – I couldn't cope with it any more.

For teachers, 'muddling through' without expert support, having to carry the burden of responsibility for children's welfare, could weigh heavily. School staff were too often left to fall back on common sense or 'instinct'. The lack of expertise and professional development in meeting a wide spectrum of needs was consistently raised by teachers, headteachers and TAs as a critical issue, if inclusion policies were to have any prospect of success: 'There is very little specialist training. You do what you can instinctively but very often that isn't good enough. It's not good enough for the assistant because they feel inadequate and it's not good enough for the child' (TA, primary school).

We were careful to celebrate the positives but they were typically bought at a cost to the heroic efforts and goodwill of teachers and school leaders, a signal failure of policy, running at cross grain to the essential purpose of inclusion. Success with challenging behaviour and complex needs is a long-term investment and highly gratifying when it finally pays off. However, as a special needs assistant pointed out, you may have to go through 'hell' to get there.

Among the many endorsements for this study from other countries, numbering close to 100, a five-page letter from the United States concluded with these two paragraphs:

> I'd also like permission, if you don't mind, to circulate your study to scholars here in the US. I know a number of nationally famous and respected inclusion (pro inclusion) scholars who would find your study extremely interesting and challenging.

Thank you for this work. I cancelled my Saturday outing today to stay home and read it, and after having done so, think I made a very good decision. As an aside – maybe it's just because you are English – but I find your paper to be extremely well thought out and beautifully written.
Dee Alpert, Publisher
*The Special Education Muckraker*

## Learning and learning how to

There was no sense of constraint imposed by political masters of any hue in the independently-funded ESRC study *Learning How to Learn*. Yet even here there were micropolitical issues to be considered. A case in point was a chapter in one of the books published at the end of the project. While I had written a critical depiction of leadership in Seven Kings School, after editorial sanitisation it would have required an astute reading between the lines to spot the critique. Perhaps my bias was too much in evidence, but the celebration of the school's success ran counter to everything that I believed, researched, and had written about. The headteacher's prescription of seating plans and patrolling classrooms to ensure that all desks faced the front (otherwise how could children learn?) was so patently at odds with the power of peer learning that I had observed at its finest in Caldecote Primary School in Cambridgeshire. In Seven Kings the headteacher's heroic leadership style ran counter to the distributed sharing of leadership, which was so significant a feature of successful schools in other studies. The headteacher was not hesitant in claiming ownership of policy and strategy and confessed to his personal addiction – 'control freakery': 'This policy has got a lot of me in it. It's largely me.' 'That wasn't from the staff. That was from myself.' Nor was the pressure disguised as collegiality or support: 'It was quite brutal. It was tough. It was me.' And the hand of steel in the velvet glove: 'I think teachers have got to feel that they're making decisions but what I suppose I'm forcing them to do is making those decisions.' Words like 'tough', 'brutal', 'forcing' are expressions of what is widely referred to as 'strong' leadership, raising the stakes, creating willing followership. My pen portrait ended with a telling anecdote from a resentful ex-student, returning to say how unprepared for university he was as a result of a regime that had never given him scope to question received wisdom or think for himself.

Although somewhat resentful at the doctoring of my case study, I could, on the other hand, grasp the delicacy of the situation. The headteacher of Seven Kings was Sir Alan Steer, not only a government 'luvvy' but running a school that was one of the most improved in the country, at least as measured by exam passes. Sir Alan was also a constant and supportive presence in the LH2L project, attending every research meeting and making a positive contribution. The following profile from *The Guardian* following his appointment as Government Tsar is a wonderfully nuanced portrayal:

You can imagine Sir Alan Steer, bearded, ample of figure, jolly in demeanour (what he says is frequently drowned out by gales of laughter), as an old-fashioned pub landlord, making convivial conversation over the bar as he pulls the pints. You can imagine, too, a flash of steel as he ejects from the premises an over-inebriated and troublesome customer. You could, I think, have a very good time in Steer's pub as long as you obeyed the rules.

(Peter Wilby, The Guardian, 23 September 2008)

Funded by the Economic and Social Research Council *LH2L* was itself an important learning experience for me. It was a challenging task for its Director, Mary James, to marshal the disparate talents that came together for long weekends, much of which was spent on trying to agree on what learning how to learn actually meant. Indeed was such a concept useful? What seemed fairly unproblematic to me became the subject of endless papers and much disputation. I am still trying to come to terms with activity theory ('a powerful and clarifying descriptive tool rather than a strongly predictive theory'), embraced with such enthusiasm by other members of the team whose intellectual acuity and academic pedigree was not open to debate.[2] I remained a stubborn sceptic, failing to see how these emperors' clothes deepened my understanding, re-inventing for their own esoteric use terms such as 'rules', 'community', 'division of labour', 'subject', 'object', 'outcomes' with meanings only accessible to inside traders. Half a decade on I am none the wiser.

## Improving school effectiveness

The meeting point of policymakers and research purists may eschew compromise but it will inevitably shape the way the story is eventually told and how it is told to different audiences. For the Scottish Office, what came to be known as the International School Effectiveness Project (ISEP) was the most ambitious study ever undertaken in Scotland, £500,000 funding in 1996 representing an unprecedented investment in research and, therefore, high stakes in policy terms. In a *Times Education Supplement* article in 1998 Peter Mortimore described ISEP as a unique initiative, never having been attempted in any other country. It promised to marry effectiveness and improvement in a way not undertaken before with clear implications for policy direction in the future.

### *Political football*

The story begins with the intrepid traveller searching for a Scottish town called Raith. There is, unfortunately, no such place as the once-famous football team, Raith Rovers, is actually to be found in Kirkcaldy, on the east coast of Scotland in the kingdom of Fife. It was, after attending a match between the Rovers and Glasgow Rangers on 6 November 1996 (Raith 2 Rangers 2), followed by dinner with HMCI Archie McGlynn, that I raised the issues of the imminent tendering process for ISEP. Archie, the soul of discretion, kept his counsel.

On the day of the tender being announced I was phoned by David Reynolds suggesting that we submit a bid along with David Hopkins for one of the trilogy of studies (School Ethos, Leadership, and Curriculum). The USP (Unique Selling Point) would, David suggested, be the opportunity to trawl some of the best pubs and sample real ales in Edinburgh. I agreed, with some enthusiasm, to a meeting, as the two Davids were not only good company but also two of the twin proponents of effectiveness and improvement. They were, however, to be trumped a day later. In the middle of a workshop in Inverness I was handed an urgent note asking me to phone the London Institute of Education. I eventually called from a payphone in Inverness station and spoke on a static line to Peter Mortimore, whose audacious suggestion was that we go for all three projects, promising a dream team of Louise Stoll, Sally Thomas, Barbara McGilchrist and Pam Sammons (all later to become professors in their own right). I had to make a painful apologetic phone call to the Davids. The rest is now history.

### Ground-breaking, high profile, and expensive

Policymakers in Scotland had been quick to embrace the effectiveness movement and, throughout the 1970s and 1980s, the Scottish Office kept a close watching brief on seminal school effects research being undertaken by the Centre for Educational Sociology (CES) at Edinburgh University. John Gray, erstwhile one of CES' leading researchers, was appointed as advisor to help shape and steer what would be a ground-breaking, high profile, and expensive study.

The study, undertaken during a period of teachers' boycott managed to enlist 80 schools, with teams from the University of Strathclyde and the Institute of Education in London gathering data – surveys and interviews with 7,100 pupils, 2,540 teachers and 5,400 parents. Value-added attainment data was gathered in Maths and English in Primary 4 and Secondary 2 in 1995, following up progress two years later. The S4 group in 1997 also included pupils' average scores from their seven best Standard grade results. The most novel aspect of the study was to designate 24 case study schools. While the research employed a fairly orthodox effectiveness methodology, collecting value-added achievement and attitudinal data, together with individual and focus-group interviews, in the 24 case study schools the critical friend was a less traditional element. On an ongoing basis he or she fed back data to school staff to help staff address key issues – in learning and teaching, the ethos that enhances teaching and learning, and the form of transformational planning that arises from new ways of seeing. A change profile instrument and a behavioural event interview were used to take staff through key events, a dialogic process in which the challenges of change were explored and documented. Feedback sessions, with small groups and sometimes a whole staff, problematised the data, its very ambiguity providing the space for differing interpretations and understandings.

In this sense the ISEP study went beyond the conventions of effectiveness to follow where the dialogue led and began to open up questions as to the limitations of school effectiveness orthodoxy and its continuing relevance for the future. The support of the critical friend proved to be vital as the attitudinal data very often came as a shock to the headteacher, with somewhat traumatic effects – in one Highland primary school requiring therapeutic intervention on my part. One primary headteacher phoned our office to inform us that the data was clearly all wrong as she had personally asked every member of staff, 'Did you say that?' to which the response had been, hand on heart, 'No, Miss, not me'.

### I didn't know he was ill

St Gerard's Secondary School in Govan, home to television's Rab C. Nesbitt, was the lowest performing school in the country and headlined by the *Evening Times* as 'The Worst School in Scotland'. It was to prove one of the most challenging and ultimately successful of schools in the study. In a first meeting with the whole staff I was introduced as the critical friend, prompting a staff wag to loudly observe, 'I didn't know he was ill'. This was followed by the union rep standing up and giving a short speech on consultation and addressing me, 'In deference to you, sir, it is something to which I, and some of my colleagues, have never given agreement'. The group of colleagues in question were the inhabitants of the upper staffroom, a small attic enclave at the top of the building which Louise Stoll and I were later challenged to visit. This was to set the tone for the first and many subsequent visits. As we described it at the time:

> On our second day in the school we made the conscious decision to make an uninvited visit to the 'top staffroom'. The dead teabag in the sink, the congealed sugar and the archeological layers of caffeine on the glass cups told their own story. One member of staff was asleep with his feet on the mantelpiece, apparently oblivious to our presence, but his occasional smiles betrayed his careful monitoring of the conversation. The conversation (no dialogue here) was the 'top staffroom' perspective on the school, on school effectiveness and on the value of researchers in particular. Making friends with this group of staff might, with a little ingratiation, have been easy, but attempting to engage in a productive critical dialogue might not have been so easy, or the wisest investment of time and energy. The aphorism 'don't water the rocks' sprang simultaneously to the lips of researcher and critical friend.
>
> (MacBeath and Mortimore, *Improving School Effectiveness*, 2001, p158)

It was Matthew Boyle, the youngest and newly appointed teacher in the school, who was to confront the divisive nature of the upper staffroom and to press for its closure. He is also due the credit for the most improved school in the project, inspiring his senior colleagues to confront the low expectations of children, the exhortation on his classroom wall bearing the words – If at first you fail, try again, fail better. The head of the English department and the deputy headteacher were frequent visitors to his Physics class, happy to emulate his inspired pedagogy. The evidence of persistence and resilience overflowed into the passageway outside the lab where exhibits of children's experiments could be viewed with accompanying motifs – I tried this thirteen times before I got it to work!

### *The boy with half a brain:* Home from School

An independent study *Home from School* might have been free of political influence but it proved to be of considerable interest to Michael Forsyth, the Conservative Secretary of State in the Thatcher Government. Issues of parental choice and voice had obvious political mileage with a Tory Government and *Home from School* was, in many respects, a seminal document and a life-changing experience for three of us who led it – Dave Mearns, Maureen Smith and myself, visiting homes across Scotland over the course of a year. We had offered parents the choice of venue, our office, their home, or a neutral venue such a café or community centre. In the event, nine out of ten chose their own homes, leading us to explore the significance of 'territory' as a determinant of what is said and heard, and the nature of the 'passport' that gains entry for educational researchers into living rooms and kitchens. These visits were sometimes attended with considerable apprehension on our part as to what might lay behind the heavily fortified and graffiti-adorned tenement door, not to mention the statutory Alsatian waiting to greet us. The home visit from which I learned most and remains burned into memory two decades later, was to spend much more time than I had planned in a house in a run-down council estate in Dumfries. The nature of my 'passport' remained for most of the visit a mystery to the family with whom I was to pass the next three and half hours. Only gradually, as it dawned that I was not there 'from the social', nor that I was a 'trick cyclist', nor about to remove their children, did they open up to allow me entry to their world. It was one of warm hospitality and frightening ignorance.

For the full three-plus hours the interview was conducted with mother and father and, intermittently, with one or both children present. The older of the two boys was constantly referred to as the clever one, the favoured son, while the younger was described as a problem child who needed 'correction' from time to time with the father's leather belt, which I was privileged to be shown. The younger son, I was told in his apparently oblivious presence, had 'only half a brain', so explaining his repeated stupidity. It was many years later before it came to me that this was a literal rather than a metaphoric description. I turned down the offer to stay the night and left with a quandary as to what to disclose to the school, having promised the family confidentiality. It was a hard lesson for the researcher when extravagant promises may have to be broken. A further important lesson for researchers, one to which many of my colleagues do not prescribe, is the responsibility one owes to respondents to engage at a human level with the issues, to advise or offer help where there is a conspicuous need. I could not adopt the posture of the neutral observer and note taker, exploiting the family's openness and good will on the one hand and ignoring requests for guidance on the other.

My colleague Dave Mearns' descriptions of home life in Wester Hailes on the outskirts of Edinburgh were equally harrowing – interviews conducted in a squalid room bereft of all furniture, except for the tin bath in the middle of the floor, in which a twelve-year-old boy was embarrassedly being given his weekly wash.

## A detour around racism

Even more harrowing were accounts from Pakistani and Indian families of intimidation, fire raising, racist abuse and terrorisation. Many young people and their families had become so inured to it that there seemed little point in complaining – as was a constant refrain, 'you just bottle it up and keep quiet'. Very often, as in the following instance, the school response was a detour around the issue.

> Balginder and I had to walk under this bridge on the way to school. There would be boys up on the bridge and they would throw things down on us and after one time when Balginder was hit by a stone we went to Mr Gray (assistant head) and he said we should go a different way to school.

Extending our research from schools to employment agencies and the workplace, we found institutional racism to be deeply embedded in language, body language and stereotypes, often at an unconscious level, attended by immediate denial of prejudice of any kind. The study was conducted in 1986 and two a half decades later much has changed by way of information and legislation, while for some children and families, very little has changed. The final irony of our studied inclusion of life stories from minority ethnic groups was to open us to attack from the more militant wing of the anti-racist lobby who questioned my credentials, as a white man, to interview black people. I ought, by virtue of my 'race' (and inherent racism as a white person), to have been disqualified from entering such contentious and precious territory, regardless of the powerful stories that put issues of discrimination and racism centre stage on the policy agenda.

## On reflection

Can policy ideologues, research purists and pragmatists ever agree on a common cause and an 'entente cordiale' that might promote genuine improvement? What latitude exists, or might exist, to open to question the orthodoxies and heresies that have proved so divisive both within, and between the arcane worlds of policy and research? In every sphere – inclusion, school effectiveness, leadership, the home–school interface, racism and anti-racism – there often appears to be little common ground between the big enders and little enders, or common cause between the dutifully compliant and the defiant risk-takers. The series of studies with Maurice Galton, which we entitled *A Life in Teaching?*, was attended by a question mark, the answer dependent on how far policymakers will be willing to go to give credence to important messages from research findings at the front line.

## Notes

1   MacBeath, J., Gronn, P., Opfer, D., Lowden, K., Forde, C., Cowie, M. and O'Brien, J. (2009) *The Recruitment and Retention of Headteachers in Scotland: Report to the Scottish Government*, Edinburgh, Scottish Government Social Research.
2   From King's College, Paul Black, Dylan Wiliam, Bethan Marshall, Joanna Swan; from the Open University, Bob McCormick; from Reading University, Patrick Carmichael, Geoff Southworh, Les Honor; from Cambridge, Mary James, Colin Conner, Sue Swaffield, David Pedder and myself.

# Part III
# The third lens

# 5 International agencies and agents provocateurs

To what extent are the lives of children, their teachers and their parents enriched or diminished by globalisation and its agents – the OECD, the European Union, the World Bank, Commonwealth organisations and other international entrepreneurs? How do we find and identify the best school in the world – the task given to us by the world's largest publishing company and philanthropic organisation. And what of the self-appointed gurus and 'agents provocateurs' who promise to change our lives by grasping our unlimited potential, constrained only by our lack of self belief? Through this third lens we may, perhaps, see less darkly the powerful forces that give shape to our educational experience, social lives and decision making.

## People watching on the left bank

If you are lucky enough to find an empty table at Les Deux Magots on Boulevard St Germain you can join in the favoured pastime of people watching, a constant procession of elegant 'dames', toy dogs, eccentrics and badly dressed tourists. If you spend enough time at the Deux Magots ('Magot', not what you think – 'a stocky figurine from the Far East'), you are bound to see someone you know or, as the website has it, 'you are sure to come across a personality from the art world, literature, fashion, entertainment and politics'. You may be seated where James Joyce, Bertold Brecht, Stefan Sweig, Verlaine, Rimbaud and Mallarmé, and Hemingway once sat. You may of course choose to take your pastis next door at the Café Flore where Sartre, Camus and Picasso were regular clients. At either of your chosen venues you are a short stroll from the Luxembourg gardens, Saint Suplice (the unlikely site for the filming of *Angels and Demons*), the bookstores on Boulevard Saint Michel, the bouqinistes on the Quai, the Sorbonne and the Musee d'Orsay, home to a stunning collection of the impressionists. It is here, just in front of the museum on Rue Bellechasse, that you can catch the bus to a leafy residential area in which the OECD headquarters are located.

The Organisation for Economic Co-operation and Development is now perhaps the single most influential source on government policy worldwide, its impact is felt by a five year old, unaware that her failure to read may be the cause of her teacher's anxiety, who may in turn be equally unaware that her angst stems from the pressures on her senior managers to respond to the politicians, who in turn are paying close attention to international comparative data emerging from the OECD. The comparative statistics serve not only to create international 'league tables', but are treated as 'indicators' of a nation's educational health. The OECD has captured the market on indicators, and is now the singular most authoritative source on the quality and performance of educational systems internationally.

Andreas Schleicher, Division Head and coordinator of the OECD Programme for International Student Assessment (PISA) and the OECD Indicators of Education Systems Programme, is currently the most celebrated, widely travelled speaker on the international conference circuit. 'The World's Schoolmaster', the title awarded him by Amanda Ripley in *Atlantic* magazine (July/August 2011), is an apt description of his style, his authority and the lessons with which no one in his class would dare to dissent. Who could take issue with compass, detail or reliability of the dazzling array of data he presents? Ripley writes:

> Arne Duncan, President Obama's secretary of education, consults with Schleicher and uses his work to compel change at the federal and state levels. 'He understands the global issues and challenges as well as or better than anyone I've met,' Duncan said to me. 'And he tells me the truth.' This year, U.K. Education Secretary Michael Gove called Schleicher 'the most important man in English education' – never mind that Schleicher is German and lives in France.

To 'compel' change and 'to tell the truth' are worrisome in equal measure, but so compelling was Schleicher's appearance at the New York Summit in 2011 that he was to do a repeat performance the following year, with Arne Duncan, US Secretary of Education, a constant presence over the two days – Michael Gove, Education Minister, preferring to spend time in Washington with bigger fish than 'the most important man in English education'! This unique event, organised by the US Department of Education, OECD and Education International, brought together teacher unions and education ministers from 23 countries,[1] agreeing on the need to reform and improve standards and teaching quality. This was the second summit organised by the US Department of Education, OECD and Education International, with agreement that over the two summits an important step forward had been made by establishing an international dialogue between education unions and education ministers on a range of professional issues.

Arne Duncan was applauded for his support and endorsement over two successive conferences, staying throughout to respond to questions and contributors from within the US and from other country delegations. There was none of the dissent or rancour to be found in other political arenas where teacher unions have been less celebrated. Attending the second World

Education Summit in New York, I politely queried some of the data, or at least their implications, recalling Schleicher's own contribution to our Routledge book *Re-inventing Schools, Reforming Teaching*, in which he said that 'without longitudinal studies we will never sufficiently understand what is cause and what is effect' (p143).

## Escape under cover of darkness

March 2012 was an aberration. In New York it was 70 degrees for most of the week, which meant that much time was spent in the Stygian gloom of the windowless Hilton conference centre while delegates' partners disported themselves in the sun-kissed Central Park a few city blocks north. During some of the more tedious perorations I was able to escape, as strategic seating near the rear entrance allowed discreet entrance and egress aided by the cover of darkness.

In the final session, each of the twenty-three countries presented the lessons they would take forward into national policy. A third of them mentioned some form of differential performance pay. An intervention by Ben Levin, for me a highlight of the proceedings, was an elegant and succinct demythologizing of performance pay, summarising an impressive body of international evidence, convincing enough for those countries' representatives to return to the table to promise a policy review. Hopefully some would have read my own critique in the book *The Future of the Teaching Profession* – thanks to Guntar Catlaks, 200 copies of which were available free to delegates.

## The conception, birth and delivery of education indicators

Indicators were, from their inception and protracted delivery, to become a 'cause célèbre' with the OECD. Its love affair with indicators may be dated to 1991 when the General Assembly met in Lugano, Switzerland in a balmy September. I had attended the gestation and birth of the OECD programme, presenting a paper on 'ethos indictors' that we were then developing in Scotland. It received a mixed reception, failing to impress the hard-line attainment junkies. The dashboard became the adopted metaphor for indicators, a blinking orange or red light denoting that something required closer attention. While policymakers wanted hard measures, it was widely agreed that indicators should not be taken simply at face value and that distinctions be made between indicators as 'measures', as 'pointers' and as 'can openers'. The notion of 'can openers' has, for me, been their primary value and been integral to research and development work in numerous international forums since.

Following the Lugano conference, the development of indicators was to be put in hands of four development groups, imaginatively entitled Networks A, B, C, D. Network A was alphabetically and substantively the most 'serious', concerned as it was with 'hard' attainment data on a student learning outcomes. Network B was devoted to labour market destinations, Network C to schools and school processes. The 'soft', and clearly least 'sérieux' of networks, was D, chaired by the Dutch, and originally comprising seven countries – the UK, the US, Denmark, Belgium, Portugal and Spain as well as the Dutch. The Network was, however, so laboriously chaired by the Dutch delegate ('I now give the floor to Denmark'), that after three successive meetings in which nothing had moved forward, rumbles of discontent began over coffee breaks and evening meals, the United States delegates threatening to withdraw their patronage. To avert such a disaster, the US being key players in all four networks, hatched a cunning plan over lunch. I was nominated to ask the chair's indulgence for a brainstorming session that I would lead for the entire afternoon. We made such dramatic process in one session that we were able to map a project. The chair was passed gratefully from the Netherlands to Scotland.

## A time and place for conviviality

It not only proved to be a fruitful partnership, as the study took progressive shape in travel to Lahti in Finland, Copenhagen, El Escorial in Spain and Washington DC, but there was also a lesson in decision making in international ventures such as this. With exquisite timing, Washington DC was chosen at the time of the football World Cup. I had the opportunity to attend the USA–Colombia match with Roel Bosker, at which the 'the Gentleman of Football', Andrés Escobar Saldarriaga, was to score a fateful own goal. On return home to Medellín, he would pay for it with his life. It is widely believed that he was murdered due to his luckless goal having caused gambling losses to several powerful drug lords.

Our cultural education was further enriched by a subsequent well-researched site visit – El Escorial in Spain. The high point of the informal agenda was a visit to the sumptuous palace of the Bourbons, with paintings by Titian, Tintoretto, Veronese, Luca Girodano, Ribera, Zurbaran, El Greco, Van der Weyden and Velazquez. The burial vaults of all the kings of Spain since Charles V was a stunning display of wealth that these former monarchs would never be able to witness. Equally impressive is the library housing 45,000 books from the fifteenth and sixteenth centuries, as well as 5,000 manuscripts in Arabic, Latin, and Spanish, all bathed in a warm light from the surrounding high-vaulted windows.

A ritual occasion in all of our meetings was the celebration of national drinks, inaugurated by Archie McGlynn, HMCI who would, with the aid of a flipchart and a map of Scotland, close the first day session with a short lesson on Scottish malt whiskies, tasting of various malts included. Emulating this modeling behavior, delegates began to bring their own national drinks. I captured this ritual on video, a lesson in ethos creation and international bonding but, with mistaken judgment, replayed this piece of bonhomie at an OECD conference in Edinburgh. Archie was taken aside and reprimanded by his immediate superiors, but it was I who had spilled the beans.

Back on task, the remit of Network D was to develop indicators of public expectations and satisfaction that would serve as international comparative measures. Comparing attainment data across school systems was clearly a less ambiguous remit than trying to define what we might understand as 'public', 'expectations' and 'satisfaction', and then gathering data that would be reliable and comparable in English, French, Danish, Dutch, Finnish, Portuguese, Spanish and Swedish, not to mention the challenge in each of these countries of defining and finding a representative sample.

The instrument we settled on eventually was a questionnaire. The debate over whether to structure it with four or five categories of response was theological and protracted. Four response categories such as *strongly agree, agree, disagree, strongly disagree* would push people in one direction, while a fifth middle category (*neither agree nor disagree*) could allow a cop out, so diminishing the value of the data. Where the fifth category might sit within the scale (middle or end) could arouse heated passions. The adoption of a double-sided format was accepted after more extended discussion. It would require two responses to each statement, on the one hand the agreement options, and on the other hand a matching set of responses – *not at all important, quite important, important* or *very important*. With two scales, one on practice and one on importance, it would offer us a gap analysis, measuring the distance between 'where we are' and 'where we would like to be'. It became quickly apparent that on virtually every item 'very important' would be chosen, so preventing any meaningful disaggregation. I was despatched to visit a polling company in London to draw on their expertise. It proved to be a hugely valuable experience, not simply solving the problem and informing the OECD study, but providing a questionnaire template for research studies that would use this format over the next two decades. The simple solution was to skew the right-hand (importance) scale to discriminate among the positives – 'important', 'very important' and 'crucial'.

The translation of these response categories into other languages might seem fairly unproblematic, but there was a vital lesson to be learned as to how meanings are constructed in different cultural and linguistic settings. For example, the questionnaire response category 'quite important' was rendered as 'bastant importante' (Portuguese) and 'bastante importante' (Spanish). However, when the data came back from Portugal and Spain it became belatedly apparent that 'bastant' and 'bastante' are quite significantly different in meaning.

## The OECD revisited

My re-acquaintance with the OECD came in 2010 when I was invited to be a member of a team undertaking country reviews, in this case about as far as one can travel while remaining on the same planet – to Wellington, New Zealand. In late August we visited schools and held over thirty-three focus groups with young people, parents, teachers, school principals, professional associations and unions, Pacifika and Maori stakeholders. These took place over the course of eight consecutive days (Sunday off for good behaviour), often beginning at 8am and finishing at 9pm, working through lunch and dinner. The four-person team comprised Danny Laveault from Ottawa and myself as the external consultants and Deborah Nusche and Paolo Santiago from the OECD, much practised in the art of country reviews, intensive work and political diplomacy.

Country reviews, carried out by an OECD team, offer an analysis of evaluation and assessment policies in the country, and recommendations for policy development and implementation from an international perspective. A country review involves 'an intensive country visit to fully understand the country's context, policies and practices and includes meetings with all major stakeholders. After the visit, the review team prepares a Country Review report'. The scope and focus of each review is determined by the country, in consultation with the Secretariat, depending on the present arrangements, their strengths and challenges, and country priorities. By providing an external perspective on evaluation and assessment issues, the country reviews are also intended to contribute to national discussions and inform other countries about policy innovations underway.

Of the fourteen countries signing up to such a review the choice of New Zealand was a valuable opportunity to gain an in-depth understanding of policy and practice. New Zealand has probably gone furthest among countries internationally towards a collaborative school evaluation model, incorporating at the same time a sequential process. In the sequential model, schools conduct their own internal review followed by a visit from the external team. New Zealand's approach is collaborative in the sense that both parties attempt to work together to agree on a rounded picture of the school in which there is mutual recognition of its strengths and consensus on areas for development. 'Building a picture of the school', according to Education Review Office (ERO) staff, relies on an integration of school self-review and external review, taking the most useful aspects from both. The choice of success criteria, indicators and evaluative questions, provide the framework and tools for the creation of a collaborative portrait.

The role of students in self-evaluation is explicitly commented on in the final report.[2] Students have a part to play in evaluating the quality of their school as well as contributing to external review. Including them requires that they are party to the language of assessment, evaluation and review and that they have the confidence to articulate their views as well as their concerns. There is exemplary evidence from schools visited by the OECD team that school leaders and teachers have taken this issue seriously and have equipped their students with the skills and vocabulary to talk to external visitors on achievement and quality issues. External review works on the principle that schools' own self-review should be so embedded in its daily practice that the visit of an external body is neither disruptive nor unwelcome. The apparent receptivity of schools to external review does suggest that the earlier apprehension of 'inspection' has been removed or at least attenuated. The generally positive response to reviews by school staff and teacher organisations may be explained by its non-threatening nature, its positive focus on good practice, its receptivity to the school's own efforts at improvement and its primarily formative character. Unlike many other systems, review reports do not attach labels or numerical categories and there is no rhetoric of failing schools.

In common with systems elsewhere that are moving toward proportional review, New Zealand's differentiated review cycle is exemplary. Reviews may occur over the course of one to two years, or every three or four to five years, depending on a number of judgments about the school's performance across the six dimensions of good practice. The key is whether the school has developed a high-quality and useful self-review framework and practice across the key six dimensions.

Essential to any collaborative model is a high level of trust on both sides. Seen as low in threat, it does not provoke high anxiety and is formative in intent. This assumes particular importance in Māori-medium schools where imposition of a set of standardised criteria would be an anathema, failing to take account of the peculiar culture and history of Māori communities.

## Flirting with the gurus

On return from the intensity of the New Zealand experience I received an email that required a dramatic conceptual shift from the world of measurement and scientific 'truth' to a world of truths cast in a diametrically different mould. It would be a challenge of a high order to find the common ground between the OECD's pursuit of rational objectivity on the one hand and the highly subjective, emotionally charged, world of the self-help gurus on the other. How I came to inhabit both universes for a short period is, in retrospect, something of a mystery, but to be an insider in these two irreconcilable domains of human endeavor proved to be a valuable learning experience. The email came from one Michael Heppell, with whom I had collaborated in schools and educational conferences before his rise to international stardom. Michael, a one-time roofing tradesman, had serendiptitously found himself in the employ of Mindstore – a Glasgow-based company with a mission to change hearts and minds, primarily the former. The email from Michael read as follows:

> I think it's only fair to warn you of my communication plans for August. I'm going to send you five (weekly) emails rather than fortnightly ones. And each one will contain some information about my new book which is due to be published on 3rd September.
>
> I'm going to do everything I can to whet your appetite and encourage you to buy it. There will be samples of the book, special offers and lots of incentives for you to invest a few pounds on what I think is my best book yet.
>
> It's called *The Edge: How the Best Get Better*.
> Be Brilliant[3]

## Meet Jack Black

My introduction to Michael had been through a Strathclyde colleague who campaigned over a period of weeks for me to get in touch with one Jack Black, who was filling theatres and the Glasgow Concert Hall on a regular basis with a stage performance that was sustained over two full days. As someone who was loathe to give a lecture that lasted more than fifty minutes I could not help but be impressed by someone who could hold an audience's attention for two days. My assumption that fifty minutes was about the length of human endurance was a legacy of sitting weekly through Sunday sermons that fell only a little short of the full hour, complemented by almost equally lengthy and tedium-inducing prayers.

Following an invited audience with Jack at Glasgow's Rogano restaurant, where I was careful to eat only salad and water (having previously been counseled to abjure harmful drugs such as coffee or tea), I was invited to a two-day BlackFest at which Jack would hold the stage for six hours at a stretch. The centerpiece of Jack's presentation was a virtual visit to the house on the right (or was it left?) bank. With eyes closed Jack would transport us to the virtual house and take us through the rooms, shedding preconceptions, hang-ups and anxieties as we travelled deeper into the Alpha state of brain activity, while exercising care not to be crass enough to fall asleep. Jack introduced me to things I ought perhaps to have read or known about such as the Alpha, Beta, Delta and Gamma brain rhythms, NLP, or neuro-linguistic programming, and the attendant power of words to disenfranchise the brain and emotional intelligence. A lexicon of terms was expressively forbidden, so the mandated response to the invitation 'how are you?' was 'fantastic' as the standard Glasgow retort 'no bad' was, he informed us, a virulent toxin. One of Jack's proof of this particular pudding was to invite someone on stage – the bigger stronger and more powerful the better – and to get the victim to hold out his preferred arm, to think of a word such as 'fantastic' while Jack would exert pressure on the arm and try to push it down, the volunteer often ending up hanging off a close imitation of a steel beam. This was followed by asking the subject to imagine, or say a negative word such as 'tired' or 'bored', at which the steel beam would miraculously become a floppy appendage that a could be overcome by the mere application of a gentle push. This could equally be demonstrated by the victim holding a cup or coffee or even thinking of coffee, so proving that caffeine could be just as powerful as the word. I have to admit that I shamelessly plagiarised this trick on a number of occasions, even with Cambridge PhD students, and on no occasion did it ever let me down.

The idea of packaging Jack into a series of manuals and accompanying video seemed like a good idea at the time and, attracted by the challenge, I embarked on writing modules that would take people through some of the big ideas with accompanying theoretical underpinnings and challenging questions. The pack was to include a series of intimate conversations with Jack, to be shot on the bonny banks of Loch Lomond with long shots of us both walking the shores and close ups of us standing by some scenic rock formations looking across the sun-dappled waters. In the event it started to snow about halfway through our Socratic dialogues and Jack, who had begun to shiver and lose his usual fluency, decided to call it a day. After a couple of days in the editing studio, mixing the Lochside conversazione with footage from the Jack's stand-up presentations it became obvious that whoever had been hired to shoot the conference hall footage could not match the quality of the Loch Lomond walkabout and the whole enterprise was regrettably shelved.

My last meeting with Jack was in Glasgow airport as I returned from Singapore with his wife Norma and the young pretender Michael Heppell (soon to acquire guru status on his own account). Norma, a former teacher, had been working on a parallel track to her husband, conducting inspirational seminars for teachers and life-enhancing workshops for children. These were framed around Mindstore's self-help principles and self-affirming language. In a Glasgow culture, where self-deprecation and fatalism was the common currency, Norma's relentlessly upbeat workshops were designed to offer an antithesis to the downbeat 'cannae' ('cannot do') world view. Jack's toolbox of Mindstore instruments were applied to a school and classroom context with some demonstrable success. The bell jar, for example, could be deployed as an antidote to bullying or negativity in general. Lowering the bell jar around oneself at any given moment meant that personal insults and censored words bounced off the imaginary surface leaving self-esteem and a positive Weltanshauung intact.

One of Jack's less successful outings was to a secondary school in the deepest parts of Lanarkshire where, despite being the birthplace of David Livingstone, missionary work had previously perished on the rocks of a 'cannae' culture. For two days Jack would lead the whole staff through his repertoire while I would act as evaluator on behalf of the local authority who were footing the bill. The house on the right (or was it 'left') bank was where the occasion began to unravel. It was a revelation to me that fundamentalist religious groups such as the Brethren would not enter into a virtual adventure that involved closing one's eyes, as it is at these moments that the devil may sneak in. Nor did everyone take kindly to the injunction that no coffee should pass their lips over the two days. While Jack did enlist a number of new converts, my evaluation never saw the light of day.

## Finding the hero inside yourself

Michael, by nature an exuberant optimist, has never been short of self belief and when the opportunity arose to attend and present a 'paper' at the Thinking Skills Conference in Singapore in 1997 he was quick to grasp the moment. The ninety-minute seminar involved a presentation by myself (academic theory) and Michael (exuberant showmanship). It was so successful that there were numerous complaints from those that had been unable to gain entry to the small room in which our seminar was being held. Michael managed to convince the organisers to arrange a further session which, to Michael's delight and my consternation, was held in the main plenary hall with over 150 people. While addressing 150 academics or teachers had never fazed me, evangelising on the curative properties of positive thinking was not something I was prepared for, even as the supporting cast, but Michael carried the day. It was a seminal moment. It was enough to convince Michael that he could be just as charismatic and persuasive as his erstwhile employer, Jack Black, and to be convinced that there was a ready-made market for his role in changing people's lives. And so it has proved.

Fast forward to 2013. Michael is author of six books, three of which have become best-sellers, plus an audio book. On Radio Two the broadcaster Chris Evans ran out of superlatives, recommending Michael's life-enhancing book as his Christmas choice – 'a great, great read'. Over the last decade Michael has worked with international corporations, his clients and advocates including Microsoft, Vauxhall, RBS, O2, WH Smith, Virgin Atlantic, Little Chef, Morgan Sindall, AXA, Scottish Power, Association of Colleges, NHS Scotland, Asda, the Metropolitan Police, Argos, Pearson and EDF Energy.

Finding the hero inside yourself is the mantra at the heart of the self-help industry. There is, we are to be persuaded, a dormant genius inside ourselves waiting to be released by the power of positive thinking. Where there is failure, in education, in life, it is down to a lack of self belief . Where there is success it is through the embrace of a 'can do' outlook, a triumph of the will that precedes and lays the groundwork for the skill. Richard Branson, Steve Jobs, Anita and a host of 'self made' men and women are proof of the possible.

This school of thought can claim empirical validation for the power of positive thinking with highly-respected psychologists and educationists such as Seligman, with his treatise on 'learned helplessness', the now widely-known 'self fulfilling prophecy', and Carol Dweck's identification of positive and negative 'mindsets'. NLP, although treated with scepticism by academics, holds that it is the very power of the words we choose that creates or diminishes mental capacity and approach to life's challenges.

Michael had always been generous to me as his inspiration, and a few years ago he invited me to run a one-day workshop for 100 disciples, preceded by an extravagant introduction, raising expectation well beyond what I was capable of fulfilling. In the event I was to crash and burn on the rocks of inflated anticipation. I was not able to provide 'the cure to an average life' or play the role of 'shot-gunning a bucket of espresso' as Michael himself has been described. What could have been a challenging workshop (a repeat of what had been well received by an alternate 100, less religious, participants) was too cerebral. Happy clappy, standing on chairs and reciting affirmations was not within my all too serious and staid repertoire.

It is tempting to dismiss the evangelism and to take refuge in one's own academic rigour, but it is more difficult to gainsay the numerous individuals whose lives have been changed by an injection of self belief or the companies that have been re-invented by a change in mindset. I remain an ambivalent sceptic caught between the dismissive world of academe and the world of the evangelicals, of which my father was, unashamedly, devoutly one.

## On reflection

For a proper academic it would a shameful confession to reveal that one had flirted with the gurus of the self-help industry. Changing hearts and minds is their business, with an emphasis on the former, while for academics it is only the mind that counts. As Sir Ken Robinson famously observed at a Cambridge seminar, academics appear to believe that their bodies are simply vehicles to take their heads from one venue to the next. As was shown in numerous studies for the OECD, minds are only genuinely receptive to policy initiatives when the prospect of change is seen as low in threat, does not provoke high anxiety and when there is a measure of trust on both sides. There may, after all, be some meeting ground of the affective domain and the domain of 'hard' data.

## Notes

1   Participating countries and regions were: Belgium, Canada, Denmark, Estonia, Finland, Germany, Hong Kong SAR, Hungary, Iceland, Indonesia, Japan, the Netherlands, New Zealand, Norway, the People's Republic of China, Poland, the Republic of Korea, Singapore, Slovenia, Sweden, Switzerland, the United Kingdom and the United States.
2   Nusche, D., Laveault, D., MacBeath, J. and Santiago, P. (2011) *OECD Reviews of Evaluation and Assessment in Education: New Zealand*, Paris, OECD
3   Online. Available at http://michaelheppell.com/ (accessed 9 September 2012).

# 6  Cogitamus ergo sumus
## We think therefore we are

Carpe Vitam (seize life) is the name of the Stockholm-based organization that sponsored a programme and set of principles which would travel globally – a reminder of how we are divided not only by differing linguistic conventions but also by a common language. The second half of this chapter tells the story of an equally far-travelled project, involving 101 schools in twenty-one countries, in which school students played a central role, none more so than Serena, who was to become the heroine of a book, in German translation bearing the title *Serena, or: how people can change their school*. This chapter opens with the legacy of fascism and closes with a historic reminder of its devastating impact.

## The Wallenberg dynasty

In Raoul Wallenberg Place, close to the Baltic Sea and in the centre of old Stockholm, there is a statue in honour of Raoul Wallenberg, the Swedish diplomat whose courage, spirit and ingenuity saved the lives of over 100,000 Jews in Budapest during the Second World War. Raoul Wallenberg has no grave. Arrested by Russian troops in January 1945, his fate has since remained a mystery. The lives of those he rescued are his greatest memorial – the tens of thousands of Hungarian Jews he saved from the Nazi machine. He remains a controversial figure in Swedish mythology, the Wallenberg family itself a continuing subject for debate.

Perhaps less well known but also never too far from making history, Peder Wallenberg is a legend in his own lifetime, a visionary for whom no world-changing project is beyond his imagination. He is disappointed that his plan to revolutionise the Stockholm transport system, with train-cum-bus services running under the lakes connecting Stockholm's islands, never came to fruition, but he can point to other significant enterprises that are changing the lives of generations to come. A Google search, for example, describes him as owner and designer of the Mövenpick Resort in Qusseir in Egypt, one of seventy-two projects including a vocational centre, a women's development centre and a waste-recycling project, in addition to numerous efforts to renovate historical buildings. Excavation behind the Mövenpick revealed that this is the site of the Roman Empire's most important port in the East. Through his irresistible persuasion he encouraged the mayor of Qusseir to create a new corniche, and First Lady Mubarak to donate a library to the town and Radisson to build a new hotel. Just over a decade ago, as Peder describes it, 'The city was utterly dirty and all the men were doing was sitting in the streets chewing herbs to clean their teeth'.

Peder's keenest interest is in education and, on his own estate outside Stockholm, he built a school that was inevitably unconventional, embodying his belief that 'by listening to the children they can pass all standard exams despite learning difficulties. It proves that they do not have learning difficulties – the difficulties are with someone else.' And it was through Peder's good offices that eighty teachers from six countries found themselves in Copenhagen in May 2004.

## A play in four acts

The Danish artist Gruntvig may be little known outside his own country, but he is celebrated in Copenhagen with a statue in his honour. It stands in the courtyard of a conference centre, quintessentially Danish, its main rooms minimalist, light wood floors, its simple Nordic furnishing allowing attention to be given to the paintings on the three walls. The room and the adjoining open spaces lend themselves well to table groups and the three days of interactive sessions, in which cross-country groups begin to shape the five Leadership for Learning principles that are destined to travel internationally many years into the future. This is the venue for the third Carpe Vitam conference, a seminal juncture in the project, captured by one of Grundtvig's masterpieces, a figure pointing in both directions, to the past and to the future – perhaps.

## In the beginning

It began in Stockholm with a meeting of an expert panel brought together to review our proposal for a LfL research programme which would, in the first instance, be a collaboration of five sites in four countries – the US (Seattle and New Jersey), Denmark, England and Austria. Its common purpose would be to explore the three concepts of 'leadership', 'learning' and their interconnections as they played out in differing cultural contexts. Three research questions, derived from cross-country conversations prior to the beginning of our study, were intended to reflect what, for all of us, were common concerns.

- How is leadership understood in different contexts?
- How is learning understood and promoted within different schools and policy contexts?
- What is the relationship between leadership and learning?

Each country would comprise teams of school leaders, teachers, parents and (where possible) students from three schools, willing to research their own practice and commit themselves to three years that would, as it transpired, take them to Cambridge, Innsbruck, Copenhagen and Athens. With the later addition of Greece, Norway and Australia, there were twenty-four schools and just short of eighty participant 'researchers'. Built into the project from the outset was the ongoing support and consultancy of a critical friend, one of the University team with the remit of helping to carry the momentum, acting as a bridge between the research and development processes. Drawing on the experience of other projects in which critical friends had worked alongside researchers, the intention was to build a relationship of trust such that teachers would feel supported in critical analyses of current practice and feel confidence in venturing into new ways of thinking about their roles as learners and leaders.

Travelling and learning together, through the highs and lows, contention and celebration, we characterised Carpe Vitam as a journey in the four classic stages of storming, forming, norming and performing. Was it inevitable that we would have to progress inexorably through these four stages? That we could do nothing to accelerate their progress to their final resolution? While language and its conceptual underpinnings was one of the Rubicons to be crossed, there were also deeper issues of relationships, of authority, historical and cultural convention.

In Cambridge (Act I) when teachers, principals and parents from four countries came together for the first time, a predominating characteristic of the occasion was brainstorming, puzzlement, frustration over linguistic conventions, struggles with researchers' terminology and considerable reluctance to embrace the term 'research'. Much of the time was invested in trying to come to terms with different conceptions of learning and leadership, let alone the link between them.

A year on in Innsbruck (Act II), storming, although not left behind, had given way to greater 'norming'. There were beginnings of a common language and some notable examples of sharing of practice that had taken place over the intervening twelve months. Teachers and headteachers had begun to share leadership dilemmas, acting as critical friends across national boundaries. Incipient networks were beginning to take shape and cross-country exchanges and visits were negotiated. To depict a neat linear progression from storming to norming would, however, be simplistic. Many participants continued to struggle to make the leadership-learning connections and to see their applications within the policy context in which they worked. There was a continuing restlessness among the English group, measuring the cost-benefit equation of a week away from the intensity of school life in Newham and Tower Hamlets – with unforgiving targets to be met, time invested in thinking and talking needing to be repaid by some tangible takeaway.

We characterised Act III, one year on in Copenhagen, as 'performing'. Participants brought to their third meeting deeper experiences of inter-country exchanges and ongoing conversations. Workshops were led by teachers, documenting their learning, in an atmosphere of greater trust, opening up leadership issues to greater scrutiny, offering vignettes to illustrate the connection between learning and leadership. Visits to Danish schools had, for some, a profound impact on their thinking. For some of the English group these visits began to dispel much of the anxiety, as they were confronted with practice so removed from the high pressure environment of their own schools that it gave pause for revisiting of previous assumptions and, for some, a determination to return to their own schools with new vision and commitment. So exhilarated was one Newham assistant headteacher that he vowed then and there to move to Denmark.

Act IV, Athens, was portrayed as 'reforming'. Change was tangible and exhilarating. Research was no longer something to be viewed with apprehension but rather as integral to learning and leadership. The research teams' 'manifesto', presented as our emerging theory, was dissected and re-presented by country groups with sharp and sometimes, for us, uncomfortable critique. Our emerging theoretical principles of Leadership for Learning, accepted in Copenhagen without much demur, were now shredded creatively and critically as each country group came up to present their views. The written reflections after each of these four conferences bear testimony to the impact of the intellectual distance travelled.

This process captures something of what happens in an international project, although not in a simple linear sequence, but in small cycles or eddies of dissonance and resolution, disequilibrium and stability. There were peaks of enthusiasm and embrace of new ideas when school principals and teachers came together for extended conferencing and workshops to exchange stories and theories of practice. There were troughs when they returned to their schools to be met with other pressing priorities and impatient government mandates. One of the most tangible exemplars of change was in a return visit to Greek schools. An English headteacher who had visited one of the Greek schools two years before said this in a feedback session on the visits:

> I could not believe this was the same school I visited a couple of years back. The change was phenomenal and visible everywhere you went. It was like people were speaking a different language, thinking differently, doing things differently. The whole ethos of the place had changed beyond recognition.

## Questionnaires as tin openers

A baseline questionnaire was constructed to give us a set of perspectives on schools at the outset of the project so that over time we might be able to assess changes in thinking about practice, re-administering the questionnaire three years on to give a picture of change. It took two days of laboured discussion in Cambridge to discuss and frame each individual question so the intent would be the same in each of the five languages, starting with the term 'leader' itself, as *Führer* had too many unhappy resonances in an Austrian context. 'Learning' was hardly less problematic, as in Danish, Norwegian, German and Greek there were unique cultural constructions to be shared and a common language found to share them in. And for the English the American term 'instruction' sat uncomfortably with 'teaching', or better still 'pedagogy'.

While subjecting questionnaire data to factor analysis, the validity of items and clusters of items really only began to be tested in the process of dialogue, when findings were fed back to schools, to clusters of schools nationally and internationally at conference workshops. These held up a mirror to current practice, setting in train a dialogue and engaging differing understandings of school priorities within and between schools. Opportunities for reflection on the data allowed participating school staff to discover meaning in the bland statistics at school, school cluster and cross-country levels. Problematising these data in conversations raised the question of whether these were measures of school effects, or were indicators of something more deeply embedded in national and local cultures – or in the nature of scholastic discourse in these varying linguistic contexts. While sense-making came in part through interrogation of the data within and across country groups, an important complement to this were qualitative data – interviews, shadowing, portraits, workshops and school visits and recording of the discussions that took place at the four international conferences.

### A critical friend

In Athens the presence, and prescience, of Harvard's David Perkins as our critical friend lent a sharper edge to the collective endeavour. He brought with him visible thinking routines – 'simple patterns of thinking that can be used over and over again and folded easily into learning in the subject areas. They have a public nature, so that they make thinking visible, and students quickly get used to them'. The depth and power of the simple routine such as 'What makes you say that?' was exemplified by presenting a work of art that we are invited to study for a protracted period. Accustomed to glancing at, rather than studying, works of art, participants became a little impatient, wondering if there was anything else to see. Debriefing our perceptions, the simple question 'What's going on here?' and the subsequent probe 'What makes you say that?' were to generate a conversation that lasted well into the morning. I was reminded of the dictum by Abraham Heschel in his book *The Prophets*[1] – 'We must learn to know what we see rather than seeing what we already know'. It also brought to mind one of the Geert Hofstede's principles – of ambiguity – the discomfort and engagement that come from uncertainty and lack of closure, from the need to the complete the crossword, the Sudoku or insert the missing piece in the jigsaw. Together with his colleague Shari Tishman. David Perkins had written:

> Using the language of thinking is one element of something more important: being a model of thoughtfulness for one's students. Teachers

who do not expect instant answers, who display their own honest uncertainties, who take a moment to think about 'What if' or 'What if not' or 'How else could this be done?' or 'What's the other side of the case?' express respect for the process of thought and implicitly encourage students to notice problems and opportunities and think them through.

LfL thinking routines were destined to travel widely and powerfully. The furthest travelled perhaps (Hong Kong, the US, Argentina, Chile, Slovenia, Poland, Malaysia, Ghana) is Think-Pair-Share, its very simplicity commending itself to teachers, whether in primary, secondary and special schools, as well as in universities and colleges of education. The routine involves posing a question, asking students to take a few minutes of thinking time and then to share their thoughts with a partner, perhaps writing down or sketching/doodling their thoughts before sharing.

In between the annual Carpe Vitam conferences, interim national conferences were held in order to keep alive the principles, their applications and teachers' commitment to the enterprise. On a number of visits to Princeton, the American contingent were strong supporters and advocates for Carpe Vitam and the ever resourceful David Green introduced us to Deidre, graffiti connoisseur, her moving tableau of words and images capturing the ongoing dialogue on a rolling wallpaper tableau.

I needed little inducement from Brad Portin to attend the three-day Seattle conference to be held, not in that most hospitable of American cities, but in a spectacular resort named after the mountain under which its sits in sybaritic isolation – Sleeping Lady.

### A sleeping lady, a wedding cake and a wide awake Alsatian

A Google search for 'sleeping lady' will take you to some predictable images, but the top hit is of spectacular vistas of snow covered peaks, luxuriously appointed log cabins, and inviting log fires in the bars and restaurants. As the website informs the would-be visitor:

> Nestled in the Cascade Mountains on the banks of Icicle Creek, just outside Leavenworth, WA. Sleeping Lady offers a distinct Northwest experience accented by sustainable gourmet cuisine and cozy accommodations.
>
> (www.sleepinglady.com)

One of the lasting contributions of the three-day workshop was the 'wedding cake'. It is depicted visually by three tiers – at its base student learning, at a second level professional learning and at the top layer system learning. Each layer is interconnected and interdependent, so that we come to grasp the nature of student learning through professional learning, while system learning is, in turn, dependent on, and feeds into, professional learning. It is a model that has since travelled widely and helped to frame our thinking not only within Carpe Vitam but in many other subsequent venues.

Phoning to confirm one's flight is something I had never done before but, perhaps in a flash of precognition, I phoned Northwest to be told that our flight to Amsterdam had been rerouted, as George W. Bush had commandeered all available 747s as troop carriers to Iraq. This, therefore, entailed an internal flight to Minneapolis and a connecting flight to Amsterdam. It was on the second leg from Minneapolis that I was to meet a most friendly, but also unusually large, Alsatian. He/it was sitting in my seat. Although we had paid a rather substantial sum for two business class seats, a somewhat brusque Northwest flight attendant informed us that there was only available one seat in business. While the only other available seat on the plane was the bulkhead aisle seat in economy. I gallantly proposed that my wife, Sandra, take the posh seat while I slummed it in economy. As the window seat was occupied by a generously proportioned black lady, whose equally well-proportioned legs left no room in front of her for the accompanying guide dog, it had taken up residence in my seat. Were it even to be persuaded to sit on the floor in front of me there would have been no room left for my legs. My complaint to the flight attendant fell on stony ground. It was abundantly clear she could not have cared less. The only solution was to invite lady and dog to change places with Sandra. The offer of a business class seat was accepted graciously and merited an enveloping bear hug and the immortal words, 'You are an angel'. The last I saw of my new-found canine friend it was introducing itself to the Business Class passenger Sandra had been sitting beside.

## *The beautiful project*

Carpe Vitam was to benefit from an ambitious international self-evaluation project that had taken place a few years earlier. Sponsored by the European Commission, 21 countries and 101 schools took part in the study designed to illustrate the power of three, juxtaposing the voices of young people, their parents and their teachers, each offering a lens through which to tell the story of their schools. Each of the 101 participating schools was provided with a toolbox of self-evaluation techniques and strategies, the centrepiece of which was the School Self Evaluation Form (SEF). As a prelude to using the tool-box, separate groups of students, teachers and parents would each rate their school according to the twelve criteria, then send two or three emissaries to a school evaluation group, which would then try to reach agreement on the ratings. This latter stage of the process was, as it transpired, to open up a rich and protracted discussion. Included in the group, the task of the critical friend was to push for evidence on judgments made. This was always more contentious than anticipated, but also proved highly revealing. Reconciling the differing perspectives that each stakeholder group brought to the discussion was both challenging and prolonged. The next stage of the process was to identify one or more of the twelve areas in relation to which the group would pursue further in-depth inquiry in their school over the coming year, reporting back in Vienna one year on.

The book that was published by Routledge following the project was unfortunately entitled *Self Evaluation in European Schools*, so failing to capture the ground-breaking nature of 'the beautiful project', as it was called by Anders Hinkel, European Head of Section in the EU. The German language version came much closer to the spirit of the endeavor – *Serena's Story*.

## Serena's story: where the bodies are buried

The stage setting for the creation of Serena's Story is a restaurant in Brussels. It is winter and a fire burns in the handsome stone fireplace. Having finished their meal with a generous accompaniment of red wine, the four project directors Michael Schratz from Austria, Denis Meuret from France, Lars Bo Jakobsen from the EU Directorate, and myself, are discussing how to tell the story of the project in a forthcoming book. While from four different countries, all four are fluent in English and have worked together for two years on the self-evaluation venture. There is shared enthusiasm for a fictionalised account of the project, with Eliot Eisner's American Education Research Association (AERA) Presidential address in 1993 still a resonant influence. He had argued, holding his own a against a powerful line-up of critics, that a novel may provide a more truthful account of the human condition than the most carefully honed research study.

As in Andre Brink's captivating book *A Chain of Voices*, the idea was that each chapter would take the narrative further with a different voice – Serena herself, Serena's mother, her teacher, the school principal, the project's critical friend and finally the researcher, a French sage modeled on our French team member, Denis Meuret. Each chapter would offer a different perspective on the objective and the subjective, what is 'real' and what is perceived. We might, had we read him then, have referred to Oscar Wilde's reference to the 'drab truth of an academic'. He had written, 'I prefer the other truth. Between the two truths the falser is the truer'.

Drawing on the current best-seller, *Sophie's World*, our Sophie would be Serena, the sole student to attend the previous Luxembourg conference, a representative from Sarah Bonnell School in Newham. She had stood up bravely to a not altogether friendly question-and-answer session, facing challenges from the European Association of Teachers. She described how self-evaluation could provide a more searching insight into the life of classrooms than an OFSTED inspection. She described how, in her school, students had loyally rallied round before the OFSTED inspection to help 'bury the bodies', characterising self-evaluation as 'leading you to where the bodies are buried'.

Half a year on, a much larger group of students would play a more substantive role in the Vienna conference and pave the way for the book. Our proposal to Routledge was for an upside-down book, one that could be turned over and read from either end – the fictionalised account or, alternatively, the more conventional description of the project. As this proposal proved to be a non-starter, the first six chapters were given to the chain of voices and the final six to more academic 'truthful' account, outlining the methodology, approach, tools and findings.

### Bridges across boundaries

'The beautiful project' so inspired an Italian policy advisor, Francesca Brotto, that she put forward a proposal for a further European Commission project to be entitled *Bridges Across Boundaries*, resulting in the further translation of the book into Italian, Greek, Polish, Slovakian, Czech, Hungarian and Portuguese, together with the previously published German version. Its scope and long-term benefits received a particular accolade from the European Union:

> The project worked with schools, and other 'end users', whereby these were testing and piloting the approach among themselves. Potential exploiters were engaged in the project. In terms of exploitation, there is evidence of continued use of the methodology as well as enquiries from new territories. There is ample evidence of a multiplier effect in terms of take-up by schools. There is also evidence of exploitation in terms of the project promoting policy debates in the partner countries. Interest in the project results continues, suggesting a longer term impact in terms of exploitation.
>
> (Cost-effectiveness Analysis of Dissemination and
> Exploitation Actions, European Commission, 2008: 22)

Francesca Brotto is not an archetypal Italian, indeed so untypical and so larger than life as to defy any categorization. Tall, willowy, blond and exuding self confidence, she is restlessly on the move, here one moment somewhere else the next, making it almost impossible to follow her whirlwind passage through a room. She speaks in immaculate unaccented English, the flow of her narrative hard to catch up with as new ambitious ventures and outrageous ideas unfold. She will take charge of ordering the wine and not allow her impatient colleagues to taste it until she judges it has been adequately chambréd.

### Lost in translation

The well-chambréd Syrah is our reward for a long day, struggling to find meaning in words and ideas lost in translation. It is a salutary lesson to discover how so much of our taken-for-granted ideas and assumptions are often simply incomprehensible to our audience. Two classic examples are the use of the words 'ethos' and 'agency'. Derived from the Greek, 'ethos' has a totally different meaning in that country and when we spoke at length about ethos and 'ethos indicators', what the Greeks audience heard was 'ethics'. In the Carpe Vitam project we had returned on repeated occasions to try to convey what was meant by 'agency', for some still a concept too far. Our Danish colleagues would not agree to any translation of 'Bildung' because, they argued, it has such a peculiar resonance that it would be compromised by any attempt at rendering it in another verbal currency.

Working at the translation on *Self Evaluation in European Schools* over two eight-hour days in Athens, the Czechs and Slovaks found a problem with 'academic achievement' as there appeared to be no equivalent term for this in their languages. 'Results as a consequence of study' could mislead as possibly referring to homework or home study. 'Acquisition of knowledge' proved to be a much broader and misleading equivalent. In Italian this idea has been rendered in the past as *profitto scolastico*, meaning how much you profit from being at school, but now translated as *rendimento scolastico*, it implied a return on investment made in schooling. Even 'education' carries very different meanings as the Hungarians tried to grapple with what it means in English, so often taken as synonymous with what happens in schools. This was, of course, over a decade ago and, thanks to the OECD and PISA, schools are getting accustomed to a common language, so that while the Czechs struggled with the notion of 'curriculum', that problem has apparently been solved by the adoption of the English terminology. This trend to a common language has, as Lejf Moos argues, complexified, rather than solved, the problem. The 'cultural isomorphs', as he calls them, are theories or concepts that look alike but are structured of quite different elements.

More than three years after the project's final conference in Budapest, wrote Francesca, undergraduate, postgraduate, teacher and headship education courses were being revised on the basis of the key *Bridges* principles. As she wrote:

> Dissertations have been based on them, academic circles, research institutes and practitioners refer to them and in Greece, Hungary and Slovakia new projects on self-evaluation and/or school leadership have built on the process. The new versions of the book have been influential in all the participating countries, and especially so in the Czech Republic, Greece and Portugal. Many of the schools that participated in the project are engaged in improving their understanding of self-evaluation, as are some of the translators.

The project also helped trigger the *Proyecto Escuelas de Avanzada*, engaging about thirty schools, set in poverty-ridden areas of Peru affected by lead pollution and severe learning difficulties. Chapters of the book were translated into Spanish to facilitate the work of the schools involved.

The sustainability and continuing impact, long after *Bridges* had been put to bed, is also owed to Gzregorz Mazurkiewicz in Poland and to Milan Pol in the Czech Republic, for whom the project and the EU endorsement gave impetus to major policy thrusts in those countries, while in Slovenia, Andrej Koren continues to play a leading role in advocacy and implementation of self-evaluation. Self-evaluation in that country continues to be a growing movement, widely welcomed by teachers and by policymakers eager to find a quality assurance mechanism with impact and cost-benefit.

## Enter grey shorts

One of the lasting legacies of *Bridges across Boundaries* for me was to meet Grzegorz Mazurkiewicz who, at our first seminar in Slovakia in 1996 introduced himself as 'grey shorts' since, he claimed, no one could pronounce his name. This was obviously a challenge to a linguist and in the ten years since then I have worked with Grzegorz and have learned to pronounce his name just about as well as the Poles do. In the leadership literature Grzegorz would be described as a hero innovator, making things happen by the force of his personal authority, his entrepreneurial instincts and his determination to let no potential opportunity pass him by. Over the last decade he has continued to build on self-evaluation and expand the boundaries to encompass a wider all-embracing approach to school transformation.

On my most recent visit to Krakow in March 2012, the lady at the bar who greeted me as a long-forgotten friend looked familiar with more than ten years of maturing, on both sides, defying instant recall of her name. Over the first five or so minutes of dissimulation the cloud gradually lifted to reveal Isobel Macgregor, former HMI in Scotland, last seen in El Escorial in Spain.

Outside the weather alternated between frost and snow one day and brilliant sunshine the next, obligingly choosing the last day of the conference to allow us to wander round the largest town square in Europe. It also has to be one of the most entertaining, with musicians, artists, a cavalcade of eccentric characters and human statues competing for zlotys, the biggest crowd-puller the young veiled woman apparently suspended in mid-air. Among the gathered crowd theories abounded as to how this apparently impossible feat was accomplished. After half a dozen theories Grzegorz was obliged to admit defeat.

The no-expense-spared conference brought around 200 participants and speakers from the US, Germany and the UK. The lavishness of the hospitality, simultaneous translation over four days and abundant goodies in the conference pack was owed to the generosity of the European Social Fund. John, from Wisconsin, told me in a taxi on the way to the airport that on one of the many cultural visits made by Polish teachers, in this case to New York, no one blinked an eye at the 27 dollar breakfast (exclusive of service and sales tax of course).

### *A pause for reflection*

Auschwitz lies forty two and a half miles west of Krakow, a coach drive of one hour and seven minutes through a succession of the Polish villages of Rzqza, Chrzanov and Oswiecim, outside of which the most inappropriately named 'camp' lies. While much of the village was cleared of its residents, those who remained were later to give testimony to the stench that came from the smoke that drifted over their village.

There was a pervasive silence on the coach drive back to Krakow, too many images burned into consciousness – room after room of human hair, mountains of shoes each with their own story, names and addresses optimistically painted on suitcases, their owners destined never to retrieve them. As visitors to the site all report, only the experience at first hand can have the emotional and cerebral impact that was conspicuously absent in my own arid school history, a series of dates and battle marching sequentially and bloodlessly to the present. What misconceived nostalgia for school history prompts Conservative ministers to advocate the memorisation of dates as an essential component of the school curriculum? Equally bizarre is the naming of rivers, a feat as a Cambridge professor I am still unable to do unless I have travelled in or across them, fished them or fallen into them. As we had found earlier in Hiroshima with a group of international students, there is little adequate substitute for the profound impact of the human story told at first hand.

## On reflection

There are few more challenging opportunities to reflect on school practice and its underlying assumptions than through collaborative international studies. Attempts to find the bridge across boundaries of language, historical and cultural convention have, through successive cross-country studies, tested the shallowness of policy borrowing and of simplistic notions of 'transfer'. We have learned, and continue to learn, more powerfully through difference than similarity, and through an openness to challenging 'the way we do things round here'. We have learned, and continue to learn, that schools improve not through prescriptive detail but through getting hold of big ideas, by scaffolding of key principles and by generative frameworks such as the multi-layered 'wedding cake', each layer interconnected and interdependent. We come to grasp the nature of student learning through professional and system learning and, in David Perkins' words 'being a model of thoughtfulness for one's students'.

## Note

1   Heschel, A.J. (1962) *The Prophets*, New York, Harper Collins

# Part IV
# The fourth lens

# 7   Academics conferring and the power of place

One of the compensations of the academic life is having an excuse to travel to exotic locations, and some less exotic, ostensibly 'conferring' while also compensating for the disembodied dullness of geography lessons in school. Starting with AERA's annual pilgrimage around American cities, offering an education outside of the windowless conference rooms, in this first of two parts some 'urban myths' are explored (Trepidation in Trenton, Safe in Soweto, Insouciant in Bangkok, Unimpressed in Uzbekistan, Sabotaged in Sacramento, Learning In Latin America), in each case highlighting the power of context in shaping the nature of learning and teaching and the nature of 'danger', real or perceived. The chapter concludes with the International Leadership Research Network (ILERN) project and the inspirational leadership of South Africa's first black dean – an uplifting account of meeting racism with tough-minded humility.

## A place to confer

A conference – a place to confer, 'a formal meeting that typically takes place over a number of days and involves people with a shared interest, esp. one held regularly by an association or organization' (Wikipedia). This benign dictionary definition conceals more than it reveals. As well as collegial sharing, consumption of alcohol and general bonhomie, conferences are also occasions for self promotion, academic rivalry, denigration of others' work, with a leavening of plagiarism and opportunism. As C.P. Snow's, Kingsley Amis' and David Lodge's satirical essays, too close to the bone, reveal, a congruence of academics can at its worst constitute a vicious assembly. Academics could spend much of their lives speaking at, preparing for, or attending conferences – the alphabet soup of major annual big events – BELMAS, BERA, SERA, ECER, AERA, IPDA, ICET, ICSEI[1] – plus those run by local authorities, universities, private enterprise and, in England, the National College. Plus the many one-off and weekend events that could account for the interstices in the rest of the calendar year. Many an hour could be whiled away at Westminster briefings, to which I am invited (never as a speaker) on a virtually weekly basis.

## Travels with AERA

Getting a paper accepted at the AERA is always a lottery, especially for a Brit. When a paper submitted by Peter Mortimore and myself was deemed unworthy it was the point at which Peter withdrew his patronage. The paper, which described one of the largest school effectiveness studies ever undertaken, ticked all the boxes and more, but was rejected because its American reviewers did not understand, or were not interested in, what was happening on some remote island in the Atlantic (or was it the Pacific?). In the event, paperless, I sat through the most turgid, badly presented and badly researched studies that would not have passed muster from a Cambridge undergraduate. To find the rare gems within the 'programme', twice the size of an average phone book, requires devoted study. Choice tends to depend on names one recognises, only to discover that his or her paper is being presented by a graduate student. The great man, or woman, is elsewhere, perhaps preparing for one of the invited plenary sessions that attract a few hundred people, the latecomers having to crowd around the doors, unless small, bold, or rude enough to push to the front in order to hear what may prove to be a disappointing rehash of what one has heard, or read, before.

When the AERA annual conference rolls into town the tenor of sidewalk conversations, snatched in passing, assumes new esoteric forms. 12,000 academics fill the hotels but beyond the windowless rooms of the Marriot, Hilton, Sheraton, Renaissance, there are cities to explore, disturbing one's preconceptions and conventional stereotypes. Perhaps inside one of those rooms a researcher is presenting a paper on ecological niches or behaviour settings. Someone will be contriving, within their allotted ten minutes, to propound a theory of urban drift or white flight. You can travel across corridors and hurried passage between hotels to catch a paper on social or economic capital, or engage in controversies over the correctness of language – inequality, inequity, disadvantage, or deprivation. Outside these airless rooms, however, these issues can be studied at first hand. If nothing else, AERA's loyal fellow travellers can benefit from a historical and cultural education, but not without an open mind and enlightened eye.

The real educational benefits of conferences such as AERA lie in discovering 'the power of place'. Each venue has something to teach about the nature of learning and how much it owes to the country, city or neighbourhood that maps life chances and shapes the future. As a thirteen year old I had the misfortune to represent my school on the Canadian equivalent of 'Top of the Form'. The humiliation still lives with me after naming the capital of the United States as New York, only partially retrieving family honour by naming Reykjavik as the capital of Iceland – the latter acquired from a bubblegum card, the former a lack of attention when capitals were being taught in class. At best, I might have been able to place these cities on a two-dimensional atlas but devoid of meaning or significance – a land of ice somewhere in the Atlantic, or was it the Pacific?

It was to be conferences that took me to all of these cities and helped me to understand the power of place, not only between cities but within cities – Harlem or Long Island, the stark contrast of life to the east or west of K Street in Washington, and in Reykjavik, 2012 the corollary to ostentatious wealth – a daily queue to receive free food from Icelandic Aid to families.

## New York New York

The New York story may not be on the agenda of the AERA conference that is held in four of its uptown and upmarket hotels, but to be there stimulates a desire to know more about the remarkable social transformation of this city. It is of itself an education as the power of place. *No longer the bonfire of the Vanities* as Anne Bernard entitled her 2007 essay. She wrote:

> The white population is no longer shrinking, and diverse immigration has made the city less black-and-white. The Bronx neighborhoods near the site of Sherman McCoy's accident[2] are now dotted with owner-occupied row houses and apartments. Artists have moved into Mott Haven lofts.

The New York of 'Bonfire' that might well have shocked people in 1987, no longer exists. Not in reality, and not in the collective imagination. New York is on track to have fewer than 500 homicides this year, down from 2,245 in 1990. The robbery rate went down 84 per cent, incidence of rape rate down by more than three quarters, burglary by 85 per cent while auto theft rate was, by 2010, 7 per cent of what it was in 1990, when we ventured with some trepidation from the Marriot Hotel in Times Square. A decade later the crime drop in 42nd Street around Times Square is 90 per cent less than then, but Times Square itself is a vastly different place.

How and why New York pulled back from the brink in 1987, torn between new heights of wealth and decadence on Wall Street and the draining of jobs and taxpayers from the rest of the city, may be a matter of conjecture and dispute, writes Anne Bernard, but there are some powerful sociological and psychological lessons to be learned. It turns out that crime is situational and contingent: depending on whom I meet today and what they want to do; depending on how good it looks to commit a crime. What hotspots policing tells you is that crime is intensely concentrated, and it's concentrated in places where it keeps happening.

Mending a broken window, attending to the incipient signs of dereliction, arresting the downward spiral, writes Malcolm Gladwell,[3] is the micro event that stimulates macro change. If a neighborhood has a broken window, it instills a sense of lawlessness among the residents of the neighborhood that leads to a breakdown of civilization:

> If you fix the window, then everybody was on board with the idea that we're all in this together, and we are all going to live in a peaceful society.

If you can reduce the robbery rate on Tuesday, you've probably reduced the robbery rate this year. And if you can make a robbery that was going to happen on 125th Street, not happen there, it probably won't happen.

It is that kind of vulnerability of crime and danger to situational and contingent and temporary solutions which is, writes Bernard, the most important lesson from the New York story.

## The world's safest and most dangerous cities: a brief treatise

To visit the world's safest, as well as its most dangerous, cities is an education in itself. New York is home to the Whitney, MOMA (the Museum of Modern Art), the New York Philharmonic, Broadway, the Mets (baseball) and the New York Rangers (ice hockey). While a decade or two ago you might have been unwise to travel on the New York subway, today is it safe, fast and relatively comfortable.

San Diego, San Francisco (Montreal and Vancouver, the two Canadian cities latterly invited into the AERA club) are all walking cities in which it feels safe to venture. Chicago, once synonymous with a gangster culture, now one of the most elegant of American cities, requires you to look around and up at the architecture and the stunning Art Institute on South Michigan Avenue. In Atlanta, the legacy of its turbulent racial history means that to journey most safely is by overhead walkways. While in Montreal when it is still winter you can avoid seeing anything of the city by travelling underground through miles of shops, banks, restaurants and wine bars.

San Francisco, to which AERA is drawn back on a regular basis, earns the accolade of the US' safest city. On the long walk from Union Square and the downtown conference hotels up the notoriously steep hills, through Chinatown, Nob Hill, through the Castro, the gay district from Market Street to 19th Street, and on to the Fisherman's Wharf, there is an endless juxtaposition of busy sidewalks, small shops, parks, business people mixing with hippies, tourists and shopkeepers on their lunch break. Here, at first hand, you can observe theory-in-practice – Jane Jacobs' compelling study *The Life and Death of American Cities*[4], in which she explores the relationship of housing, shops, streets, traffic, workplaces and the organic relationship of these one to another. The death of American cities is owed in large part to the failure to grasp the profound significance of Jane Jacobs' insight. Modernist urban planning has, she argues, failed human beings, the planners' greatest error lying in separation of uses (residential, industrial, commercial), creating 'unnatural urban spaces', a misunderstanding of 'community', characterised by layered complexity and congenial chaos.

Factored into the equation has to be the availability and nature of work and its susceptibility to global trends. Nowhere are there more powerful lessons to be learned about the lingering death of cities than Detroit, consistently ranked as the most dangerous city in the United States. Once an industrial boom town in the 1950s, when its population rose from 250,000 to 1.8 million, it was to become the victim of economic outsourcing and the inexorable rise of Japan's auto makers. As Detroit's car factories fought a losing battle against the East, progressively accelerating unemployment brought in its wake white flight to the more affluent suburbs, leaving behind entire swathes of what was once a vibrant bustling city, now depressed blocks of abandoned buildings, stray animals foraging among garbage simply thrown into the streets, a breeding ground for property theft and violent crime.

The impact on schooling is immediate and devastating. As middle-class families move progressively from the inner city to the outer city and to the suburbs, the gap between the rich and poor, white and black widens. One of my least memorable experiences was to address the whole staff in Trenton High School. What did I know about the lives of young people and the challenges of their teachers in one of Americas' most crime-ridden inner cities?

## Trepidation in Trenton

Inner-city Trenton is not a welcoming place. Year on year it wins an accolade as one of the most dangerous cities in the United States, most of the thirty or so annual homicides being gang related – a substantial number for a city of 84,000 people. Once described by James Madison as a 'dismembered torso bleeding into Philadelphia and New York', the city sits almost halfway between these two metropolises and is less than half an hour away by car or train from the idyllic pastoral village of Princeton. The contrast with the inner city, sitting cheek by jowl with surrounding affluence, adds to the sense of embattlement. It seems much safer to drive to the school than run the silently watchful gauntlet of young men who occupy every street corner.

Trenton High is an archetypical American high school. Its ancient brick building, fronted by tall white colonial pillars, consumes a large city block, a building large enough to house 4,000 of Trenton's youth who, out of school time, and often in school time as well, take up their positions on street corners. They may extend goodwill to those who pass by, but to the wary pedestrian they are a threatening presence.

The main campus of the high school occupies a symbolic space and the clock in the impressive white central tower marks the exact time. It was an expensive repair to restore the clock to its proper function after years of neglect, but the new principal Priscilla Dawson, in 2000, saw it as a statement to the community that she and her staff meant business.

In common with all inner-city schools, entrance is via a metal detector, the main target of which is knives and guns, a familiar armoury for young people for whom carrying arms is seen as a necessary form of defence and a badge of membership. This is, of course, not true for all Trenton High students, many of whom excel in one of the award, scholarship and honor programmes. Nonetheless, a serious minority are affiliated to one of the fifty or so gangs that inhabit the local community. Despite the hallway guard, Trenton Central High is a hospitable place. Efforts have been made to brighten the long traditional, otherwise bleak, tiled hallways that stretch into the middle distance and echo with the metallic banging of locker doors in between periods as students make the repetitive journey from one end of the building to the other. There is a vibrant atmosphere, with students' work displayed in corridors, together with posters bearing homilies and injunctions to strive and to excel. Teachers work hard to engage their students' interest in face of an often uninspiring curricular diet within the core subjects, and pressure to succeed within the draconian strictures of *No Child Left Behind*. In tenth grade they choose one of nine small learning communities which range from the Renaissance Academy to the Law and Justice Academy, all of these with a strong vocational bias. From a plethora of clubs students can choose hip hop, Bible club, basic Spanish dancing or a model UN club.

Of the students, 67 per cent are African American and 27 per cent Latino. You are never far from reminders of race, racism and anti-racism. This is a predominantly African-American school and you better watch your language and your choice of iconography. On a conference day, teachers pack the main hall and the visiting speaker makes the mistake of showing a video of an English school with all white children. I am kindly informed afterwards by three elderly female members of staff that this kind of fare does not go down well in Trenton Central High.

Trenton School District, 'committed to excellence and equity within an environment conducive to learning', enjoyed, up until 2006, the superintendency of Torch Lyttle, so-named for the luminosity of his red hair. An enlightened and unorthodox leader, he not only presided over a complex school district but invested a lot of time in educational matters. He wanted to keep abreast of thinking and encouraged his teaching force to read educational texts, convening regular 'book club' meetings to discuss a set reading.

Unlike in many schools in other countries, management is not devolved to school sites, so allowing staffing decisions to be made at district level. So, Torch would pore over lists of senior school staff with his latest district intelligence, shuffling principals and vice-principals around to create the best blend of experience and opportunities for mentoring and professional development. It underlines some of the benefits of system leadership, an opportunity lost by Trenton's marketised counterpart in England. The downside is, however, felt at school level where staff express a desire for more local control over decision making.

In visits to cities such as Trenton, New Orleans or Washington, these cities bear testimony to the impact of urban migration and white flight. K Street in Washington divides the majesty of the monumental city from black housing 'projects', where to be the lone white face is a disturbing and a deeply educative experience for the unwary traveller. In New Orleans, turning right rather than left off the highway we suddenly found ourselves in a dead end, in a neighbourhood of squalid housing and incipient threat. The wisdom of not renting an open top Pontiac convertible was suddenly apparent. A similar educational experience in Atlanta – a wrong turn out of the hotel, in this case right instead of left – found me walking at quickened pace, looking around and reading into the faces of teenagers and young black men a latent hostility. Racism or realism?

## The nature of danger

Danger, we are told weekly on television's 'Crimewatch', is more in perceptions and apprehension than in reality. The large majority of violent crimes are committed within the family or by people known to the victim. On the other hand, it is wise to heed the warnings of one's conference hosts. In Mexico City we were advised not walk the 400 yards back from the restaurant at night, nor to believe that we were safe in the company of the police, described colourfully, and probably unfairly, as 'highwaymen in uniform', yet it was a pertinent health warning. In Johannesburg, one of the top ten most-dangerous of cities, my morning walks were advisedly confined to the compound of the hotel. On a brief excursion beyond the hotel we were advised of the ritual of keeping doors locked and car windows tightly shut to avoid the traffic-light opportunists for whom the unwary traveller offers rich pickings. Another website informs me that Cape Town earns pride of place over Johannesburg and counsels against the most hostile areas of the city – Greenpoint, Salt River, Seapoint, the last of these where I spent the first five years of my life and began my school career.

As a five year old with a black maid, Dinah, and manservant, Gideon, who was to become my closest confidant, I was uneasy with the deference of these adults to the white folk and their all-too-reverent attitude, even to a five year old. In my all-white primary school these issues were not on the curriculum, nor things to be talked about, and young questioning minds would soon learn that there were taboo areas best left unexplored. Racism was not a term in my vocabulary until a good few decades later when it was to become a hot and divisive topic, often bound up in theoretical disputes between the little-enders and big-enders so that its history and day-to-day impact was obscured.

## Safe in Soweto

It was at a conference in Soweto that I was to gain an insight into the impact of racism at its most virulent. The event was held in Regina Mundi church, the largest Roman Catholic church in South Africa. The opening keynote – a powerful and moving account of South Africa's struggle against apartheid, and the role played by Soweto and the church as would-be sanctuary – made reference to the bullet holes on walls and ceilings, testifying to the breach of the sanctuary principle. Since political meetings in most public places were banned, the church became the main place where Soweto people could meet and share experiences. During the events of June 1976, when students were shot by the police, many of the demonstrators took refuge in Regina Mundi.

The police entered the church, firing live ammunitions, incurring multiple injuries and damage to the marble altar and, poignantly, to the statue of Christ. After apartheid, meetings of the Truth and Reconciliation Commission were held in the church, presided over by Archbishop Desmond Tutu.

Ironically, it was in a visit to a shanty town in Soweto that I felt most safe, escorted by a local teacher (white) who was known and respected in the community. It is an indelible learning experience to witness at first hand lives lived out in the most basic levels of subsistence imaginable – sheets of corrugated iron against a tree serving as home, women foraging for sticks to build a fire, men sitting idly watching them with little else to do but see out the day. The teacher who accompanied me came with a safe passport, having worked for years to help build schools, however primitive, their corrugated roofs making them uninhabitable in the hottest weather as well as subject to leaks in the rainy season when the hammering of heavy rain makes speech inaudible. In the local hospital, Baragwanath, surgeons (among whom was, for many years, my elder brother Len), spent much of their time treating knife wounds on an endless stream of casualties.

In the early days of Mugabe's reign as a benevolent dictator I also felt at ease in streets, street markets and parks of Zimbabwe's capital city, Harare. I had been told that there was something unique in the air of this most beautiful of countries and I savoured it to the full, perhaps only because I could see it through a white man's eyes. While a heavy price had already been paid for its shameful colonial history, the Mugabe terror was yet to come.

## Insouciant in Bangkok

Perhaps, in retrospect, I ought to have felt less insouciant in Bangkok where I blithely wandered the streets and haggled in street markets – a short walk from the conference hotel. This sprawling city competes for a place in the top ten dangerous venues, as it is the major transit site for Thailand's pre-eminent place as producer of opium and heroin. In 2010 there were 20,000 assaults, 13,500 burglaries, and 5,000 murders, the highest in south east Asia.

Yet I could not have anticipated the nature of the school I was to visit on the Mekong Delta, looking across a slow-moving stretch of greenish water to Vietnam, a place from which so many young American men were never to return. Working my way across the grass and rubble, scattering the chickens and avoiding the occasional undiscovered eggs, I found myself on the open deck facing the three classrooms that constituted the school. Outside each classroom was a chart on the wall with ratings by children of their enjoyment and learning, together with formative comments for their teachers. I was invited to the headteacher's office where, on an ancient computer she took me through the data, collected over the years, showing the strengths and weaknesses of her staff and some of the recommendations as to how teaching, and more importantly learning, might be improved. She had, I regret to say, never read any of my treatises on self-evaluation or student voice. She had invented them herself.

## Sabotaged in Sacramento

It seemed like a good idea at the time. The proposition from Bill Clark HMCI was for himself, John Bangs and myself to meet with California legislature in the state capital Sacramento over the course of two days, and convince them of the need for a statewide self-evaluation system for their schools. Bill's introductory pitch, drawing on Scotland's success story, appeared to go down well with the legislative panel and the invited audience. My own slightly less evangelical presentation describing the NUT's adoption of self-evaluation in England was followed by John Bangs, his devastating critique of top–down government policy leaving Bill speechless with dismay.

The legislature's response in the vein of 'don't call us, we'll call you' came, in the event, as no surprise. The case against the two Johns for sabotage of the event was never re-opened and peace broke out on the long car ride back to San Francisco, followed by a memorable evening in Chinatown where our waitress assumed the sixty dollars in change was intended as a tip. We were too embarrassed to ask for it back. There was worse to come as the putative flight back to Stansted airport was no longer. The budget business class airline Maxjet had, during my brief absence, gone into receivership.

## Unimpressed in Uzbekistan

There are three people seated at a table in the courtyard of an Uzbek restaurant expectantly awaiting their dinner. They are a Scottish HMI, a Dean of the Faculty at Strathclyde University and Director of the Quality in Education Centre. A young woman appears in layers of diaphanous veils and proceeds to remove them one by one as she dances towards the table and invites the three gentlemen to insert Uzbek soms (or better still American dollars) into her garter. No sooner has she disappeared than another emerges to repeat the process. Five dances and three depleted wallets later an inedible dinner is served.

A visit to Uzbekistan to run workshops for school leaders seemed like a good idea at the time and Ian Smith, Bob Young HMCI and myself found ourselves having to make some rapid adjustments to our cultural assumptions. Our first introduction to these new cultural mores was for our car to be stopped at every intersection while police examined tyres, lights and windscreen wipers and declared them unsafe and therefore subject to a fine, cash on the spot. As police earn no salary this is their payment by results. The same must be true of the airport staff who weigh your bag on check in and declare a virtual handbag to be overweight, pointing to a remarkable set of scales that shows the bag to have mysteriously gained ten pounds since leaving my hand. The once-moving walkway is now so rusted so that, like the trolleys, nothing moves. Waiting two hours for a plane one is obliged to 'hold on' as the single toilet is three feet deep in water and other unmentionable objects. It was to be seven years before the bug contracted by Bob was eventually flushed from his system.

These events took place a decade and half ago and much has changed since, as many of the world's once poor are now the *nouveau riche*, as two of

Cambridge's most recent projects testify. A multi-million pound contract with Kazakhstan engages members of the Faculty in regular well-resourced visits, while Mongolia, equally generous in its hospitality to visiting academics, provides, as a by-product, a rich source of anthropological insights.

## A guide to national protocols

I had learned the hard way about art of bathing in Japanese households, the protocols of food and drink, forms of dress, address and table manners, the ignominy of ordering a glass of wine in Dubai with six sheiks present at the table, and attempting to shake hands with the lady Minister in Abu Dhabi.

In Nara in Japan a week with an extended family, including grandma, was a series of lessons in etiquette – not to let out the bath water as you should clean yourself before bathing; to keep both hands above the table (in case you might be hiding a weapon); to not hover undecided over food with your chopsticks (rude to the hostess) but to make up your mind and go directly to the food; finish everything on your plate down to the last grain of rice and remember to slurp – a sign of enjoyment. If you bring a bottle of wine (or two) don't expect it to be served! And, whether wine or any other beverage, never serve yourself. Serve others and let them serve you. Too late I learned to say *tadakimasu* before the meal, and *gochisosama (deshita)* afterwards.

## Learning in Latin America

I did have occasion to visit Mexico City, the first of four invitations to address the Latin American Heads Conference (LAHC), held annually in different venues in South and Central America. Three cultural peculiarities of Mexico City are lodged forever in my memory – the bodega in which a gutter ran along the base of the bar so that drinkers need not interrupt their drinking by the onerous duty of visiting the loo. I did suggest that simply pouring the drink straight into the gutter would 'cut out the middle man'. The second observation was in my hotel room, in which the entire ceiling was comprised of one extremely all-embracing mirror. I should have known better than to ask its purpose as the hotel did offer rooms by the hour. The third 'learning experience' lay in moving to another hotel and asking for a room facing the grand square. The Mariachi band would regale me until well after midnight, resuming at first light in the morning. It was my first encounter with insomnia.

Travels with Latin American headteachers contributed much to my international education, both geographically and culturally – these expatriate English, Scottish, Irish and Welsh headteachers running their schools to 'reflect British practice throughout Latin America' with 'criteria for membership based on the degree to which the schools concerned reflected that practice and on the level of 'Britishness' to which the Head could lay claim'. In 1997 a reformulation of its mission was an attempt to moderate its full-on Britishness. LAHC is a network of headteachers and leaders of schools based on British educational principles and with an international focus. The membership is dedicated to sharing good practice and to mutual support through the provision of professional development opportunities.

My visit to Mexico City included the invitation to run a two-day workshop for staff of the Lancaster School whose headteacher, Alan Downie, was keen to embed self-evaluation into the school's priorities and development planning. It was to be the complement to inspection or external review. It proved to be a challenging two days, bridging the two cultures of the English and Spanish speaking staff, and bringing to the surface some of the inherent tensions that lie behind linguistic and cultural conventions.

## The Switzerland of Argentina

The keynote that I gave in Mexico City earned me a revisit the following year to Baroliche, where I was invited to manage the whole three days of the conference along with a colleague who I could choose to bring with me. I invited Archie McGlynn HMCI, a devotee of international travel and always welcoming of new cultural experiences. Bariloche, known as the Switzerland of Argentina, lies near the very southernmost tip of the continent, the point at which Argentina is separated from Peru only by the tail end of the Andes. The following description is taken from the LAHC website – 'idyllic' is too understated a term for a place of such breathtaking beauty:

> The members' conference in 2002, held in the idyllic location of Bariloche, marked a significant departure from previous such occasions, in that, instead of having a number of presenters, these were limited to two, John MacBeath and Archie McGlynn. Professor MacBeath was invited in response to the popular request from the membership that he should be invited after the previous year's conference had given him only limited exposure. He and Dr McGlynn proved immensely popular, and the conference, which addressed the subject of self-assessment, was marked by their combined wisdom, infectious sense of humour and the involvement of those present in a number of activities that stretched their artistic and dramatic skills. After the conference, LAHC took out affiliation with the University of Cambridge 'Leadership for Learning' Institute.

There is an interesting footnote to the Baroliche story and its place in history. It was reputed to be the hideout for Adolf Hitler and Eva Braun and the home of the former SS *Hauptsturmführer* Erich Priebke, who was director of the German School of Bariloche for a number of years before the war. When tracked down in 1995, Piebke was flown directly from Bariloche to Germany where he stood trial and re-trial, but was eventually released as his plea that he had been simply acting under orders was accepted.

My third invitation to run the LAHC conference, together with Jim O'Brien, was an opportunity to explore Buenos Aires, another walking city, wide leafy boulevards earning it the title of the Paris of South America, with its cafés, theatres, bookstores, stately homes, world-famous zoo and botanical garden, and architecturally noteworthy churches. We dined out, literally, on the exchange rate that valued the American dollar at three times its Argentinian equivalent, so making a meal of the best steak in the world and a bottle of the best Malbec only marginally more expensive than Joe's Caff in Brixton.

Perhaps there can be too much of a good thing and the third LAHC conference was met with slightly diminished enthusiasm. This was no reflection on my compatriot, Jim O' Brien, but there was a need for new faces and I was not invited back until 2012, at which point I had been long enough forgotten or forgiven to merit a further invitation, on this occasion to Santiago in Chile, a city that I had previously explored extensively on foot, never aware of threat.

## The devil drink

The invitation to publish a translation of MacBeath's collected wisdom in Spanish (*Liderar el aprendizae dentro y fuera de la escuela*) and to launch it in that stately city was irresistible. The visit to Santiago and Valparaiso included a guided tour of one of the world's largest vineyards, home to *Casillero del Diablo,* and was a further reminder of how people perceive and respond to 'danger'. The name given to the vast wine collection has, for a century, guarded it from intruders and infidels by the story of the phantom that haunts the cellars. When, in the middle of our tour, the lights went out and ghostly images appeared on the walls of the crypt, the apprehension among some of our party was testimony to the power of myth. On the Casillero del Diablo website you can find the evidence in Emilio Contereras' tragic tale.

> For the locals say that in the depths of the cellar lives the Devil himself. A tale so infamous, they named the wine, the Devil's Cellar. He may have worked the vineyards of the Rapel Valley all his life, but Emilio's old eyes have never seen into the depths of the cellar. Stories of the darkness that protects the barrels have been enough to keep him away. A friend once told him about a cousin who went down there many years ago. She never came back.

## I learn

What do Boston, Johannesburg and Nottingham have in common? One of the many possible answers to that question is the ILERN Project, conceived by Andy Hargreaves of Boston College and Geoff Southworth of the National College of School Leadership. The big idea was to select academics in the leadership field from around the world and accompany them on three journeys, over the course of which they would create a new paradigm in leadership across national boundaries. The group brought together to share the physical and intellectual journeys was a heady mix of luminaries from Harvard, Boston

College, Stanford and Northwestern universities, from Australia, New Zealand, Hong Kong, South Africa, Denmark and Norway and, from the UK, Nottingham, Warwick and Cambridge universities.[5]

The first of three construction sites was Johannesburg and a night-time barbecue in Kruger National Park. The second venue was Boston, the day on which a defeated Democrat, John Kerry, shared our waterfront restaurant, while the third and final conference, payback time, was at the National College (NCSL) in Nottingham, at which key documents would be produced, changing forever the way we thought and talked about leadership. Well, that was the grand plan.

Each of the six publications were produced by small writing groups and expensively packaged under the generic title of *Positive Leadership*. Collaborative writing is always a challenge and never more so than within the triad of myself, K.C. Wong from Hong Kong and Ben Levin from Canada, tasked with the theme 'Context as opportunity'. Through a simulation of a school meeting in which a teacher, headteacher and parent try to find some common ground, we tried to illustrate the differing perspectives these three protagonists represented, and how through a genuinely dialogic approach new ways of seeing – 'in-sight' – might emerge. The interested reader may search fruitlessly on Google to trace these seminal compositions which, in the end, didn't change the nature of leadership forever, but it was fun while it lasted.

The most enduring legacy of the ILERN was the continuing relationship with one of the education's most inspirational leaders. Jonathan Jansen's experience as the first black Dean in a climate of racist intimidation is retold in his book *Knowledge in the Blood*.[6] The title depicts a way of knowing the world that is passed from generation to generation. With deeply entrenched 'knowledge' of white, black and 'coloureds', stretching back over generations and insitutionalised in schools and universities, the challenges facing Jonathan as first black Dean are a sobering reminder of the virulence of racism. It was a huge privilege to host him at the Faculty of Education and for him to lead a lunchtime seminar. His responses to some of the questions put to him tell their own story.

**From your experience as leader in a hugely challenging context what is the most important lesson you have learned?**
That leading through the open acknowledgement of your own brokenness (as opposed to moral self-righteousness) finds enormous resonance among young and indeed older South Africans as we struggle to deal with our woundedness from the past and our mutual vulnerability in the present.

**You entitled your book Knowledge in the Blood. What underlies the choice of that title?**
The title comes from an Irish poem by Macdara Woods, referring to the deep emotional, spiritual, psychic and bodily roots of knowledge – a knowledge not easily changed or transformed, and which from time to

time keeps holding us back from doing the right things, and propelling us forward towards what is good: 'for there is no respite from the knowledge in the blood' (Woods). It is a reminder, in pedagogical terms, that simple instructional or curricular remedies for complex problems do not yield easily to the logic of those who teach.

**Theories of organizational change abound. For you as a new Dean or VC what was the very first step?**
The first step is understanding. Politics hates complexity, and in the overcharged politics of South Africa, there is little room for deep understanding of how society and its institutions came to be the way they are. You cannot change something without investing time (and resources) in 'getting to the bottom of things', in a manner of speaking. Wherever I have been asked to lead, always in complex circumstances, I spend three months saying nothing except in trying to understand the cultures, traditions, histories, practices and beliefs of the organization I am entering. It works.

**What have been the most formidable obstacles you have faced in trying to achieve your vision?**
Dealing with myself. I do not lead outside of my own emotions, hurts, experiences and troubles. Leading is a deeply personal and indeed emotional experience. Knowing yourself, being open to change and adjustment even as you lead, and yet knowing what is worth pursuing, are critical elements in credible and effective leadership. I often find myself "surprised by joy" (CS Lewis) as the people I am privileged to lead respond with enthusiasm to what we set out to do. The problem is not the followers.

**Your willingness to understand and forgive bigoted students guilty of outrageous behaviour to black students could be seen by many as 'soft' on racism. Is there a limit to 'understanding' and a place for tough sanctions 'pour encourager les autres'?**
The charge ('soft on racism') would stick if that (forgiveness) is the only thing you do. But when forgiveness is part of a collective of actions that deal with personal and institutional and societal transformation, then it is a first step, not the only one. Institutional forgiveness (remember students still went through the criminal trial) brings students back into the university so that their bitter knowledge can be engaged and their angry knowledge intercepted; this is exactly what happened. One of the students now teaches others, like him, about the dangers of racism and the possibilities of a life that embraces others. Forgiveness of course also helps the perpetrator overcome the burden of unresolved hurt and the restoration of human relations.

By going counter-cultural, in this way, the door is opened for other white South Africans to 'come clean' and re-join the project of social change and renewal knowing that the finger of judgment will not (again) be shoved in their faces; we now have more white students coming to the UFS than before, for this reason. You cannot deal with racism in an all-black university, which is what the UFS was on its way to becoming. But this simple act of forgiveness, in a country still hurting deeply with past wounds, enabled a national dialogue to break out in civil society which is quite unprecedented, not only in churches and synagogues and mosques. More and more South Africans now claim to understand the deeper meaning of that initial act of forgiveness; of course Desmond Tutu understood it right away.

## On reflection

Knowledge is 'in the blood', writes Jonathan Jansen. We may come to new experiences with our expectations and prejudices intact but, as Jonathan told a Cambridge audience, as a new Dean he was to spend three months 'saying nothing except trying to understand the cultures, traditions, histories, practices and beliefs of the organization he was entering'. ILERN was the title of the international project in which he played a seminal part, pointing to the challenges of unlearning, seeing things through a new lens, as if for the first time. In New York, Bangkok, Soweto, Trenton, Sacramento, Mexico City, beyond the windows of the conference centres, preconceptions and conventional stereotypes may be forever disturbed, when we travel with optimism and insight.

## Notes

1   The British Educational Research Association, the Scottish Educational Research Association, The European Council for Educational Research, The American Educational Research Association, The International Congress of School Effectiveness and Improvement, The International Professional Development Association, The International Council on Educational Technology .

2   Accidental hero of the book *Bonfire of the Vanities* by Tom Wolfe (1987) whose unwitting stray into alien Harlem territory begins the book, and his education.

3   Gladwell, M. (2000) *The Tipping Point: How Little Things Can Make a Big Difference*, New York, Little Brown.

4   Jacobs, J. (1992) *The Life and Death of American Cities*, New York, Random House.

5   Andy Hargreaves, Geoff Southworth, Richard Elmore, Ann Lieberman, Jonathan Jansen, Ben Levin, Lejf Moos, Jim Spillane, Ciaran Sugrue, Susan Moore Johnson, Jorunn Miller, Juan Manuel Moreno, Bill Mulford, K.C., Hidenori Fujita, Wong, Ken Stott, John MacBeath, Jan Roberson, Alma Harris.

6   Jansen, J. (2009) *Knowledge in the Blood*, Stanford, Stanford University Press.

# 8 In pursuit of congress

## True believers, pragmatists and heretics

While ICSEI (the International Congress for School Effectiveness and Improvement) wins the prize for global adventuring, from Auckland to Vancouver Island via Hong Kong and Belarus, those it brings together for annual debate do not always agree, sometimes even with rancour, as to the premises on which its core mission rests. Finding the common ground among the true believers, pragmatists and heretics may be viewed through a half empty or half full glass, the maturity of the movement measured by its ability to embrace difference. Through this lens the histories of dissent and reconciliation are retold, offering an insight into a movement of ideas, the impact of which on policy and practice is not immediately evident but may be profound. One outcome from the debate was a Commission from Education International to demythologise 'effectiveness' and to provide a book for attendees at the Education Summit in New York. The 'Sunnier' uplands with which this chapter ends is a remarkable story of the power of money and Presidential patronage.

### Recycling and tetraphobia: a newcomer's guide to Hong Kong

At the exit from the MTR underground in Hong Kong you are likely to find a group of three of four ladies standing with canvas shopping bags. You might well assume they are waiting for a friend but if you stand long enough you will notice that from time to time a passenger will hand one of them a newspaper. They may stand there for many hours of the day in order to collect enough papers to take for recycling, for which they will receive perhaps ten Hong Kong dollars (less than one pound sterling). Ironically, not ten feet away there will be a news vendor pressing the free daily newspaper into the hands of passersby. I could not resist taking a free newspaper and handing it to a slightly built, kindly looking lady who reminded me too much of my mother. She thanked me profusely in English. This 'green' transaction is a further lesson on 'cutting out the middle man'.

That I did not discover this small but telling facet of a culture until my twentieth visit to Hong Kong is a reminder of how long it can take to get inside another culture, to see things with an inquiring eye, reminding us how easy it is to allow things to pass you by. It was also only after twenty visits that I noticed that hotels often did not have a fourth floor. Is the 28th floor the 28th floor of the hotel? With my new-found knowledge I could not wait to challenge my colleague, Jim O'Brien, who had been staying on the 28th and top floor of the Butterfly Hotel with me for the past week. I was confident in offering to pay the restaurant meal if he got the answer right as to the number of floors in the hotel. The answer – it is the 25th floor, as there are three missing floors, the 4th, 14th and 24th.

For fifteen years this aspect of my education had simply been a closed book. When eventually pointed out to me, I went to the dictionary and discovered tetraphobia (from Greek τετράς – *tetras*, 'four' and φόβος – *phobos*, 'fear' is an aversion to, or fear of, the number four). It is, says the dictionary, a superstition most common in East Asian regions such as Mainland China, Taiwan, Japan, Korea and Vietnam. The Chinese word for *four* (四, pinyin: sì, jyutping: sei), sounds quite similar to the word for *death* (死, pinyin: sǐ, jyutping: sei), in many varieties of Chinese. Similarly, the Sino-Japanese, Sino-Korean, and Sino-Vietnamese words for *four* sound similar or identical to *death* in each language. Not only are these floor numbers often skipped in buildings, ranging from hotels to offices to apartments and hospitals, but table numbers 4, 14, 24, 42, etc are also often left out in wedding dinners or other social gatherings.

## A not always happy valley

The top floor of the Butterfly Hotel offers unimpeded views of Happy Valley racecourse. Lit up spectacularly on a Wednesday evening, it is an awesome spectacle. Happy Valley (not always deserving of that name for some its most reckless punters) plays host to some of the world's finest horses and jockeys. If you are lucky enough to be invited to one of the upper floors you can indulge yourself from an extravagant buffet, carvery and fine wines at surprisingly modest prices. That I have now enjoyed its hospitality as a ritual duty on every Hong Kong visit is due to a small, now white-haired, man, who claims to know something about racing but tends to lose about as often as I, although more extravagantly. S.M. was, in a previous life a Chief Executive of the Education Bureau and the reason for my presence in Hong Kong.

S.M. was the prime mover and responsible for my first visit to Hong Kong in 1997 as a VIP. I had never counted myself as a very important person and at first took the invitation to be a cruel joke. S.M. was, however, to become a good friend and despite our shared addiction to losing money we spent many pleasurable evenings not only failing to spot the winners but dreaming up international projects, only some of which ever came to fruition.

The schedule S.M. had arranged for me on my initiation into the Hong Kong culture was, as well as a private suite at the Jockey Club, to include a helicopter ride to the Chinese border, a visit to Macau, a suite in the Mandarin Oriental hotel, my private chauffeur for a week, twice-daily banquets and meetings with all the key agencies and power brokers in Hong Kong. Each visit ended with a small gift, prompting a visit to the famous Temple Street night market to buy an extra suitcase.

In 2001 I was to give the first of many speeches to come, my exposition on self-evaluation possibly the least well-received in history. I spoke about pupil voice, the part young people could play in evaluating teaching and learning, showing some of the data from our NUT study in which pupils described the qualities of good teachers, and less good teachers. The polite, and at best lukewarm, reception for the substance of the talk was explained to me later as simply untenable in a Hong Kong culture. I was duly chastened and ought to have learned the lesson from a similar misreading of authority and status in Singapore a few years earlier.

Fast forward to 2012. I found myself counseling senior school managers and teachers that students' assessment of their teachers, conducted so systematically and transparently (for example, once yearly in a hall under exam conditions) could prove inimical to teacher morale. In one secondary school, a highly demoralised headteacher confessed to being on the point of retirement after a series of less than fulsome commentaries from her students. In another school, students offer individual feedback to their teachers at the end of the academic year, filling out a ten-item questionnaire. These evaluations are returned directly and confidentiality to the individual member of staff. A teacher with five or six different classes might then receive 150 to 200 such evaluation forms. Not only is the teacher rated, but is provided with their standing in relation to the norm.

Questioned as to whether finding yourself below the norm might be dispiriting, teachers claimed to find such feedback helpful. Although feedback forms are described as 'confidential', feedback in this school was also read by the Vice-principal and Principal, together with comparative findings from the previous year. A visit to a Buddhist school a few days later offered a sharp contrast. In an interview with a group of students I was discussing how they gave feedback to their teachers. One explained that there was a suggestion box in the ground floor corridor into which you could post anonymous comments addressed to individual teachers. So what kind of comment have you made?, I asked. The reply – 'thank you for being such a good teacher'.

These revelations were made in the course of interviews, conducted as the third and final phase of reporting on the impact of school self-evaluation. The Impact Study, ongoing from 2005 to 2013, has gathered a large body of longitudinal data from students, teachers, middle managers, headteachers, external review teams, School Sponsoring Bodies, and Education Bureau officials. The data set includes more than 50,000 questionnaire responses with accompanying open-ended commentaries, around 200 group interviews in schools, and 50 two-and-half-hour focus groups with key groups of stake-holders. The evidence from three successive studies is consistent and compelling.

The progressive embedding of school self-evaluation (SSE) and External School Review (ESR) has played a significant role in helping schools to develop a more reflective culture, lessening apprehension about the use of data, encouraging greater self-scrutiny, reflection and collegial dialogue. School self-evaluation and attention to student voice is credited with giving school staff a greater sense of ownership, improved team spirit, and heightened visibility of schools' accomplishments, both affirming good practice and lending a more critical edge to views of teachers' own efficacy. SSE tools provided by Education Development Bureau (EDB), have helped schools to make the transition from an 'impressionistic' to an 'evidence-based' approach to the evaluation of school performance. Greater transparency of classroom teaching, peer observation and collaborative lesson planning have given impetus to lessons becoming more engaging and student-centred. Recommendations from successive reports have encouraged school leaders to put in place structural supports and opportunities for reflection, dialogue, and shared pedagogy.

After a keynote in Hong Kong in 2011, a sixteen-year-old student introduced me to his headteacher who he had brought with him to the conference. He described to me how he had, entirely on his own initiative, created and carried out school self-evaluation, led by a group of internal 'inspectors' – his peers.

## Accessing leading-edge practice online

OIR stands for Online Interactive Resource. It can be accessed at http://hk.sitc.co.uk/, where both English and Chinese versions may be navigated. Two-and-a-half years in the making, it was intended as a user-friendly site for principals, teachers and School Improvement Teams to engage with leading-edge practice, to download tools of self-evaluation, to structure professional development workshops or use as prompts to seminars. Highlights of the resource are testimonies from children and young people reflecting critically on their learning, as Kylie, aged ten testifies:

> When we get older, teachers don't tell us the answers. They ask questions, and let us find the answers by ourselves. We may surf the Internet, and go to the library to find some books. When we do it in this way, we can learn how to learn. We will be more interested in the things we learn. We also think that if teachers just stand in the classroom and talk and talk, it will be so boring. This is active education and we like it very much. We keep on learning, maybe just watch the news, it's so useful for our learning. We may care (about) our world, our home Hong Kong, and China, and to know more about our society.
>
> (Lui Chiu Yee, Kylie, Plover Cove Primary School)

## War and peace

Hong Kong hosted the 13th International Congress for School Effectiveness and Improvement (ICSEI) in 2000, setting an attendance benchmark that has not been matched since. In January 2012 'ixy', as it is known to its friends, celebrated its 25th birthday in Malmö. It is a movement which, for more than of a quarter of a century, has provided a barometer of educational policy and school practice on an international scale. Founded as a forum in which to report and discuss a growing body of research on the school effect, it has succeeded in bringing together some of the world's leading researchers in that continuously developing field of inquiry.

The transition from ICSE to ICSEI, in the early 1990s, from effectiveness to improvement, had not been without controversy as 'improvement' was seen by the true believers as a more flaccid concept than 'effectiveness', the latter regarded as a science. In each stage of its global travels from its modest beginnings in Cardiff in 1987 to Santiago in Chile in 2013, the movement has been constantly re-inventing itself as these two key ideas have been contested and reframed.

Toronto had marked the nadir of the movement. Any mention of effectiveness had all but disappeared from the line up of speakers that included self-declared heretics. Heated discussions were conducted in small enclaves and meetings were called to explore what had gone wrong and where the movement would go in the future. Such was the lasting schism that, at an ICSEI board dinner in Seattle, during the AERA conference a few months later, two empty chairs were a token of protest.

Malmö was an occasion to lay to rest the tensions and rancour that had lain barely concealed below the surface of the movement. An avid reader of Henning Mankel's detective books and his jaded hero, Wallander, might have assumed that Malmö in Sweden was hardly the place to effect reconciliation, given the litany of dismembered bodies that turn up in and around that city. It was no disincentive to the 400 attendees at the ICSEI conference in early January 2012, strolling through its picturesque squares and taking refuge from the cold in its ambient bars and restaurants, nor to those now gathered in the Vollmeer's restaurant to celebrate its 25th birthday.

The restaurant, carefully researched by Dale Mann, was the site selected for a celebratory meeting of ICSEI's glitterati, its founding fathers, luminaries and past presidents. The meeting was an occasion for nostalgia, for a revisiting of ICSEI's history and impact on policy and practice. The challenge for the assembled alumnae was to list in chronological order the dates and sites of ICSEI's annual conferences beginning with its inception in Cardiff in 1987, in which fifty or so participants enjoyed a sandwich and a meat pie served in a brown paper bag, to the year 2000 and a banquet in Hong Kong's Regal Hotel attended by over 1,000 guests.

## The march of the ducks and the runaway dog

The nostalgia contest was a demonstration of distributed intelligence, as memories were pooled, disputed, revised and a chronology eventually agreed, from Cardiff to Malmö via Leuwarden, Memphis, Belarus, Portoroz, Auckland and Kuala Lumpur, among many other exotic (and less exotic) venues. High points were nostalgically recreated, the hospitality benchmark set by Tony

Townsend in Melbourne, and the most bizarre – the daily march of the ducks from their penthouse suite to the fountain in the lobby of Memphis' historic Peabody Hotel.

Each ICSEI setting was an occasion to not only visit schools in these host countries but to engage with policymakers, to hopefully contribute to the shaping of policy direction as ministers, advisers and researchers were invited to share in state-of-the-art research on school effectiveness and improvement.

Each of the sixteen present at the Malmö dinner was invited to offer their own personal reminiscence of the ICSEI journey, starting with its founders, Dale Mann, David Reynolds and Bert Creemers (symbolic of the movement, an American, an Englishman and a Dutchman). I was the last speaker, benefiting from the amount of wine consumed by that late hour not only by my audience but also fuelling my own loquacity. I began with my first ICSEI conference, in Victoria, British Columbia, in the sumptuous Canadian Pacific Hotel, the Empress, and the introductory welcome by Larry Sackney from Saskatoon. My only memory of that speech, or any that were to follow, was of Larry describing the endless horizons of Saskatoon, which allow one to sit on the back porch and watch your dog running away for three days. Such is the power of anecdote and imagery!

Snowbound Norköpping in Sweden was fresh in people's memories. Empty trams rattling through deserted streets, hamburgers on New Year's Day, with MacDonalds the only place to eat, the Grand Hotel where we were staying not even rising to a cup of tea or coffee. Finding Norköpping's only restaurant open in the evening we phoned to book a table. Yes, it transpired after some wait, they could fit us in – a table for two. Would near the orchestra be ok? Eight o'clock and the orchestra was playing for us, the lone diners. By nine, since nobody else had appeared, the orchestra packed up and retired to their homes and families. Swedes, we were told, but not by the person who took our booking, rarely venture out on the first night of the new year.

I recalled the prelude to the Norköpping gathering at which HMCI, Bill Clark, had persuaded us to book a table at a New Year's Eve celebration. The setting, which after considerable searching we managed to track down, was an ice hockey stadium with long tables laid out on what normally served as the rink. The four of us, Bill, his wife Ann, myself and my wife, Sandra, were seated at a table with a motley collection of eight other Swedes. One of this lugubrious collection included a lonely gent who broke into tears, prompting Sandra to go and put an arm around him and try to say something comforting between his deep mournful sobs. The evening was to become even more lively as Bill landed a well-aimed punch on the jaw of a fellow diner who had made some sort of advance to his wife, Ann.

Everyone present at the Malmö dinner was also able to recall the opening session in Leeuwarden's main church. Bert Creemers struggling to erect a screen and operate a Powerpoint™ projector in a pulpit of not more than a meter and half in diameter, facing the third of the audience who had a direct line of sight, while in the two trancepts, left and right, not only were the slides not visible but the acoustics defied all attempts engage with the content. The main entertainment was provided by the 'mad woman of Leeuwarden' who wandered around the church, not simply to get a better view of the screen but to cast her eye over the assembled congregation. Her penchant for stuffing as much food as she could into takeaway plastic bags was also a conference low point. She was eventually ejected from the conference.

Bert, good sport, laughed as uproariously as the others in recollection of his finest hour, at least the most bizarre. I recalled the sybaritic high point a year earlier in Limassol in Cyprus. Such was the splendour of my executive suite at the Le Méridien Spa hotel – complimentary champagne and hors d'oeuvres, my balconies (plural), sunbeds overlooking the Mediterranean, a kingly sized four-poster bed, televisions (plural), and bathrooms (plural) – that I held a party for the glitterati of ICSEI and icons of the publishing world.

In my reminiscence in Malmö the following year I did not wish to dampen the mood with recollections of other ICSEIs past, the heated and not always amicable debates, the vitriol and deep resentment among those who saw the treasured traditions of ICSEI being sold to the philistines, among whose number I had been counted. I had never been a true believer in the church of effectiveness. In Slovenia I had entitled my presidential address 'ICSEI: a broad church' and I had argued for the need to embrace the agnostics and sceptics as well as the true believers and the evangelicals. I was met afterwards by an incandescent Sam Stringfield, uncompromising in his insistence that ICSEI was not a broad church but a broad science.

## Broad church or broad science?

The second year of my ICSEI presidency was in Auckland where I re-engaged with the issues that had so bothered Sam. The following, an extract from that speech, was an attempt to capture the very nature of a 'movement', its breadth and challenge, embracing the scientists and the heretics alike.

> Last year in Slovenia we enjoyed one of the best ICSEIs. In my speech on assuming the presidency I referred to ICSEI as a broad church. I am grateful to Sam Stringfield for his challenge to that statement, arguing that ICSEI is, in fact, a 'broad science'. Sam set in train a current of ideas that has, for me, been a source of intermittent puzzlement over the intervening year and led me back to Thomas Kuhn whose work on paradigms has been highly influential in social science. It furnished the theme for these few opening thoughts in Auckland. In 2008 in Auckland where is ICSEI as 'movement'? It is a term we use to describe ourselves but one with strong theological connotations. Voltaire's reference to being 'baptized into the Newtonian religion' was at the time an act of faith.
>
> Today it is pertinent to ask whether, as movement, we share a common faith? Do we subscribe to a broadly similar scientific approach to the study

of schools? In fact, it seems to me, we represent a broad spectrum of 'believers' who we might classify as founding fathers (and mothers), true believers, pragmatists, agnostics and heretics.

In the first group are the founders and architects of this 'movement' to whom we owe a considerable debt. Without them we would be somewhere else, perhaps sitting in the Scottish rain or Vancouver snow or on Bondi beach. This group represents a core continuing strand that has run through ICSEI for over two decades. They have leant heavily on the tools of social science, which has, at its best, been rigorous, exploratory and uncompromising in its respect for evidence, cautious in its inferences and reluctant to overinterpret or overclaim its findings. They built the ICSEI house or at least laid its foundations.

Then there are the true believers have who kept the faith, some of whom have maybe come late to ICSEI. Within this group are school improvers, for whom 'improvement' is rooted in effectiveness, and 'improvement' is defined within that paradigm, and evaluating improvement by reference to a number by conventional measures, primarily (but not exclusively) student attainment or value-added.

The third group are also improvers but they take a broader, perhaps less scientific or systematic approach. They want to make schools better places for kids, and classrooms better places for learning. They are pragmatists and comprise a large proportion of those who attend conferences. They approach keynotes and sessions with an open and selective orientation because they include policymakers and practitioners who live with the day-today tensions between policy and practice, and understand the art of compromise.

The fourth group, the agnostics, bring a sceptical view to the effectiveness tradition. They want to work within the movement but also want to open to question what they see as the limitations of the 'scientific' paradigm. They are not antagonistic but rather a bit like doubting Thomas, needing to see the evidence that there is life after effectiveness. Their perspective is captured, to quote Judith Little, by 'aggressive curiosity and healthy scepticism'.

Then there are those genuinely antagonistic. They are the heretics, perhaps not within ICSEI but represented by 'outsiders', invited (often unwelcome) speakers, their challenges deeply rooted in a view of society, adopting a critical theorist's view of the essential functions and purposes of schools and highly critical of the effectiveness and improvement paradigms. Some of them are the structuralists to whom Russell Bishop refers.

I would argue that, whether a broad church or a broad science, we are nourished by that wide spectrum of participants. We engage with the pragmatists and agnostics and we thrive on the challenge of the heretics. Because we are, above all, a learning organisation.

Thomas Kuhn, who invented the term 'paradigm', defined it as a collection of beliefs shared by scientists, a set of agreements about how problems are to be understood, essential tenets of scientific inquiry. Improvement occurs, he argued, when 'mature science' develops through the transition from one paradigm to another. When a paradigm shift takes place, 'a scientist's world is qualitatively transformed [and] quantitatively enriched by fundamental novelties of either fact or theory.

Rather than relying on what is already known and applying knowledge to solving the problems that their theories dictate, scientists are open to ideas that may threaten the existing paradigm, but may in fact trigger the development of a new and competing paradigm. This is the 'broad' science. It is not afraid of, but rises to, the challenge. The way in which we respond to heretics is a salient litmus of the ICSEI 'movement'.

At its best the movement has been characterised by a social science that has been circumspect in treating 'effective schools' as a relative concept, in other words 'effective' as against 'less effective' schools. Nonetheless, it has at times been difficult to avoid a conceptual slide into conflation of the 'effective' and the 'good', slipping imperceptibly from science to theology. What a good school 'is' not only remains a contested notion but is becoming even harder to perceive in the current policy climate in virtually every country represented within the ICSEI body politic. I wonder if we have been guilty in the past of looking so closely within the black box of school we miss the true significance of what lies outside it?

## A 'plaice' to remember

Numbered among the effectiveness sceptics is Guntars Catlaks, Research Co-ordinator at Education International, the world's largest federation of teacher unions, representing thirty million education employees in about 400 organisations in 170 countries and territories worldwide. At a meeting in John Bang's much favoured 'Fish and Chip Plaice', just behind the NUT headquarters in Camden, Guntars commissioned me to write a book that would demystify 'effectiveness' and its insidious impact on educational policy. While the book enlarged its scope to become a treatise on the future of the teaching profession, I devoted a chapter to a critique of the effectiveness paradigm. I questioned by what statistical wizardry it is possible to disentangle the emotional lifes of young people lived out in the push and pull of peer and parental influence. What constitutes homework or 'home work', encompassing the tedious ritual of yet more sums at one extreme to the challenging dialogue with informed parents – a rich source of social capital? What to make of the term 'parental involvement', a strange concept to describe children's first and foremost educator, for good or ill, their 'involvement' in their children's learning, with the school or with a teacher, or with a multiplicity of teachers, lost in translation to a completely meaningless two digit figure? Television, a negative correlation (−0.12) may, for some, give rise to stimulating conversation, may ignite interest for further exploration and may, at its best, offer a veritable fund of information and inspiration. Why, after all, did schools so avidly embrace 'educational television'?

'Fishing for correlations' is how Coe and Fitz-Gibbon characterise an approach in which 'more of this is associated with more of that' does not help to tease out the intricate relationship among these 'variables', nor help to explain the hidden and deeper factors that underlie these relationships.

## A land of union members, university graduates and elves

The Guntars book, which had found its way from the Education Summit in New York to Reykjavik, found a particular resonance in Iceland where the impact of effectiveness is more implicit than explicit. In common with everywhere else, teachers are working longer hours for less pay and are uneasy with the 'hard' performance data. During a week's visit in October 2012, teachers and university academics welcomed the challenge to 'effectiveness' and to the 'hard' comparative data on which it rested. They welcomed the affirmation of their professional agency and status that too often is lost in political mandate and international comparison.

On an Icelandair flight, preparing to talk about the book, I learned that 30 per cent of the population has university degrees and that 50 per cent believe in elves. It did not mention that 100 per cent of teachers are members of a union and that their collective professional identity is a bulwark against the depridations of divisive politicians. There was, in discussion with students and teachers in Iceland, an echo of the theme for Ibraham Bajunid's opening keynote at the ICSEI conference in Malaysia, where he had spoken of the impatience of politics. 'In their rush to modernise and bureaucratise political leaders failed to build on the cultural legacy in which teachers learned, in the Socratic tradition of asking questions, in the Prophetic tradition of emphasizing self knowledge, in the community tradition of learning by doing, and in the storytelling tradition by listening'. Lifelong learning had, he argued, indigenous roots in Malaysian culture but been displaced by a politicised model of schooling that devalued the collective power of teachers and teaching. There were close resonances with experience in Iceland.

## A school education pays off at last

As the presidency of the European Union moved every six months from one country to the next I was, for a time, invited to follow its journey. Under the French Presidency, Poitiers was the site for the 2008 EU Conference entitled *Gouvernance et Performance d'écoles en Europe*. Its projected outcomes were: a) to show that increased autonomy of institutions and growing accountability of school partners constitute key factors for good governance based on the students' success; and b) to highlight the need to intensify the culture of results and accountability within the educational institution by involving teachers and educational leaders in educational performance evaluation devices. Invited as the opening keynote to 'frame the problematics of the conference and introduction of key aspects of governance and performance', I wondered if they had mistaken me for someone else as I had little sympathy with the two key aims of the conference. With some trepidation I addressed the problematics of autonomy of results, of accountability and what is too often mistakenly counted as 'student success', and the consequences of intensification. I had not expected that the two respondents, Joao Barraso, Professor at the University of Educational Sciences in Lisbon, and Per Tullberg, General Director of the National Direction of School and Pre-school Education in Sweden, would find so little to disagree with and would be so generous in their endorsement of what was, in the circumstances, patent heresy. I had won some sympathy for stepping down after fifteen minutes of my peroration to allow the late-coming minister to have his platform, departing as soon as I resumed my fractured talk. It did, however, give me the opportunity to take to task, however politely, some of the main assumptions of his rhetoric. I got the feeling there were of the audience more on my side than that of the minister. In Frascati in Italy shortly afterwards my heresies were less well received. The respondent on that occasion, Anders Hinkel of the European Commission, was less than impressed by my anti-thesis.

My vocation as a teacher of French had served me well not only in conferences in France but in French Canada. Invited by the Ministry in Quebec to speak at conferences in Montreal, Quebec and Trois-Rivières they had not anticipated that I would conduct these workshops in French. Regardless of content it earned me enormous credits in a part of the world hugely jealous of its Francophone identity. McGill University in Montreal was also the habitat of Bill Smith who had written the policy document *Schools Speaking to Stakeholders* and was delighted to discover that somewhere across the Atlantic a fellow traveller was composing a very similar thesis, *Schools Must Speak for Themselves*. The coincidence, or co-incidence of ideas that are given birth in two unconnected places is of itself a subject of numerous theoretical treatises.

## An intimate family

The smallest and most intimate of family conferences, at least in its early incarnation, is SERA – the Scottish Educational Research Association. In the heady days of the 1970s it was located in a suite of rooms directly overlooking the ocean in St Andrews. A strategically-placed seat during the more tedious of presentations allowed an unimpeded view of the waves rolling on to one of Scotland's finest beaches and one of the world's most famous of golf courses.

In the family tradition, evenings were given over to games, quizzes, occasional indiscretions and flirtations. It was less than wise for Her Majesty's Inspectors to be guilty of both those lapses of good taste. On one infamous occasion we lost our young researcher whom we didn't rediscover until well after midnight.

We learned that two of Scotland's most eminent academics had fallen in love with this callow youth and had enticed him to participate in a naked midnight swim.

## Sunny stories

Sunny Varkey is a Middle East multi-millionaire. To enter his grand house, or mini palace, one has to navigate past the Porsches, Bentleys and Rolls Royces. It is hard not to feel the poor relation confronted with Sunny's Saville Row suits and shirts that (according to reliable sources) never cost less than £200. He looks at my shoes and embarrassment deepens as I'm told, you know a man by his shoes. Lunch, served on gold-plated dishes and attended by hovering waiters, has to be ungraciously rushed as I am due back at the conference venue for the afternoon session.

Sunny, cited on the rich list as being worth £950 million, entrepreneur extraordinaire and founder of Global Education Management Services (GEMS), has been the recipient of numerous awards, many from India, his home country. His ambitions extend beyond the UAE to the appointment of Bill Clinton as the Honorary Chair of the Varkey GEMS Foundation. In September 2011 UNESCO announced the largest school principals' training programme involving a private foundation, GEMS, in their history. It was announced by President Clinton at the Clinton Global Initiative annual meeting in New York. A news item announced:

> The '10,000 Principals Leadership Programme' was announced by President Clinton as a 'commitment to action' at the Clinton Global Initiative annual meeting in New York today. By uniting parents, educators and governments under the cause of equal opportunity to schooling, Sunny Varkey is not only influencing teaching methods, but also helping to provide greater access to education, especially in Africa. An on-going collaboration between UNESCO and GEMS Education is training more than 10,000 school principals in Kenya, Ghana and India, while yet another programme is helping to improve STEM (science, technology, engineering and maths) education in Lesotho and Kenya.[1]

My Sunny story began at a conference in Dubai in 1998 when I was about to address around 500 people, the majority hidden behind the full burka, the only external appendage a mobile phone clamped to what could be assumed to be the right ear. Talking to an audience whom you cannot see and who spend much of the time on the phone does not do much for the fluency and confidence of delivery. A wave of laughter at one point – not for a joke but for an idiosyncratic Arabic translation – was a little unsettling and made me wonder what other forms of gobbledygook were being transmitted to my half-attentive audience. The front two rows of golden-robed sheiks had by this time left after their grand entrance, wreathed in coloured smoke and a sound and light show. There are probably many more exciting things to do in the Emirates than listen to what I was about to say. This may also hold true for the mobile phoners or those who might well have been catching a discrete nap behind their veils.

My invitation to Sunny's house for lunch with him, his wife and his two sons was: a) to bestow on me a lavish gift; b) to inspect my shoes; and c) to inquire if I would be interested in some form of consultancy for which I would enjoy a retainer that would help to subsidise more acceptable footwear.

This was the beginning of a two-and-a-half year relationship with GEMS. My schedule of visits to Dubai included leading workshops on self-evaluation, together with John Collins who headed the Quality Assurance Division of GEMS. It also included keynote speeches at conferences and in schools on parent evenings, attended by young people as well as their parents and teachers. My treatise on pupil voice found a particularly receptive audience with school students who engaged me in impromptu seminars following the talk. My attempt not to be too subversive was needless as my ex-Cambridge student, Jasmin Dannawy, whose MEd thesis had been on pupil voice, was now putting this to the test in a Dubai secondary school, her pupils holding the conference stage with aplomb and conviction.

The most challenging of presentations was at a highly formal dinner held round the swimming pool at the Varkey mansions with 100 prestigious guests, almost equaled by the number of dinner-suited waiters attendant with anticipation. There was a pulpit for me to give my after-dinner speech, admonished to be short on the jokes and long on homage and protocol. Forgetting this counsel, the first joke fell flat, met by a palpable and disconcerting silence. Over-enthusiastic embrace of the fine wines was perhaps a mistake.

The most lavish of occasions was the wedding of Sunny's eldest son, held in the Medinat Jumeirah hotel, more like a small town with its alleyways of shops, souks, restaurants and cafés, and gondolas that transport guests from one part of the sprawling complex to another. The menu for the evening banquet came in the shape of a small book, each section offering a choice from the Indian, French, Japanese or Middle East confection, each individual serving area occupying a different room in the hotel. For the ample constitution it was possible to sample all of the above. The after-dinner entertainment was provided by international artistes from trapeze acrobats and clowns to magicians and musicians. A gondola carried us after midnight back to our suite, the balcony of which looked across to the continually changing sequence of colours that light up the facade of the Berj, from pink to mauve to pale yellow.

On a later visit I was to enjoy a lunch in that outrageously decadent hotel, the very symbol of Dubai, with its helicopter pad and seven-star rating. But first were further visits to schools, accompanied by Mike Tomlinson, ex-HMCI who would later be appointed chair of the advisory group of which I proved to be a too infrequent attender, their meetings falling on dates that could not accommodate my Cambridge schedule. The munificent Christmas hampers, champagnes, caviars, hams, pâtés, and tinned delicacies began to diminish in size over the course of next three years and my honorarium was replaced by a more behaviourist polity of payment by results.

## On reflection

'Effectiveness' and 'improvement' are both words with common sense meanings, but have come to acquire quite specific and technical definitions for researchers and policymakers. There are some within the ICSEI movement who claim it as a science – a potentially invidious position when embraced by conviction politicians, for whom relative 'performance' and value-added come to assume a spurious validity. As each stage takes us closer to a common effectiveness and improvement template what is being lost, asks Ibrahim Bajunid? 'In their rush to modernise and bureaucratise political leaders have failed to build on the cultural legacy', endorsing and extending international comparisons and 'high stakes' league tables. Through this fourth lens we are confronted with the cultural beliefs, religious mores, unique rituals, and 'superstitions' in the Middle East, in Hong Kong, in Iceland. I wonder, again, if we have been guilty in the past of looking so closely within the black box of school that we miss the true significance of what lies outside it?

## Note

1 *UNESCO and Varkey GEMS Foundation launch principals' training programme that will impact 10 million children*, Online. Available at www.unesco.org/new/en/media-services/single-view/news/unesco_and_varkey_gems_foundation_launch_principals_training_programme_that_will_impact_10_million_children/> (accessed 9 January 2013).

# Part V
# The fifth lens

# 9 New enlightenment and a university for children

Harvard's David Perkins contrasts learning in captivity and learning in the wild. The latter is exemplified in what came to be known as 'study support', a misnomer for out-of-school activities that were not about 'study', not even requiring much 'support'. How this transformed into something more ambitious in the shape of the Children's University (CU) and its concept of learning destinations is described, with an example of one stunning such 'destination', Glasgow's Centre for New Enlightenment. The chapter begins with the story of enthusiastic support from Prince Charles for out-of-hours learning.

## A once and a future king

Learning out of school was the common theme in seminars with the King of Sweden and with Prince Charles a decade or so ago. The conduct and content of these seminars brought sharply to the fore the nature of the monarchy in these two countries, as well as the nature of the respective monarchs themselves. On two occasions King Carl Gustav participated in one-day conferences held in the library of the Royal Palace in Stockholm. On the second occasion he was accompanied by his wife, Queen Silvia, and his two sons and daughters. In the second of these two workshops the royal family was one of eight working groups seated around a table and engaged in the tasks at hand, reporting back and happy to be pressed for clarification and evidence for their conclusions. I took great pleasure in asking the queen to remain on task, a reprimand that she accepted graciously and with good humour.

A few years earlier at a conference in Glasgow, Rebecca, aged fifteen, had taken the stage in the school hall and had been speaking about how much study support in St Leonard's School had meant to her. It was a moving tribute to the difference that it made to her life in one of Scotland's most notorious housing estates. A few years later I was to write to HRH in the following terms:

November 2nd 2002

Dear Prince Charles,

I am in the process of writing a book about out-of-hours learning or 'study support', the name given to it by The Prince's Trust and the term that has remained in vogue nationally. I am documenting in this book what many regard as the most significant achievement of the Prince's Trust, a national movement that has touched virtually every school in the country, that has had a major impact at Government level and has been responsible in many schools and authorities for the evidence of raised achievement. More importantly, it has done so much to increase the confidence and self-esteem of disadvantaged young people. Our national evaluation, inspired and initially funded by the Trust, and eventually published by DfES, attests to its achievements.

The book will describe your own visits to Sarah Bonnel School in London, to St Leonard's in Glasgow and the national conference in Edinburgh, all three occasions on which we met. Much of its success is attributable to your personal endorsement and support and much to the vitality of the work done by Arwyn Thomas and Molly Lowell and support from Tom Shebbeare. The summer school movement emerged from those initiatives and has extended its influence since. I hope, through interviews with Arwyn, Molly, Tom and others, to portray why, even in the face of constant undermining from Her Majesty's Chief Inspector, a big idea was able to survive and flourish as it has. I will dedicate the book to that excellent human being and inspiration behind the movement, Jock Barr, who remained a courageous and enthusiastic supporter to the end.

I realise it may be an impertinence to ask you for an interview with you personally but I would be grateful for your view on this extraordinary achievement against the odds, so much of which was owed to the Prince's Trust Study Support team. I believe there is a great story to be told.

Yours sincerely

Professor John MacBeath OBE

So began my disingenuous letter to HRH, careful to add the OBE as a reminder that I had been personally honoured by his mother. It was disingenuous because there was a back story.

## The story begins

The story begins with four slightly apprehensive men in suits driving through the mean unlit streets of the Ardoyne at the height of 'the troubles' in Northern Ireland. There is a sense of relief as the car turns the corner, emerging into a pool of light that spills from St Gemma's School. Inside, over 100 children and young people are engaged in reading, sharing, playing, talking with teachers, with student mentors or other adults, motivated to return to school for up to three hours of an evening to do their homework or simply to enjoy a vitally different quality of learning in a relaxed, friendly and stimulating environment. Three nights a week the school opens its doors to children of any age and any religious persuasion.

There is no system to check out the books that children borrow from the library. If they fail to return that is all to the good, says Celia McClosky, the headteacher, as that means there is at least one book in the home. Celia had been the head of St Gemma's for more years than she cared to remember and after-hours learning, or 'study support', was her own initiative. It had been sustained in the face of opposition from the IRA, unhappy with the ecumenical nature of her project.

This was my introduction to study support at the invitation of Jock Barr, a trusted emissary of Prince Charles. While in Belfast we visited a small drop-in centre on the Shankhill Road where teenagers were able to study, share their homework and play pool, provided they have divided their time wisely between work and play. A third venue, later to become something of a cause célèbre, was Hackney Downs School, closed in 1995 after a Government declaration that it was the worst school in Britain.[1] The fourth visit was to Tom Hood, Jock Barr's former school in Leytonstone in East London, more famous perhaps for its most celebrated former pupil, Bobby Moore, the West Ham and England footballer. At Tom Hood study support took the form of residential weekends. In a placid college environment students could enjoy sustained tutorial support and structured activities such as Shakespeare workshops, in which the bard was recreated and performed in East End argot.

'Trust' was, in that more innocent age, the byword, as my costed proposal to evaluate the impact of study support required no extensive paperwork, refereeing, or further justification. The four studies of out-of-hours learning were then complemented by a somewhat more elaborated proposal to evaluate Strathclyde's own version of 'supported study'. In Strathclyde, supported study mainly took the form of homework clubs or study centres, held in the youth wing or the school library from 4pm until 6pm, with volunteer teachers on hand to work with students individually or in small groups. In Doon Academy in Ayrshire, serving a cluster of deprived rural communities and being one of Strathclyde's priority areas, young people returned in the evening from 6pm until 9pm, with snacks and drinks provided at half time.

As the evaluation showed, the success of these initiatives typically rested on the enthusiasm of an individual headteacher or teacher, as in the case of St Leonard's, in the urban wilderness that is Easterhouse. Situated seven or so miles to the east of Glasgow, Easterhouse is a depressing tribute to 1950s housing policy that transported inner-city residents from their collegial neighbourhoods to high vertical 'metropolises' and endless blocks of low-rise tenements, unrelieved by gardens, parks, shops, pubs, community centres –

'dry' areas in every sense of that word. Progressive demolition, refurbishment, introduction of shopping centres and pubs had, however, done little to undo the initial social architecture.

In St Leonard's, Chris (his surname long forgotten or never known) was the architect and patron of a frenetic hive of activity, circulating in perpetual motion around his charges and declaiming its success to any visitor or evaluator. Perhaps it was this that persuaded the Princely party to pay a visit and agree to take part in a seminar with some of the Strathclyde officers, teachers and school pupils. Seated in a circle of teachers, young people, the school head and various assorted royal minders, I invited the dozen or so participants to make a 'Toblerone' – a piece of A4 paper folded over twice to make a nameplate on which people would write the name by which they would like to be addressed. His expertly folded Toblerone bore the epithet HRH.

This was HRH's third visit to celebrations of study support, a previous success story had taken place in Sarah Bonnell School in Newham in East London, one of eight schools and centres in which we were researching out-of-school-hours learning funded by the Prince's Trust. So significant was the impact of the study support that the DfE was to publish two large ring binders, running to over 300 pages, one for pupils and one for tutors. Following a glowing endorsement by Jacqui Smith, Junior Education Minister, it contained a cornucopia of tools and good ideas, including pages from our Learning File on thinking skills and self-evaluation. Like much else, these expensively produced, inspirational and highly practical documents now lie at the bottom of a cupboard, no longer used and long forgotten.

## Al and I

The headquarters of the Prince's Trust is housed in an elegant terrace facing on to Regent's Park. I was a frequent visitor for meetings, seminars, data collection and briefings with the Prince's Trust team. It was the hive of activity, with an ever-expanding team managing the study-support initiative. Among the many memorable events, two are particularly vivid. The first, as I mounted the steps to the building one morning, I was to be greeted with an almost casual aside from Molly Lowell, 'Would I like to meet Al Pacino?' That evening there would be a royal premiere preceded by a cocktail reception with Al himself in attendance. Later, he very diffidently gave a short speech before the showing of the film 'Looking For Richard'. It remains to this day one of my all-time favourite films, although I have never met anyone who has seen it. The Richard in question is Richard the Third and the film moves between readings and rehearsals and the final production. The cinema-vérité of the film is further layered by an impromptu scene in Trafalgar Square where the actors in rehearsal are moved on by a couple of London bobbies.

The second and much more weighty moment was being informed by a shocked Molly Lowell that HRH was pulling out of funding the project, which would move to the DfES.

Perhaps things might have been different if Jock Barr had not passed away, a victim of an aggressive cancer. A few days before his death, a pallid imitation of his former self, he bravely joked about the future of study support which, he assured us, would long outlive him.

## With a little help from my friends: a university for children

Learning for yourself, out of school hours and with a little help from your friends, was an idea too big to go away. The CU, originally established by Tim Brighouse (then CEO in Birmingham) and David Winkley, a leading Birmingham headteacher, was revitalised five years ago with a small handful of centres and a management team of three, based in the Royal Northern College of Music in Manchester. The major credit for the continuing growth of the CU nationally, and now internationally, is owed to Ger Graus, its creative and apparently tireless Chief Executive, only rarely to be found in his office as his diary takes him on a daily basis to CU centres around the country as well as to other countries interested in finding out more about the Children's University – Australia, Estonia, Italy, Portugal, Ireland, Malaysia, Indonesia, Singapore, South Africa, Sri Lanka, China, Belize, the USA.

By April 2012, in the UK there were 80 local CUs, accounting for 3,000 schools and academies and over 100,000 children, with a total of just over 2 million hours of attendance. While centres have grown exponentially, the Manchester management team has remained intentionally small, demonstrating that the vitality of the CU lies 'out there' in local schools, universities and communities and the many agencies and 'learning destinations' that become partners. An important principle of the CU is that participation is voluntary. It is intentionally something other than school – with a different ethos, different activities and often a different location, staff and peer group. The ultimate testament to the effectiveness of the CU is that young people give up their time to attend and that they begin to realise that learning can be 'a satellite navigation system to better places in life'. Over the past year, not only has children's participation and commitment continued to increase, but they are also now playing a much more proactive role in generating ideas for future activities and exercising their agency and leadership.

Each local CU has a link with a Higher Education Institution and is encouraged to appoint its own Chancellor. Local CU Chancellors include the authors Louis de Bernières and Gervase Phinn, BBC's Anita Bhalla, Major General Christopher Callow, High Sheriff of Northamptonshire, David Laing and Olympic medallist Nick Gillingham. The national CU Chancellor is the children's author Michael Morpurgo.

Opportunities to learn out of the classroom are a distinguishing aspect of the CU. The more the potential to learn in sites outside school is opened up, the more imaginative and unexpected the result. One of the latest additions to the repertoire of learning destinations is a cemetery. What questions might be provoked by structured and focused explorations in a cemetery? Family histories and changing family size over the years? Child mortality? Changing life expectancy and advances in medical care? The 2,750 CU learning destinations include:

- The BBC
- The Houses of Parliament
- Shakespeare 4 Kidz
- Chatsworth House in Derbyshire
- Stage Arts Warwick (SAW)
- Engineering for Life (Engineers without Borders)
- Port Vale Soccer Club
- South Yorkshire Wildlife Park
- Doncaster Minster: a detective trail
- The Plymouth Naval Base
- The Plymouth Records Office

Many of the learning destinations and out-of-hours activities are suggested by children themselves. Tutors try to accommodate suggestions as long as there are viable numbers. 'While we try to meet all good suggestions', says a tutor in Doncaster, 'We can't do Disneyland or bungee jumping'. Lectures have proved hugely popular. In Plymouth the first lecture attracted thirty young people. Now over 150 young people regularly attend, as the success of previous events spread both by advertising and by word of mouth. Lectures in different parts of the country have included:

- How insects see the world – Professor Peter Smithers
- Polar Exploration – Anthony Jinman
- A year in Madagascar – Jeremy Sabel PCC biodiversity champion
- Marine Photography – National Marine Laboratory
- Pyromania – Professor Roy Lowry
- The truth behind Finding Nemo – The National Marine Aquarium
- Geology – Professor Iain Stewart (presenter of BBCs 'Journeys from the Centre of the Earth')

On Saturday mornings the superstore B&Q offers lectures and workshops for young people. At Manchester University, under Professor of Biomedical Egyptology Rosalie David, children can take part in courses on Making a Mummy, Ancient Egyptian Gods, Writing in Hieroglyphs, the Egyptian Number System and Egyptian Jigsaws.

Local libraries sign up and display the learning destinations logo. CU passport holders can claim up to six hours of credit for reading six books, plus a further four hours for additional challenging activities related to literature. Another summer programme, promoted by Lambeth CU, is the Poetry Parnassus, with free activities such as *Eat Your Word Edible Poetry, Kid's Poetry Tea Party, Kids' Poetry Treasure Hunt*, in which children hunt for individual lines of poetry and use them to create their own poem. Also in Lambeth, and recently validated by the CU, children can engage in exploratory trails around the Natural History Museum, including hands-on family activities, animal vision workshops and explorer backpacks. Collaboration with UTV Media, based in Wigan, is an e-learning programme that enables children to create their own radio promotions, with the help of the UTV creative team, writing and recording a radio or video 'commercial'.

The creation of passports, which give entry to learning destinations and merit a stamp for every validated learning hour, has proved a major success. By March 2012, 160,000 passports had been issued, with plans to reach a quarter of a million by 2013. The prototype with squared corners was rejected by children who pointed out that real passports have rounded edges. Passports, now with rounded edges and embossed with gold, are so valued that the loss rate of around 2 per cent compares with an adult rate of nearly 20 per cent.

Graduations take place in universities, often in surroundings described by children as 'awesome' and by parents as 'breathtaking'. They are very often presided over by the Vice Chancellor himself/herself, handing out certificates to children begowned and wearing tasseled mortar boards. Ten headlines in my 2010 evaluation were:

1 **Being in the CU significantly improves school attendance.**
A recurring theme in the evaluation of the CU is children's increased attendance because, as they told researchers, they don't want to miss CU activities, however engaged, or disengaged, they may be during timetabled lessons in school.

2 **Achievement is significantly better at Key Stages 1 to 3 for children who participate in the Children's University compared with non-attenders.**
In the second reading of the Education Bill, Michael Gove pointed to the progressively widening gap between those on free school meals and those not. A gap in reading scores of 16 points at age 7 grew to 21 points by age 11 and 28 points by age 16. That gap narrows for the most disadvantaged children who participate in CU activities.

3 **The further children engage with Children's University, the better their attendance and achievement.**
As the evidence, shows, the greater and more sustained the opportunities for learning activities beyond the classroom, the higher the achievement. Engagement with CU has been shown to set in train a virtuous circle of engagement–satisfaction–raised motivation–higher aspiration–higher achievement.

**4 Children's University provides an environment for self-driven, confident and collegial learning.**

While school is, for many children, a place in which success comes easily, for others, school is an experience of struggle and failure, with very few incentives and rewards for the return on investment. For such children the CU environment has proved to offer a lifeline, restoring self-esteem and satisfaction in learning.

**5 Children's University provides a safe haven and models positive relationships.**

A sense of safety and friendship offered by CU is valued particularly by vulnerable children – a safe place to talk with teachers about bullying and racism, typically concealed and suffered in silence. Relationships forged within CU among pupils and between pupils and teachers carries over into in the main stream of school – a raised awareness and readiness to deal with incidences of bullying or intimidation.

**6 Pupils and teachers testify to life-changing experiences.**

Opportunities to complement and enrich classroom learning can be life changing. Disillusion can become ambition and failure turned to success. Often overlooked are life-changing experiences for teachers, the escape from the classroom allowing them to engage with children in a different environment, to listen free from pressures of time and impatient targets, gaining a new understanding of children's lives and learning in differing contexts.

**7 'Opportunity costs' are high for children in disadvantaged areas who do not attend Children's University.**

Young people who do not attend CU are often, by default, to be found hanging around shops and street corners, vulnerable to trouble makers, to drugs and other inducements. They are also likely to fall foul of the law. Those who do attend prove to be much less prone to trouble and police 'harassment'.

**8 Certificates, credits, Passports To Learning and graduations are valued incentives and rewards.**

Access to learning destinations validated by CU as learning sites, have proved to be highly motivational, the stamp on children's Learning Passport providing a cumulative record of their achievements, leading to the excitement of graduations and impetus to engage further.

**9 University settings help to inspire and raise aspirations for children, and their parents.**

Through CU graduations, which a majority of parents attend, through visits to universities and through a keen interest taken by vice-chancellors, children and their parents are offered a vision of what might be, raising aspirations and making a university education less beyond their reach.

**10 Children's University has helped to make learning a reality beyond academic studies.**
The range of activities encompassed within the CU helps to cultivate many of the skills and dispositions that are at a premium with employers. Initiative, self direction, reliability, ability to work in a team, willingness to learn, emotional intelligence, while less likely to be the product of direct teaching, have been shown to be the product of engagement in CU activities.

## A Centre for New Enlightenment

Glasgow's Museum and Art Galleries Centre for New Enlightenment, TCoNE for short, is set to become a CU learning destination. I was able to take Ger Graus, the CU CEO, there on a participatory visit in which, as a pair, we experienced at first hand the pupil's eye view. At the launch of the CU in Scotland in December 2012, Jean Paul, architect and champion of TCoNE, told me that 10,000 young people had now experienced its peculiar magic. Kelvingrove's Centre for New Enlightenment is a dedicated space that children visit, initially as a school class, or on a return visit with their parents or friends. The entry portal is a six-foot eye that eerily follows you round and, for young people, it is the first sense of intrigue before entering the futuristic white space, captured by one twelve-year-old girl as 'The room looked like a cyberman ship'.

Before entering, children have their photo taken in pairs, heightening the sense of mystery and expectation. Once seated, a panoramic screen immerses the audience in a journey into the future. As pairs of photos are flashed up on the screen young people join their appointed partner. Each pair is then equipped with earphones and a handheld computer that will help them navigate the museum. Finding the exhibit and following the clues, in a maze as large as the museum, is frequently cited as the most rewarding challenge. It begins to build a sense of self-confidence as pupils successfully locate the item and then follow instructions without the help of an adult. While turning to an adult for help is OK, it is not the same as being told what to do. Problem-solving activities are designed to engage one of the four key objectives of compassion, trust, endurance and determination. For example, seated by a statue of a widowed mother with child, pairs are asked to consider the circumstances and what to say to the bereaved mother. The objective of empathy proved to be so powerful that, in some cases, teachers accompanying the pupils were advised to be aware and to use these occasions for follow up in the classroom.

At each of the selected sites there is a camera recording young people's reactions so that when they return to base their photos and reactions are flashed up on the screen, generating excitement and sharing of anecdote.

The evaluation demonstrated the benefits for children of working with someone they didn't know. Children said it was a good way of getting to know someone, adding that some pairs had become friendlier afterwards. One boy said he was surprised that he had learned so much from his appointed partner. Working with people you didn't know very well proved to be an unexpected bonus.

The Centre grew out of the Hunter Foundation's ambition for children and young to 'find the hero inside themselves', to believe that they were not victims of circumstance but architects of their own futures. It was recognised that Scotland's achievements were owed to the much-vaunted 'canny' Scot, but that the 'cannae' (cannot) Scot was a much more familiar figure to teachers in Scottish schools. In interviews leading to the design of TCoNE it was found that young people said it was much easier to talk about failure than success. Failure in exams was the most frequent theme, with unemployment, addiction and dependency recurring as salient aspects of the discourse. Inevitability and fatalism were prevalent themes in these conversations. These findings gave impetus to confronting the 'cannae' and bringing out the buried sense of agency that lies at the centre of the TCoNE's purpose. Problem-solving activities around the various exhibits, children working in pairs with a handheld PDA, engaging in a learning experience so different from school, is a consistent theme in the evaluation, in which children wrote fulsomely about the new lease of life it had given them as to their capacity as learners. The navigation with the handheld PDA was integral to the experience – no paper and pencil, no adult direction or supervision, but a demonstration of trust – that you are capable of learning on your own, capable of helping your partner, capable of looking after expensive technology and behaving considerately in a public space.

Being trusted to work independently, to solve problems on your own without a teacher directing you, were cited by a number of young people as helping to build confidence in their own resourcefulness and self-efficacy. Most of those interviewed in both primary and secondary schools would like to go back and many said they would like to take their parents or friends with them. The following are words used in the evaluation, conspicuously devoid of any negatives:

| | | | |
|---|---|---|---|
| New | Great | Exciting | Problem solving |
| Different | Excellent | Dynamic | Riddles |
| Special | Gigantic | Fun | Adventurist |
| Good | Marvellous | Cool | Teamwork |
| Enjoyable | Fantastic | Brill | Independent |
| Entertaining | Fabulous | Happy | Partnership |
| Praiseworthy | Spectacular | Funny | Communication |
| Positive | Super | Weird | Hi-tech |
| Informative | Enthusing | | Liked the gadgets |
| Great knowledge | | | Want to go again |

## On reflection

Schools are places for enlightenment, in Plato's famous metaphor leading us from seeing the shadows on the wall as reality, to coming to understand the shadows as merely pallid imitations of truth, values and virtue. In the 'new enlightenment', as illustrated in Glasgow's Kelvingrove museum, children are trusted to find truth and beauty in unexpected places. Perhaps this is what David Perkins had in mind when he contrasted learning 'in captivity' with learning 'in the wild'. As with Glasgow's TCoNE, the CU exemplifies what Perkins refers to as 'wilding of the tame', taking children and young people out of their comfort zone, freed from the captivity of teaching to become leaders of their own and others' learning.

## Note

1   The decision remains controversial to this day, opponents of the closure pointing out that Hackney Downs was singled out for special treatment by the government (presumably *pour encourager les autres*) and that its academic results were not significantly worse than many other inner-city comprehensives, especially considering the problems it had inherited, including the steady 'decanting' of problem pupils – who had frequently been expelled from their original schools – to Hackney Downs.

# 10 'Notschool'

## Freeing the children ... and other political prisoners

The free schools of the Coalition Government bear little resemblance to those that flourished in the heady days of the 1970s. Their inspiration, A.S. Neill's Summerhill School, was to become something of a cause célèbre, defying the combined might of OFSTED and the DfE. While Summerhill spectacularly survives, its imitators have largely disappeared and been co-opted into the mainstream. Schools without walls, which flourished in the same era, may enjoy something of a renaissance, as school buildings can no longer contain the learning that takes place increasingly in the virtual world.

### Justice in the Royal Courts

In March 2000 the Royal Courts in the Strand were the site for Summerhill School's appeal against a notice of complaint issued by the Education Secretary, David Blunkett. A highly critical OFSTED report had said pupils were allowed to 'mistake idleness for the exercise of personal liberty'. If the notice were to be upheld, the school would be closed after seventy-nine years. Inexplicably, I was appointed as one of two independent witnesses in the case against Summerhill brought by OFSTED, determined to bring this unruly miscreant to book. Summerhill and OFSTED could not easily be accommodated in the same sentence. Summerhill, sometimes described as 'the do as you please school' and OFSTED, the 'do as we say' enforcers.

I was to visit Summerhill on a number of occasions and to visit many of its American imitators in the heady flower power days of the 1970s. In that era there weren't many people in education who weren't acquainted with the legend of Summerhill School or had not read the works of its founding father, A.S. Neill. I had corresponded with Neill up until his death and been hugely impressed by the maturity and intelligence of young people I talked to in the school, the embodiment of his values and his charisma. As a visiting Professor at the State University of New York, my first lecture on education in England had proved so eminently dull that a number of my less-than-captive audience exited at the rear theatre door. Many had come expecting me to talk about Summerhill and so when I eventually capitulated and engaged in a Q and A session on Summerhill, my erstwhile disengaged audience began to revive.

As an independent counsel for the court hearing I was to peruse a veritable mountain of documents – inspection reports, government guidelines and legalisation, responses from the school, letters to and from parents, newspaper reports, etc. I also visited the school, not for the first time, but on this occasion in the company of Ian Stronach, appointed as 'counsel for the defence'. We conducted a few informal interviews with young people whose perspicacity and individuality were hugely impressive. Less impressive was a visit to a History classroom where the teacher had prepared documentary extracts and a video excerpts only for no one to turn up. Some had decided to stay in the previous Maths lesson. Some had decided to engage in more interesting pursuits.

In my report I tried to reconcile the freedom to choose and the teacher's investment of time and efforts being disappointed. While sympathetic with the philosophy of no compulsion or coercion, I commented on the obvious dysfunction of sequential timetable periods in a traditional school mould, and the pursuit of freedom and choice. I felt it was a failure of imagination when a young person could spend weeks and months on end climbing trees and never being enticed into engaging 'lessons', projects or research. I was not persuaded by Ian Stronach's argument that climbing trees could be just as valuable a stimulus to deeper insights. The paradox of Summerhill was that in such a rich and congenial environment, classroom teaching could be so often uninspired.

As I was also required to attend for the week at the Royal Courts and give testimony, I wanted to be as supportive as possible, but at the same time honest in my critique. The first act on entering the court was to be greeted by Queen's Counsel (QC) Geoffrey Robinson, representing the school. He asked for my signature on the book resting before him on the podium, *Schools Must Speak for Themselves*.[1] Was I to be hoisted on my own petard? Despite being called as 'independent' researchers, the two independent counsels shared the room with the Government side and were, therefore, party to their discussions and alarm calls to the Department and to the Chief Inspector. By day three of the hearing there was something of a siege mentality, with the admission over afternoon coffee that 'we' were losing the case. When asked what I was going to say late on day three when I was due to be called, there were sudden alarm bells on the part of the Government team who famously observed, 'But you're not on our side'. It was a further lesson on what 'independence' can mean in a high-stakes policy arena.

The OFSTED case rested on two key demands: one, that there be separate toilets, and two, that lessons be made compulsory. These were so antithetical to the ethos and raison d'être of the school that they were beyond compromise. I was prepared to fully endorse the Summerhill rationale that was at the very heart of the case against it. By day three, however, it had become increasingly apparent, as the beleagured DfES civil servant was being given an increasingly hard time, that the Government side were not going to win. Half an hour before I was due to take the stand on the afternoon of day three, the Government side capitulated and Anna Neill (A.S. Neill's daughter) was asked to accept the verdict of the Tribunal that the Government demands be dropped. She could not make that decision, she said, as she was not 'the school' but the caretaker. The court was therefore cleared and the Tribunal bench taken over by three Summerhill pupils who asked their colleagues – all the pupils of the school in the hall – to vote on the final decision. This process lasted for one hour until finally the pupils agreed to accept the Government climb down. Celebrations followed outside the court while the Government team (without me) made a hurried exit. As reported by *The Guardian* on 23 March 2000:

> Outside court, Mrs Readhead hugged pupils and staff and said: 'This is the most wonderful triumph for us; my father always had faith in the law, and he would be delighted at how it has brought him victory and vindication over a bureaucracy which could never cope with his ideas.' She added: 'We have lived for a year under the OFSTED falsehood that we have mistaken idleness for liberty. Today's verdict refutes that defamation and shows that liberty and learning go hand in hand at Summerhill. We can now put all the pettiness and incomprehension to which we have been subjected behind us, and look forward to a sensible and productive relationship with OFSTED and the Department of Education.'

In late October 2012 Ian Stronach's support for Summerhill was spectacularly vindicated. He was to write an article entitled 'OFSTED's Opinion of Summerhill: From pariah to paragon':

### OFSTED's opinion of Summerhill School: From pariah to paragon

### Release: 27 October 2011

A. S. Neill's famous Summerhill School, the world's first 'child democracy', has received the best HMI/OFSTED report in its 90-year history. After decades of criticism and controversy at the hands of the Inspectors, the School has now been found 'outstanding' in 8 aspects of its provision and practice and 'good' in all others. Inspectors were particularly impressed by its continuing excellence in relation to pupils 'spiritual, moral, social and cultural development' (SMSCD). 'Welfare, health and safety of pupils' was also outstanding, as were all 5 aspects of boarding provision, welfare and outcomes'.

The contrast with Summerhill's 1999 Inspection is total. Then, HMI condemned its philosophy, aims and outcomes, finding its freedoms to be an 'abdication' of adult responsibility. The adjective the Inspection most often directed at its pupils was 'foul-mouthed'. The finding that it offered neither 'suitable' nor 'efficient' education meant that the school faced closure. The School had to raise a Tribunal case to prevent that outcome.

The Tribunal vindicated the School, and the Ministry withdrew in haste from the case after three days. These events were vividly portrayed in an award-winning BBC drama in 2008. The parties to the Tribunal Agreement accepted that future inspections of the School would be accompanied by an 'expert' nominated by the School. In turn the Ministry demanded a similar 'expert'. So now the Inspectors were to be inspected, and the inspector of the inspectors likewise. Thus the possible tragedy of closure became something of a farce of surveillance (hyperveillance?) – but a necessary and useful safeguard for the School.

Since then, things have looked up. The 2007 Inspection deemed the school 'satisfactory', while assessing SMSCD features 'outstanding'. Why have things turned round so dramatically? Two explanations are possible. In audit logic, a 'failing' school has been transformed. Or, from a research perspective, a 'failing' OfSTED has finally acknowledged the virtues of the school, including uncoerced learning, democratic governance led by the pupils, and freedom in relation to learning and assessment.

Professor Ian Stronach, Liverpool John Moores University, the school's 'expert' since 1999, argues that the school A.S. Neill wrote about more than fifty years ago, and the school he researched in 1999, 2007 and 2011, is 'essentially the same place, though the inspectorial surfaces are much more expertly polished.' He added, 'OfSTED deserve credit, at last, for an 'outstanding' Inspection process and outcome in 2011'. Let's hope this marks the end of Inspectorial persecution, here and elsewhere.

Ian Stronach

Professor of Educational Research, Liverpool John Moores University

## Free the children and other political prisoners

The title of Alan Graubard's book captures the spirit of an age in which freedom was the byword and policymakers the enemy within. Summerhill was the inspiration for the wave of free schools that surfaced in the early and mid 1970s. They were of their time, an era of dissent and protest. Neill himself did not approve of some of the early imitators, as licence for him was not to be equated with freedom.

In 1970 a directory of free schools across the United States was published. While of lesser substance than its telephone equivalent it was, nonetheless, testament to a burgeoning movement. Free schools resonated with the general euphoria of liberation, flower power, dropping out, Jack Kerouac, road movies, peace, mysticism and the Beatles' adoption of the Maharishi. Free schools sprang up so fast all over the States, many of these for children of middle class, predominantly white, parents. A broadside from the Left criticised such schools as the indulgent preserve of the middle class who, by opting out of the mainstream, further marginalised less-privileged children in the state sector. A particularly powerful voice at the time was that of Jonathan Kozol, who had written about systemic failure to provide a decent education for black inner-city children, documented in his moving account of Boston elementary schools, *Death at an Early Age*.[2] It described the dreary and soulless schools in inner-city Boston, which for black children meant a slow attrition of their hopes and self-esteem, as the essential message of schooling was to be resigned to one's status in an unjust society. At the same time James Herndon[3] was writing about the frustrations of trying to counter the expectations of black children for whom such radicalism threatened 'the way it spozed to be'. Such threat to the status quo was both unsettling and, as these disenfranchised black children saw it, a futile gesture.

This more politicised critique gave rise to a very different kind of free school. Kozol was to give strong support to free schools in inner cities, exclusively or predominantly for children from African–American backgrounds. These schools offered a more structured and disciplined alternative to the imperfect anarchy of their white counterparts. Leaving children to do as they pleased in the name of freedom held no appeal for families whose children had been already disadvantaged enough by a laissez-faire approach and wanted structure and support, if not the stultifying kind typified by mainstream schools. The archetypical expression of these free schools was Harlem Prep, sited in a disused supermarket in one of the most dilapidated neighbourhoods in New York city. The 'prep' was for entry to higher education, designed to raise aspirations of young people for whom a university, let alone Columbia on their very doorstep, had never entered their compass of thinking. It was to prove spectacularly successful.

During a nine-month period as Visiting Professor at the State University of New York I had spent much of my (considerable) spare time in perusing the free schools directory and paying visits to the free schools in New York State, Vermont, Massachusetts and Philadelphia. Least interesting were the free-for-all 'schools', such as one to which I paid a very cursory visit, witnessing a child riding a mini motor bike unimpeded through the 'classroom', 'expressing himself' with total disregard for those around him. The most compelling initiative was a Storefront Learning Center in Boston, established by African–American parents and teachers and funded on a social contract with bounds of behavior discussed and sanctions negotiated and agreed.

> What gets you about the Storefront Learning Center is a kind of exuberance and joy that goes into everything. You wish school had been like this when you were a kid. Wonder if your own kids are getting as much excitement out of learning. It makes that precious moment of childhood charged with meaning.
>
> (Thelma Burns, Director)

The freedom espoused by schools such as this is owed to a liberation from low expectations, from the legacy to the black community of a system in which institutional racism was only now beginning to be exposed.

In Boston I also visited Highland Park, where its commitment was to black inner-city children whose parents earned less than 1,000 dollars a month, but were willing to give their own time to helping out and coaching children in this desperately deprived inner-city enclave.

Although the United States was the mecca for free schools they were, albeit briefly, an international phenomenon. In Britain the first and most well-known free school was Scotland Road in Liverpool, run by two former community workers, John Ord and Danny Murphy. On return to the UK with my post-Brockport idealism still intact, I arranged a visit for twelve of my Jordanhill College students to visit Scotland Road, the deal being that we would take over the school for a day. This was not an entirely successful enterprise as the first lesson to be learned was that, by definition, you can't manage a free school, so finding the putative attendees, keeping hold of them and requiring them to do things was a fraught and generally thankless exercise. As the free school was not a building but an itinerant collection of children and young people, it seemed like a good idea at the time to bring them for a week to Glasgow and to Jordanhill College. The proposed visit was, unwittingly, approved by a benevolent Principal who could not have envisaged the true nature of the motley hoard that would descend on his college. The plan was for these children each to be housed with a volunteer student teacher who would also organise an educational experience for him or her in the city of Glasgow, based on the Philadelphia model of the school without walls.

General disillusion was not slow to set in. The Scotty Road youth expressed their preference not to stay with students, and John Ord, after a night chez nous, opted for a less conventional place to stay. Visits to art galleries and museums failed to ignite the enthusiasm of restless teenagers who preferred to play the juke box in the College cafeteria, resulting in a complaint to the Principal by college students tired of hearing Amazing Grace played for the twentieth successive time. A.S. Neill would not have approved. Nor did we, although in the spirit of the times the blame could be laid at the door of the stuffy rule-bound institutions unable to accommodate the free spirits released from the bonds of convention.

## Who dares to venture

One outcome of visits was the founding of Scotland's first and only free school – Barrowfield Community School – in the east end of Glasgow. Barrowfield was at one time described as the most deprived housing estate in Europe. It was a place where delivery services refused to enter, depositing furniture or other goods at an external rendezvous. Taxi drivers too dropped off their deliveries on the main London Road to the south or on the Gallowgate to the north. Barrowfield was a testament to Glasgow Council's housing policy that clustered all its most problem tenants in small and notorious bottom-of-the-heap enclaves, in effect 'ghettos', although I was to be admonished by the Jordanhill College Principal never to use that word again. For a time my head of department was obliged, with conspicuous unease, to precede my lectures with the health warning, 'Mr MacBeath's views do not reflect the views of Jordanhill College'. My extravagant language ('ghetto') somehow reached the ears of the headteacher of Riverside School, from which the Barrowfield clientele had opted out. I was, in the company of my head of department, Colin Holroyd, required to visit the school and explain myself. The tirade to which I was subjected, accused of 'seducing' little children by showing them a better life, was delivered with such invective that afterwards Colin and I had to repair to the nearest hostelry for a therapeutic drink.

## A divided community

The Barrowfield story in the 1970s is told in part by the statistics. At that time no single family in that desolate square mile had ever been to a university or experienced any form of further or higher education, indeed no single resident had obtained school-leaving qualifications, most having left at fifteen or sixteen. Lone parent households outnumbered nuclear families. Infant mortality was well above average and life expectancy alarmingly low. Crime and violence were endemic and the main street running through the estate was divided north and south by two rival gangs, the Torch and the Spur. For a period there was a police curfew that required everyone to be off the streets by 10 o'clock.

Although by 1971, when I returned from the US, I had lived in Glasgow for sixteen years, I had never heard of Barrowfield. How I got there or how it got to me remains a bit of a mystery but it was not long after my return from the United States that I was contacted to ask if I would advise the local Tenant's Association on setting up a free school. Such an outlandish thought in Glasgow in 1971 deserved at least the courtesy of a conversation and I duly found my way there and followed the counsel to park my car well away from the area and walk the rest. The children I was to meet were either expelled from school, persistent truants or simply bored and disengaged. It was a daunting prospect to envisage a free school in such a location and with such disaffected young people. In the event the pleas from this small group of committed tenants was irresistible. I was still under the heady influence of my American experience and a belief that all things were possible. However, it was apparent that I would have to do a number of things if a free school were to in any way become a reality – consult the statutes and legal provisions, locate a venue, find any teachers idealistic enough to want to teach in such a place, then to give serious thought to finance or sponsorship.

The first step was to examine the legal basis for running a school. At that time, to open a school one had to have a minimum of five children, a building that would meet safety regulations, a toilet and at least one 'teacher', although the qualifications for that role were somewhat elastic. A local church hall and a Church of Scotland Minister, Eric Cramb, hugely sympathetic to the cause, left to me the simple job of finding a teacher (or teachers) and a source of finance to pay them. I devoted much of my time to working my way through reference books on charitable foundations, writing begging letters and receiving polite rebuffs. I stood at the stage door of the Alhambra Theatre waiting to canvas the singer Lulu who had grown up near Barrowfield. I wrote to Sean Connery and Jackie Stewart and eventually got a small grant from their charitable foundation. The Calouste-Gulbenkian Foundation eventually responded to a begging letter and sent their Director Peter Brinson to look us over.

Meanwhile, Brian Addison was teaching the first cohort of five select young people, receiving no salary but living in our house for a year or so where he was fed and watered. Brian had been one of the famous few who had been part of Option H at Jordanhill, the elective for free thinkers and dissidents. When the germ of the free school idea surfaced Brian was first in line to volunteer to teach the six young people who had signed up for sessions in a barren church hall , with no prospect of income and no resources except these young people's own internal motivation and a teacher who believed in them. The continuing quest for sponsorship and the search for more suitable premises continued for the first few months, the basement in the church hall serving as a classroom. To eventually find a suite of three rooms above a taxi firm was a cause for celebration, funded by a small grant from the Scottish Education Trust.

## To each according to need: a democracy in miniature

With the promise of some financial security we were able to engage two more teachers, Roddy Thomson, another product of Option H, and Stella Coumbis, employed as a hospital night porter, but with an optimism and passion of the kind that was alive and well in the early 1970s. In the spirit of the free school, in which decisions were made by the pupils, Brian, Roddy and Stella were awarded salaries commensurate with their perceived needs. Stella already had a night job, so she was deemed to be worth nine pounds a week. Similarly Brian, lodging with us, was accorded a similar sum. Roddy with a house, wife and two children was voted the princely sum of twenty-seven pounds a week. 'To each according to need' – a democracy in miniature.

And what about a curriculum? What would these young people deem important priorities? They may not have been acquainted with the trivium or quadrivium but that was what they originally opted for – History, Maths, English, Science. What else would one learn in school after all? It took some time to open up the scope that their community, their city and their country could offer them, but gradually a more adventurous curriculum began to take shape. A vegetable plot was a big attraction and allowed Brian, a Maths graduate, to exploit the space for some basic numeracy and geometry.

The 'curriculum' is perhaps a misnomer for the range of activities that extended to all members of the community as well as young people – the setting up of a Citizen's Rights group, a Food Co-op, community transport, which ferried pensioners to clubs and helped with furniture removals and emergency transport to hospitals and vets, courts and police stations. And what about rules and sanctions? Again, school-shaped suggestions were offered – uniforms, no smoking or swearing. Obviously. Ironically, the school was later to be headlined in the tabloids and on television as 'The School where Children Smoke and Swear'. Interviewed on Newsnight and asked to comment on such outrageous behavior, I suggested that it would be difficult to find any school in the land in which pupils didn't smoke or swear, but only by devious and subversive means. Although indulged in more openly in Barrowfield, neither habit was encouraged and efforts were made to discuss alternative modes of expression and satisfaction.

One of the first of many visits was to a farm at which these young people were introduced to a potato, this knobbly brown vegetable that was the source of their chips and chip butties, children marveling at the oval shaped white objects which, they learned, were eggs. While this may seem a little apocryphal, a newspaper article in June 2012 reported on a study in which one third of sixteen to twenty-three year olds interviewed did not know that eggs came from chickens.[4]

En route to the farm in my minivan we passed Barlinnie prison. An excited contest took place behind me: 'My dad's been in there'; 'My big brother is in there the noo'; 'I have two brothers in there'. It struck me that this contest of esteem by proxy was the equivalent of middle-class children bragging about a university. George's observation that he would be there before his mates because he was the oldest of the group, confirmed the impression that this was the logical next step after school.

Brian's photo, along with his first few disciples, was to feature in numerous newspaper and television documentaries. Newspaper headlines tell the unfolding story over four years:

> Glasgow's First Free School Opens its Doors
> Pupils in a Class of their own – for making History
> School is for Living
> Lessons for Living – the Barrowfield way
> Optimism Growing
> Trying to stop the rot
> Permission to go on living
> Barrowfleld – bleak news from the East
> The School for Rebels is facing the axe

The school only finally faced the axe after a proper school building had been donated by a forgiving local authority and, a year or so later, destroyed by fire. Apparently, after one of the school's number had been sanctioned by his colleagues for theft – his punishment to be left at home while his classmates went on weekend trip – he climbed into the school via a skylight and set fire to a classroom, it spreading successfully to the rest of the building. I was phoned in the early morning with the doleful news, followed by an estimate from the local authority for the damage, and a query as to whether there were resources to rebuild. There was no such resource and little energy in reserve to start again, and in 1977 Barrowfield Community School followed the path of its predecessors into the history books.

## An aquarium for William

The 1970s was a golden age before the invention of accountability, and the freedom for college lecturers to go out and play allowed virtually unlimited time and scope to produce video programmes, with the facility of an outside broadcast van and team of producers, cameramen and sound engineers who had nothing else to do. So, months were spent filming in and around Barrowfield, capturing the neglect, the threats of violence and the dismissive treatment of its inhabitants by the local authority, by tradespeople and local businesses. Video vignettes included:

- A young woman crossing a derelict wasteland and climbing through a window to get into her flat as the front door didn't function and had no key.
- A lone parent pointing to the wallpaper sagging off the ceiling and explaining that the council workmen, in their hurry to get out, had simply taken one roll of wallpaper, slapped it up one wall, across the ceiling and down the other side.
- A grandmother confessing that her television had long since 'conked oot' but she kept it so as people wouldn't think she was too poor, adding but if she were to come into money she would by an aquarium for her grandson, William.

Our producer, Gus Macaulay, thought it would be a great idea to counterpoint the poverty in the film with images of luxury, so he recruited Jack Maclean, newspaper columnist and self-styled urban Voltaire, and filmed him speaking about poverty against a backdrop of state-of-the-art kitchens at the Modern Homes exhibition, and at the Marriot Hotel in Glasgow, sipping a lavishly-adorned cocktail. An orchestra was hired and filmed in a Glasgow pub and, when that didn't quite work as a soundtrack, a busker was brought in to record an adapted version of *The Streets of London*. An evening of free drinks with an invited comedian Billy Glasgow (the other Billy wasn't available) was recorded, Billy making would-be sympathetic jokes about life in the east end, resulting in a walk-out of insulted tenants and an article in the *Evening Times* the following day recording tenants' displeasure. Their anger was further fuelled by our filming of an interview with Carol X, the victim of a notorious assault that had dominated headlines for a number of weeks. Silhouetted against an orange curtain she talked of the endemic violence she lived with. The good people of Barrowfield did not want Carol X in their film and the sequence, powerful as it was, never saw the light of day.

The film ran for an hour and a quarter and was due to be screened at the Cosmo Arts Cinema, but for some forgotten reason this never came to pass. The happiest sequel to the film was for a Glasgow pet shop to donate an aquarium to William, his photo featured in the newspaper, proudly receiving his gift.

## Schools without walls

In many respects Barrowfield was a school without walls since much of the learning took place in the community, in the city or on travels to places that at best had only been ciphers on a two-dimensional map. Twenty years ago, before the invention of the virtual world, the 'real world' beyond the school offered an alternative arena for lifelong learning. The iconic demonstration of a powerful alternative to desk-bound learning in Philadelphia's School Without Walls had played a part in what was to take shape in Glasgow's east end.

Parkway, the central artery that runs through the heart of Philadelphia, offered the learning space for a whole curriculum, centred on the agencies that comprise the life of a city. This not only saved millions on school buildings, textbooks, administration and all the paraphernalia that consumes the lion's share of the education budget, but also was able to show that young people have a much greater capacity for initiative and agency than schools give them credit for.

Rochester, New York had its own version of a school, one which I was privileged to visit in 1972. Led by Lew Marks, an English teacher at Monroe High School, his students presented a proposal for the School Without Walls (SWW) to the District Superintendent in January 1971. Approved later that year by the Board of Education it opened in September 1971, its base soon to be the defunct Sears Automotive building not far from Monroe High School. Even schools without walls do no need a home base. In 1972 I had the opportunity to talk to young people from this not-school. Their knowledge of the city, of local and state politics, of decision-making and vested interest was humbling. These were lessons that I had never learned in school or even university, and certainly not with the immediacy of living learning at first hand and in situ. Helping young people to make sense of their experience has been described as promoting 'horizontal connectedness', making connections across areas of knowledge and beyond what school has taught us are 'subjects'. Removed from the insulation in the timetable and the abstracted classroom context, 'knowing', as these young people amply testified to, acquired new and vital meanings.

In New England a 1972 directory of schools without walls listed forty-seven in its six states. One of these, Home Base School (a suite of three rooms in a commercial site) was enough to provide the base for students venturing into community learning sites. Its co-founder, Barbara Gardner, was persuaded to come to Scotland in 1972 to test the idea in the less adventurous ethos of Strathclyde Region. It is a mystery, in retrospect, that the powers-that-were agreed to an experimental SWW initiative in two Renfrewshire secondary schools. Barbara and I were to work with two classes of young people who would enjoy the experience of learning in the city for the whole of the third term of their third secondary school year, never touching down at school but trusted to make journeys on their own across the city to their chosen learning destinations. These were young people from the bottom stream, the most expendable, those who teachers readily admitted they had simply failed to reach.

## Stuffing tigers (or was it penguins?)

Sitting down with these young people to explore what they would like to learn was a salutary experience. As in Barrowfield previously, History, Geography, Maths and Science – of course, what could be more obvious? After a little more probing and brainstorming on what they would *really* like to learn, the list included deep-sea diving, marine life, how orchestras work, space exploration, studying the stars, jam making, milking cows, stuffing tigers, car mechanics, hospitals, guns, how a city works, why monkeys are like human beings, and much more. We then sat down with the Yellow Pages and began phoning shops, hospitals, zoos, museums, astronomy departments in universities, the Scottish National Orchestra (SNO), the Royal Navy, the AA, St Andrew's Ambulance Service, Robertson's jam factory, the Chrysler factory, car workshops and car markets, manufacturers, gunsmiths, shops and farms. Every student then had an individualised, highly varied, five-day timetable that met his or her expressed interest, although the taxidermy department in Glasgow museum, clean out of tigers, could only offer the alternative of stuffing penguins.

What was both surprising and highly gratifying was the willingness of the Royal Navy, the SNO, The Glasgow University Observatory, the AA and the ambulance service not only to take on young people but to help build a coherent educational programme designed to broaden their horizons. Of the two gunsmiths in Glasgow the first simply laughed, and the second agreed to take the lad in question and teach him something about responsible gun use and ownership. An excited William went on tour with the SNO, while James became expert on submarines following his weekly visits to the Holy Loch American nuclear base.

Seminars were arranged with tutors and small student groups in parks and cafés to debrief and share experiences, probing their learning and relating it to a broader educational agenda. While much of the content learned did not fit easily within a school curricular framework, many of the insights and skills acquired exceeded what might have been gained by a third term spent in the classroom. The greatest impact was, however, the enhanced self-esteem of these young people, their newfound sense of agency and their re-engagement with learning for themselves.

While the project enjoyed success far beyond the expectations of teachers, students and the Director of Education, for the latter, Tom McCool, the potential risks involved had provided too many sleepless nights for the experiment to be continued. As he told me in November 2012, such an enterprise in the current health and safety climate would never get to first base. However, a great deal had been learned about the initiative, resilience and unseen capabilities of young people and the consequent need to take stock of where failure lay, not in the potential of the young but in the limitations of curriculum and assessment.

These issues are revisited in *The Child in the City*,[5] written by Colin Ward in 1978. His study offers valuable insights into the nature of intellectual adventuring in urban areas, experiential learning in children's street culture, the variety of sensual and spatial experiences to be found, and the creative initiatives and games that children invented, organised and managed for themselves. These new experiences and the ability to move around, to explore and invent were, wrote Ward, an important part of a child's education: 'The city is in itself an environmental education, and can be used to provide one, whether we are thinking of learning through the city, learning about the city, learning to use the city, to control the city or to change the city' (p3). It parallels Wacquant's[6] studies of adolescent culture in Paris 'banlieus'.

Experiments in alternative 'construction sites', as Weiss and Fine term them, remind us again of the power of different kinds of behaviour settings and alternative models of peer and adult–child relationships. Weiss and Fine's[7] collection of essays chronicles how young people construct meaning from their experience in differing situations, and through the interplay of the various sites in which they struggle to find meaning and coherence. The more we venture into this territory the more complex and contested becomes our knowledge of children's learning, its social and emotional character and the precarious path that young people have to tread to make sense of what schools promise them. How to help children and young people bridge their learning across these disparate construction sites continues to elude school effectiveness research.

Nearly a century ago, the visionary educator Henry Morris propounded the idea of a village college, one that would 'provide for the whole man, and abolish the duality of education and ordinary life'.

> It would not only be the training ground for the art of living, but the place in which life is lived, the environment of a genuine corporate life. The dismal dispute of vocational and non-vocational education would not arise in it. It would be a visible demonstration in stone of the continuity and never-ceasingness of education. There would be no 'leaving school'! – the child would enter at three and leave the college only in extreme old age.
>
> (Henry Morris, 1925)[8]

The Henry Morris idyll returns us to the question of purpose. What purposes do schools serve in this brave new world? How much do we lose by containment in the classroom and an unforgiving curriculum and assessment diet? With the advent of new technologies and the restless preoccupations of generation Z what new forms of intellectual adventure can we expect of schools without walls?

## On reflection

School without walls. Behind the SWW terminology lies both a literal physical description of where learning may take place, together with a more metaphorical reference to the nature of 'walls' that separate some forms of learning from others. In the Scottish initiatives described, young people initially viewed learning through the lens of 'subjects', disciplines in both senses of the word. It took time to help these young people to see through a different lens, to see 'learning' as something lying within their own province and within their own freedom to choose. In A.S. Neill's Summerhill, classrooms were seen as places you could, or could choose not to, visit, and in many of the free schools that followed the Summerhill prototype, learning was where you found it, sometimes in the most unlikely places. In England under the Coalition Government, 'free schools' have come to assume a quite different meaning but will have to come to terms with the 'free' learning that is now offered through a world-wide web of connectivity.

## Notes

1   MacBeath, J. (1999) *Schools Must Speak for Themselves*, London, Routledge.
2   Kozol, J. (1967) *Death at an Early Age*, Boston, Houghton Mifflin.
3   Herndon, J. (1968) *The Way it Spozed to Be*, New York, Wiley.
4   Metro, 14 June 2012, reported on a Linking Environment and Farming (LEAF) Report.
5   Ward, C. (1979) *The Child in the City*, London, Pantheon.
6   Wacquant, L. (2001) *The Rise of Advanced Marginality: Notes on its Nature and Implications*, Berkeley, California, *Acta Sociologica*.
7   Weiss, L. and Fine, M. (2000) *Construction Sites: Excavating Race, Class and Gender among Urban Youth*, New York, Teachers College Press.
8   *The Village College. Being a Memorandum on the Provision of Educations and Social Facilities for the Countryside, with Special Reference to Cambridgeshire* (Section XIV).

# Part VI
# The sixth lens

# 11 Being and becoming a teacher and the end of idealism

How much has changed in teaching and induction into teaching in the last half decade? 'Delivery' remains the predominant metaphor for the teaching and learning process. The major change, reflecting wider social and cultural mores, is the removal of sanctions and in particular corporal punishment, a shameful and long-standing tradition in Scottish educational history. The story of teaching in one of Scotland's most prestigious 'grammar' schools, saved from closure by Mrs Thatcher, and in a French junior secondary school, offers a lens on the nature and abuses of authority, the refocusing brought by escapes from the classroom, and the comedic and tragic in school life.

## Sitting by Nellie

Teachers will always be with us. In what we call the 'West', teachers and teaching have survived in some recognisable form from Socrates' dialogic through the punitive doctrines of the Middle Ages, the enlightenment of the Renaissance and heresies of the Reformation and through the pendulum swings of the twentieth century; all the while there has existed a dialectic of freedom and authority, 'progressive' and 'traditional', child-centred and subject-centred, as if these were antagonists rather than essentially complementary. In the East (more or less everything that is not the West) teaching was inspired by Confucian principles, until the West and the irresistible forces of globalization cast teachers and teaching in a common mould.

Teaching: ideas or principles taught by an authority. This somewhat tautological definition offered by the online dictionary tells us very little about the transactional character of teaching, its purpose, nature or effect. It says nothing about skills, attitudes or dispositions. Its reference to authority is ambiguous and contentious. Is it a reference to the exercise of control or to the nature of what the teacher knows and his or her charges don't know – the authority of knowledge? Its applicability to an information age seems quaintly dated, as what children and young people need to know lies less and less in the teacher's head and more and more in the ether, known as the World Wide Web. And what does the definition assume about context, about where and when teaching takes place, or takes effect? The discourse around teaching tends to assume a classroom, a teacher and a 'class', generally of the same age, progressing inexorably through a sequenced pre-determined curriculum, in recent times determined by politicians, bypassing the authority of the teacher.

'Sitting by Nellie' is a long-standing view of how teachers are inducted into the profession. It is an age-old tenet that appeals to governments eager not simply for economic reasons to circumvent university induction but by virtue of deeply-held suspicions of academics and their inexplicable addiction to 'theory'. The apprenticeship model serves a fundamentally conservative process, replicating from generation to generation the most profoundly ingrained of classroom habits. My colleague and Cambridge room-mate, Maurice Galton, who has studied classroom interaction for a lifetime, has found that the ratio of teacher talk to pupil talk has remained stubbornly at 80:20 for five plus decades. In similar vein, teacher questioning continues to be characterised by closed, and impatient questioning, reported Ted Wragg, who timed the typical lapse between teacher question and pupil answer as less than one second.

## The emperors' clothes revealed

The first day on which I stepped into a classroom with the mantle of authority, in both senses of the word, I was confronted by the sight of Rosalind Wood, next-door neighbor, seated in the very front row, archly expectant. It was an unwelcome intrusion of real life into this unreal space. A sudden dilemma to be confronted – what persona could I adopt that would not expose me to this most significant other who knew me for what I was in real life? I ought perhaps to have heeded the counsel of wiser colleagues to live at the furthest possible remove from where I would teach, two worlds' distance apart. One day on a visit to the dentist close to the school I was met by an incredulous first former, apparently amazed to discover that teachers too had toothache, did their shopping, and were not simply shut up in a cupboard overnight and brought out the following day.

To distance myself from 'real life', my choice of classroom persona was to 'become' Zombie, the most eccentric of French teachers who, in my uninspired school days, had enlivened the tedium of everyday routines. He was perhaps so named because he seemed to glide around the classroom, never betraying any sign of emotion, but behind the implacable mask was a surreal sense of humour and brilliantly contrived put-downs, to which none of us ever took offence. He not only kept us royally entertained but we learned some idiosyncratic French constructions and, perhaps primarily due to Mr Mcinnes (aka Zombie), I became a French teacher. This is known as the cannibalistic function of education, consuming its own products and perpetuating practice from one generation to the next.

It was about a week into teaching that I had a strange out-of-body experience. It was as if I had floated up to the corner of the classroom ceiling and seen myself down there strutting pretentiously and borrowing the Zombie glide, replicating his hand gestures and practised stance of authority. At that moment of revelation of who I wasn't, I decided to be myself. However, as being 'myself' had proved a dangerous venture in my year as an 'assistant' in France, I had to find a teacher identity, drawing on the sedimented layers of models I had been exposed to. Although not consciously, I incorporated behaviors and mannerisms, ploys and tricks from the many teachers I had been exposed to over two decades. I knew from 'Hector' MacMillan not to stand halfway down the classroom, allowing those behind his back to indulge in unscholarly activities, nor ought I to adopt Mousey Morrison's posture seated behind the desk, which left too many blind spots and invited sedition. I adopted Captain Cowper's technique of writing on the board with his back to us while admonishing the talkers by name – 'MacBeath, try paying attention for a change' – it was a skill that rarely failed to impress. I picked up the very bad habit from my Maths teacher, 'Ivy' Bell, of secreting a tennis ball in the 'arm' of a gown which could, before the age of litigation, be used to deliver a friendly swipe to the back of the head. There was the jelly baby syndrome borrowed from I can't remember who. There were three grades of jelly baby question, the toughest earning three. One red, one green and one yellow. It was amazing how even the most streetwise of kids would be seduced into competing for a jelly baby. I had also learned how to get even the least intellectually endowed through an O grade exam by providing formulaic answers to questions, the most obvious example being the short essay prompted by a sequence of six pictures, which inevitably began with: 'Par un beau jour d'été ou les oiseaux gazouillaient dans les arbres (picture 1)'; 'un petit garçon nommé Jean et sa petite soeur, Amélie, (or any other combination from the cast list) ont décidé de . . . (picture 2)' and so on with many ritual fillers such as 'Bonjour Jean, Comment allez-vous?' a dit X, 'Quelle surprise!', 'Tout est bien qui finit bien' unless, of course that wasn't the case in which the appropriate ending might be 'Hélas . . .'.

Disaster struck one year when the examiners, perhaps wise to superstitious approaches to composition, set the essay at night with the first of six frames depicting an owl in a tree and a full moon. I waited in dread as 4S1 emerged from the exam room less than enamoured with my pedagogy, one that had failed to introduce them to owls, full moons, or with invention to construct a phrase such as 'one beautiful night when the birds were no longer twittering in the trees . . .'.

While I retained a healthy scepticism as to the value of written French and, in particular, composing essays about birds and owls in trees, I tried to ensure that even acne-ridden, lazy and utterly disinterested Sinclair would have at least one certificate pass to produce for an employer or college of further education, however intrinsically worthless. Above all, I was determined never to terrorise the class or diminish children's self-esteem, never to indulge in cynical derision, a weapon used by the worst of my own High School teachers, nor to have recourse to the use the belt either to assert my authority or, more heinous still, in retribution for honest (or even dishonest) mistakes. My experience in my primary class in North Berwick, where spelling mistakes were ritually punished with the tawse, and the similar admonitions for mistakes in Latin in Glasgow High School, were indelible reminders of the most shameful legacies of a Scottish miseducation.

Equally indelible was the moment I walked into the staffroom at Eastwood High School, barely a month into my first teaching job, to ask for the loan of a belt. I will never forget the sense of rejoicing at the redemption of another offender against public decency. I can still see Alex in his familiar chair by the window and his words, which continue to resonate four decades later, 'Another young teacher loses his idealism'. Welcome to the fold. Welcome to the way we do things round here. My erstwhile behaviour had been, in a sense, a breach of professional etiquette. Was I claiming to be something they weren't? A kind of moral superiority? Eschewing corporal punishment was, of course, a statement, underpinned by a moral purpose and by values that, forty years later, would be uncontested. We no longer believe in hitting children with a very thick two-tailed leather instrument of torture, the Extra Heavy (XH) supplied by Lochgelly Beltmakers containing a metal reinforcement between the layers of seasoned leather. Times change, and sometimes irrevocably.

While hitting young people with a lethal instrument was not only legal but a matter of convention, to deliver a well-placed slap was a serious breach of professional etiquette. An obnoxious youth, whose name I have since repressed, was a constant thorn in my side, his inane interventions and rude asides I did my best to ignore. On this one and only occasion in my teaching career I did something I ought to regret but in fact recall with some satisfaction. I had asked the baleful youth a question to which he responded 'piss off'. He was in the second row of desks but I reached him in one swift move, knocking over two desks and clattering him sideways. This act of impulsive and unprecedented madness was met with stunned silence. A number of girls began to sob quietly. While I anticipated inevitable repercussions nothing ever came of it except for the reward of a much more co-operative pupil whose respect I had, apparently, gained, not so much I was assured as an authority but as a human being.

When I conducted seminars with pre-service students at Jordanhill College years later I would ask them to consider the maxim 'punish only in anger'. This was almost inevitably met by an intended corrective, 'don't you mean *never* punish in anger?' This maxim from Sanderson of Oundle is probably not a sound piece of advice for the beginning teacher, particularly in an age of litigation, but being angry at bullying, injustice or racism carries a much stronger message than the cool dispassionate hand of authority. A.S. Neill, whose Summerhill was to eventually play a role in my life, founded his school on the principle of reciprocity, the first categorical moral imperative – do unto others as you would have them do unto you.

## A brief history of violence

I have called this assault on a pupil a true 'Désautel moment' in honour of the headteacher in the Collège d'enseignement de garçons in Macon who introduced me to the unrestrained power of genuine anger and direct physical intervention. Monsieur Désautel was a generous host from day one, inviting me to his home for meals in which one course endlessly followed another, each accompanied by another fine Burgundy or Maconnais. He provided me with a two-bedroom apartment in the centre of town and paid me more than I was earning as a full-time teacher. I fear I let him down by being a terrible disciplinarian, causing him to enter my rowdy classroom and nearly choke the life out of a couple of miscreants, pinned to the wall in the best French traditions of the film noir and Jean Gabin at his ugliest.

I was to spend nine months in this town in the very heart of the Burgundy region, or more correctly the Maconnais, famed for its dry white wines. It was to be my first and possibly only occasion to experience falling down drunk when a fellow teacher took me, novice wine drinker, on a tour of vineyards, sampling (and swallowing) wine in each location so that on return to my first-floor flat it took three attempts to launch myself successfully at the staircase.

So generous was my salary that I accommodated a growing collection of impecunious house guests – my school pal Macniven, later adding Eugene John Gilfillan Duffy to the in-house menagerie, and later still Jules somethingorother whom Macniven had adopted on a side trip to Spain. We were joined on most evenings by Volker from Germany, Bruno from Switzerland, Leslie from Durham and Susan from somewhere in England. The evening entertainment, following too much Beaujolais, was provided by Bruno and myself performing daredevil tricks on our matching Vespas. It was to be Bruno's undoing. My last, poignant memory is of his departure to Switzerland across the bridge spanning the river Saone, in a hearse.

## Teaching for real

My second school, once I had trained to be a proper teacher, been certificated and eventually registered with the General Teaching Council, was Paisley Grammar School and William B. Barbour Academy. My entrée to the profession as a bona fide trained teacher occurred at a time of severe teacher shortage, which would allow me to pick and choose which school I would like to teach in, visiting Govan High, Bellahouston Academy and Paisley Grammar, a close inspection of each to decide which one I would grace with my presence and which one would make me the best offer. Paisley Grammar is a handsome red sandstone building sitting square on to the busy Glasgow Road. Today it is no longer selective as it was then, at that time admitting only the top 30 to 40 per cent of children from neighbouring primaries. The dreaded prospect among my colleagues was that one day, which they hoped never to see, it would become 'comprehensive', admitting all and sundry to those prestigious precincts. Plans to close it and amalgamate it with a secondary school in Ferguslie Park, 'the Fegie', one of Scotland's most notorious housing estates, were soon laid to rest by an unprecedented political intervention. Andrew Neill, then editor of the *Sunday Times*, TV pundit and faithful member of the

Conservative Party, had been a Paisley Grammar pupil during my four-year tenure (I never got to teach him unfortunately, or fortunately) and he appealed directly to Margaret Thatcher to save the school. Such political interference went down not at all well with the local Labour Council, especially at the hands of the blessed Margaret, who was, for any self-respecting Scot, an anathema. But her intervention was successful and, possibly, a historic first.

## The man in the pyjamas

In the Grammar, as it was known, my head of department Walter Gardner was an awesome disciplinarian, complemented by his much-discussed eccentricity of letting his pyjama bottoms appear below his trouser turnups. Walter demonstrated his faith in this neophyte teacher by giving me IA and IB in a six-stream entry. The forty children in each class were the crème de la crème in an already selective school and absorbed as much French as they could get and emitted a communal groan when the bell went at the end of the period. They were irrepressible high achievers and the rarest exemplars of what teaching can be like in the very most propitious of circumstances. For wee Neil Macdonald from the Orkney Isles, getting less than 100 per cent on any exam would have been a badge of shame. However hard working and high achieving these young people were, to stop the period ten minutes early was, in Walter's book, a cardinal sin. 3.50, on one particular afternoon was the hour for the blast off of the first space shuttle, a historic moment one might have assumed, although unfortunately not French grammar. As I inhabited the one classroom in the school with a television set I had promised the class a reward if they applied themselves assiduously for thirty-five of the forty-five minutes. At the very hour of lift off enter Walter. A gasp of horror rippled round the room. They obviously knew what to expect. I was duly chastised and the TV switched off. 'French is French, Mr MacBeath, never forget that'. Yet, I didn't have to try hard to forget that. Walter's incursion was a telling metaphor for school education, for the dislocation of learning into discrete time-bounded slices of instruction, however inefficient, ineffective or demotivating. It was one of these seminal cumulative moments that added fire to my incipient deschooling views.

The irony is, however, that Walter Gardner was a wonderful friend to me and a hugely supportive head of department. He was always ready to take my part in any dispute between myself and the Rector, on one occasion standing up for my slightly errant conduct by telling the Rector that he was categorically in the wrong and was, to put it bluntly, 'a right bustard!' We would on occasions enjoy a drink together after school and share our views on the man in the principal's office.

My most celebrated run-in with the Rector is now the stuff of legend. As a beginning teacher in those less affluent days – my first monthly salary was £49 – I was given a lift to school by the Head of Music, Nora Marshall, in her Vauxhall Viva. Due to a flat tyre and heavy traffic we were running slightly late and arrived at school five minutes after the bell as pupils were on their way to classes, watched over by the Rector standing outside his office, regal in his black gown, an imposing figure not be trifled with. The school was built in the long-standing tradition of the factory with a large open hallway, around which ran a gallery of separate classroom cells. This setup, sometimes knows as the pantecnicon, or all-seeing eye, allowed the foreman, or in this case the Rector, to spot the miscreants and 'n'er-do-wells' – on this particular morning, me. As I followed Nora towards the classroom I was arrested by the words, 'What time of the morning is this to be coming into school, Mr MacBeath?' By this time the procession around the balcony had come to a halt as pupils gathered to take in the unfolding drama below. To add further insult to what was already injurious, the next line drew everyone's attention to my carefully assembled wardrobe, 'and what kind of lurid garment is this you're wearing?' The lurid garment was, in fact a black Glasgow University blazer complemented by the inevitable grey flannel trousers. The lurid aspect were 'colours' that trimmed the edge of the blazer, a recognition of my contribution to the University basketball team. Having been dismissed in the words one addresses to loitering schoolboys – 'Get to your class' – for the first two teaching periods of the day I could barely suppress my anger. By the morning interval I was rattled enough to forego the statutory coffee and fag in the staffroom. My determination to go and see the Rector to express my feelings was met by counsel to think again if I really wanted any future in the school, or, for that matter, in teaching. 'How long have you been a teacher, John. Five minutes?' Undeterred and unshakable in my resolve, a knock on the imposing Rectorial door was met with the instruction to take a seat outside, appropriately in the company of the naughty boys. It would be nice to add that one of them inquired, 'And what have you been caught doing?', but in fact, I sat in livid silence. Eventually summoned into the august presence, I did adopt the stance of the naughty boy, stood before the imperious mahogany desk at which he sat, eyeing with unmistakable condescension and some surprise. 'And what brings you here, Mr MacBeath?' 'I'm here to ask for an apology'. It is very likely that the Rector had never apologised to anyone, let alone be asked for an apology, and certainly never by a young upstart such as myself. He seemed momentarily lost for words, aghast at the impudence, not to mention imprudence, of this overture. 'And what would you say to a third year boy who asked you for an apology Mr MacBeath?' 'I would probably say, sorry'. The improbability of such an affront to a teacher's authority seemed to leave him again momentarily speechless, leaving me the space to add: 'But I am more intrigued by the implied relationship between me and a third year boy, and the relationship between me and you'. His reply left no room for further argument: 'Mr MacBeath, I am the Rector'.

Had I at that time been familiar with Peter Senge's treatise on organisational learning disabilities, I would have added: 'Organisational learning disability number one – I am my position.' Following my summary dismissal, the Rector went straight to my head of department and, as told to me by the faithful Walter over a beer, the conversation went like this: 'I had a member of your department in here this morning holding a gun to my head!' 'Well I wish he had bloody well shot you.' Walter, nearing the end of his career, had nothing to lose and he was not one to be intimidated by someone he regarded as his inferior. However constraining of my teaching he could be at times, he was a man of great integrity and imbued with a loyalty that was not always to be in evidence among all of my colleagues.

What remains with me as an insight into the uses and abuses of authority is the willingness of teachers to submit to despotic and arbitrary behaviour of their seniors. Here was I replaying the challenges to authority that, as a pupil, had left me isolated from my peers, whose promised support vanished when brought to the test. Walter was the conspicuous exception. He had of course nothing to lose but he also had a very strong sense of values and loyalty to his colleagues.

## French isn't always French

Walter would not have approved of everything (or perhaps anything) that took place on school trips to France in the Easter holidays. That French was not simply French was to be vividly brought to life by the many lessons about life, relationships, authority, culture, and much about the vagaries of human nature. While there were a few bold attempts to converse with the locals it was the unplanned events, the critical incidents, that opened a new chapter on education without confining walls.

The Paris trip was the brainchild of my next-door-classroom neighbour, Drummond Wilson, he of my French class at Glasgow. He has the added distinction of being the only person I know able to bring an XH belt down on three parallel pieces of coloured chalk to create an instant tricolor. It took a trick with 2C anyway. The fifth and sixth years who were to volunteer for the Paris trip were young men, bursting with libido and not averse to the odd libation, or a taste for the Gauloises. My staffroom colleagues shook their prescient heads at some of the tearaways who had chosen to accompany us, among the motley crew the infamous McMinigle *et al.*. Twenty five of them let loose in Paris – it would we were promised, all end in tears.

In the event, the bond of trust that emerged among us meant that the places they chose to go they shared openly with us, however reserved we felt about some of the less apparently 'educational' of venues. Yet educational, in a less-conventional sense, they all proved to be. We joined groups of students in tentative dialogue with flea market stallholders in Saint Ouen, pavement artists in Montparnasse and the con artists around the Gare du Nord, as well as in some of the least salubrious places in the city. One site where there were opportunities to actually practise the French language was in the cafés around St Denis frequented by the ladies of the night, with stories to tell and willing to induct these young men into the vocabulary that had been missed out in school.

When Donny Orr decided on spending a night on the Quais, I accompanied him, slept only a little and spent much of the night talking to the 'other' people of Paris whose life was lived out 'sous la belle étoile'. We drank wine at dinner and on no occasion did we have to rescue drunken schoolboys like those from other schools who climbed out of, or vomited out of, windows, who smuggled drink into their hotel rooms and, like Colditz escapees, devised cunning plans to slip out below their teachers' radar.

That it did indeed end in tears for some was the greatest irony of all. It was the chosen two of the twenty five, about to be appointed as sixth-form prefects, who let us down and abused the communal trust. Over the first few days a growing number of our party were reporting money stolen from their rooms. Suspicion fell on the two, whose names I will conceal to protect the guilty, as they often stayed behind in the hotel when others went out. The ever-creative John Dickie suggested a cunning plan to confirm our suspicion. A sum of money (carefully marked) was left in his bedroom while the rest of us went out for the evening. J.D. himself hid under the bed and waited for the inevitable entrance of the duo. He did not leap out to accost them in flagrante but waited to report to me in confidence. The fact that both did go on to be prefects was that any disclosure of their perfidy might have jeoparised not only their careers but future ventures by the 'Drummond/MacBeath' cartel.

As a deschooler-in-waiting, the deep imprint left by living and learning together, by the growth and testing of trust, by the generosity of young people who reciprocated that trust, by the hidden opportunities for learning that lie within a city, sowed the seed for my involvement many years later in schools without walls, free schools and the CU.

Among that group of students, separated from me in age by only seven or eight years, I was to make two good friends. I maintained contact with Donny Orr for more than a decade, and when he became a teacher I visited his Art classroom on many occasions and co-authored a research report with him on *Social Education through Outdoor Activities* – a pursuit he found more engaging than teaching Art to apathetic young people. His interest in learning out of the classroom he attributed at least in part to the formative experience of the Parisian school without walls. My wife joined Donny's art classes at a time when adults in the classroom was a policy initiative of Strathclyde Region.

John Dickie went on to a career in education, from classroom teacher in a school for bad boys (where I was to work with him for a while) to his role as 'one of the key players in the world of ICT in Scottish education', as was written in his obituary, after his a tragically premature death in 2004. 'John was a wonderful colleague to work with and a very good friend to so many people across Scotland', it was written, and that accolade included his friendship and generosity to me. I was hugely saddened by such an unjust fate for one of the world's good guys. It was J.D. who told me on my very first day of teaching 4S1 that new-fangled things such as tape recorders would not go down well in this very serious department, presided over by the man in pyjamas. The John Dickie ICT Awards in Scotland are a continuing legacy.

## Squadron Leader Fox: flying below the radar

The friendship and generosity of John, Donny and many of the others was to pay off handsomely when my utter incompetence as a Careers Master was exposed. In that role, bestowed on me by the Rector, no doubt as an attempt at my rehabilitation, required me to organise and play host to visiting speakers and recruiters. I was deep into a French lesson with 2A one Tuesday morning when my door opened to the announcement that Squadron Leader Fox and his party were here to talk to the fifth and sixth Year, and to interview boys who had expressed an interest in the Air Force. My blood must have drained away so rapidly that the messenger of doom asked me if I was alright. I had, of course, entirely forgotten, made no arrangements let alone lined up any boys interested in life in the air. A very angry squadron leader and an equally irate rector left me in a state of such acute embarrassment that my teaching was an incoherent failure for the rest of the day.

Yet worse was to come. On the rearranged date one month later I was to repeat the felony. This time, however, I knew where and how to capitalise on my investment. Asking for the squadron leader and company to be ushered in to an interview room, I searched out the whereabouts of fifth and sixth year boys and gathered them together for a hasty briefing: 'You are all dead keen on a life of the Air Force and have volunteered for interview with the Squadron leader and you will be an audience for his inspiring talk'. 'We are? We have?' The ever-resourceful John Dickie was the first to grasp the nature of the game and entered into it with aplomb and his customary creative flair. He gave a hugely impressive performance as a would-be flier, I was later told. The squadron leader and his party left happy with so many potential recruits and a Careers Master truly rehabilitated.

## A sad epilogue

As someone whose sports were baseball, ice hockey and basketball, I had failed miserably in my only other outing, against the staff of another Glasgow school, as a guardian of the goal. Even after much coaching and shooting practice in the gym at lunchtimes, my first ten minutes in goal had proved to be an unmitigated disaster. I can still hear the words that echoed after the ball dribbled through my legs for the second time, 'The goalie's a haddie'. I was solely responsible for the drubbing that awaited us. So when challenged by the pupils to a football showdown against the staff I was posted in the least invidious place possible, I seem to recall 'left outside'.

A pint or three after school was a not uncommon preparation for such an event and on one fateful afternoon we persuaded Bob Scott, Head of PE, to play in the staff v. pupils annual football match. Thrice he did refuse and we should have known better than to pressure him into playing, but in the end he reluctantly agreed. The referee, Bob King, School Chaplain, relished the role of arbitrator and it was he who rushed the full length of the pitch blowing his whistle as Bob Scott dropped to the ground. It had been his very first sprint for the ball which brought on the massive coronary. Bob dropped literally at my feet. The experience of a whole school in shock will stay with me forever. Nothing was taught in the morning following Bob Scott's death. The complete silence that enveloped the school for the whole of the first four periods was one of the most eerie experiences of my life. Was it that fifty years ago young people were less inured to the reality of death? Was it because it overtook us so immediately? Was its impact greater because Bob was a much-liked and a vigorous presence in the school? Shock, like hysteria, has a viral quality. It seemed to course through the halls from classroom to classroom. Like many of my colleagues I was unable to teach all morning and there was no appetite among the pupils for a French lesson at that time, so irrelevant did it seem in face of the precarious balance between life and death. In a sense the bond of grief that bound pupils and staff together captured school in its finest hour.

Schools come together in times of grief and in times of celebration. One of the high points of the school year was (and continues to be) the school drama production, the musical, the play, the Christmas concert. What distinguishes these occasions is the investment in an end product, an audience, a progression of accomplishment, recovering from setback, positive reinforcement, teamwork, and a hugely satisfying sense of achievement. It occurred to me that schools would be much more satisfying places if they abandoned the curriculum and were organised around a series of productions – plays, concerts, newspaper and magazine productions, radio and TV news and features, exhibitions of work, sporting events, visits and community projects. With a little imagination all of these could incorporate every subject of the curriculum. Perhaps that was what Dewey and the 'progressives' really had in mind.

## On reflection

'A deschooler-in-waiting'? For many teachers life is lived in the containment of the school and the classroom, leaving an even deeper imprint on them than on their pupils who, after all, spend no more than ten to twelve years in that cloistered environment. The escape from the classroom to live for a week together in a city such as Paris proved to be much more than a cultural tour of monuments. It was an opportunity to learn together, about relationships, trust, authority, boundaries and reciprocal accountabilities, to explore the hidden opportunities for learning that lie within a city, but also within ourselves.

# 12 Back to the future
## A new storyline

Learning to teach in higher education had clearly bypassed university lectures, which were delivered unencumbered by any theory of pedagogy or andragogy. The re-invention of teaching, described in this chapter, is owed to the brilliance of Storyline, which has travelled internationally to incredible effect. Together with the genius of Priestley and Macguire's cornucopia of interactive approaches to teaching and learning, for me the beneficiaries would extend from children to teachers, social workers, home helps and Strathclyde Police. Beginning with a year in Provence and a sometimes painful induction into teaching grown-ups, the chapter ends with the highly contested issues of sex, sexism, race and racism in the classroom.

## A year in Provence

Aix-en-Provence is often referred to as the city of a thousand fountains. Among the most notable are the seventeenth-century Fontaine des Quatre Dauphins, in the Quartier Mazarin, designed by Jean-Claude Rambot, together with three of the fountains down the central Cours Mirabeau. The Cours Mirabeau, which has been described as the most beautiful street in the world, is a wide thoroughfare, planted with double rows of plane trees, bordered by elegant houses. Along this avenue, which is lined on one side with banks and on the other with cafés, is the Deux Garçons, a world-famous brasserie, built in 1792 and unchanged since the day of its most prestigious clientele – Paul Cézanne, Émile Zola and Ernest Hemingway.

Before realising my ambition to return to the place of my induction into the profession, Jordanhill College, this time as a lecturer, I took a year out for my MEd. thesis, combined with a teaching job at the Institute for American Universities in Aix-en-Provence. It was a job Professor Nisbet had found for me to complement the William Boyd Scholarship of £500. The job entailed a couple of weekly lectures on Comparative Education to undergraduates, so receptive and engaged that it was eerily unsettling. I did not have long to worry though as another job came through as Lecteur at the Technological University of Marseille where I was to receive a sharp reminder of French students who never seem to grow up. These young people were a rowdy bunch for whom listening or sitting still were unreasonable demands. As I travelled weekly between my American and French students I could not inhibit my impulse to make cultural generalisations, so mature were the American students and so juvenile their French counterparts. Could it be attributed to the authoritarian and often repressive schooling, on the one hand, and a more liberal and democratic regime on the other? Or was it just me?

A six-hour teaching week could be effected within one day, comprised of a three-hour morning class and a three-hour afternoon class, separated by a generous intermission for a leisurely French repast. A three-course lunch with a bottle of Beaujolais in the Café du Port, partaken in the affable company of my departmental head, Monsieur Merle, brought a pleasant haze over the afternoon session and a greater tolerance for the antics of my grown-up adolescents.

## Becoming a teacher

Having taught for two years in France and also a year in Scotland, I was convinced I had little to learn from nine long months in a teacher education college. In Scotland I had learned to administer the tawse without breaking wrists and in the first of my years in France I had been introduced to institutionalised violence by Monsieur Désautel. To be required to attend a college of education was, at that time, a ritual deeply resented by many university graduates who felt it an offense to their dignity to have to be 'trained'. This antipathy was fostered by apocryphal tales of arcane psychological and educational theory, infantalising teaching methods and a daily timetable more redolent of schools than of universities, in which you were able to do what you liked rather than do what you were told. Some of my mother's favourite anecdotes were how, in the early 1920s as a student at Jordanhill College, she got so much into role that she regressed to five-year-old behaviour.

I was, therefore, by virtue of rumour and anecdote, firmly opposed to attending a college of education, especially since I had already taught for two years and believed I had little to learn about the realities of the classroom. So I entered Jordanhill College with my prejudices intact. It took me less than my first week for those préjugés to be blown away. I attended lectures on teaching of Mathematics that opened a whole new pedagogy to me. I was captivated by theories of education, lecturers who could have taught university staff a thing or two about how to teach, and I profited from my methods classes and, although indeed casting me in the role of a pupil, introduced me to things I ought to have known and been able to do as a teacher.

Although I had a degree pass from Glasgow University in Psychology, its content had been primarily about rats running mazes, pigeons playing table tennis, Konrad Lorenz's ducks imprinted on human beings, Kohler's apes and cybernetics (why toilets fill up again after flushing and planes stay aloft rather than spinning out of control). I had, until Jordanhill College, never heard of Piaget, Vygtosky, Erikson, Bruner or how children learn. So impressed was I by the nine months I spent learning about learning that my ambition was to one day graduate from school teaching to teaching at Jordanhill.

Education lectures by two inspired teachers, Leslie Hunter and Desmond Morrow, made me realise just how bad university teaching had been. In Psychology seminars we explored our own thinking, encouraged to read and take responsibility for leading the class. I discovered the wonders of hypnagogic and hynapompic imagery, those voices and images that flit through your semi-conscious mind just before sleep or prior to waking. They continue to fascinate me forty years later, although I have as yet to meet anyone who is familiar with those two technical terms.

In Education seminars we each took turns in presenting papers so the tutor had very little to do, adopting the prevalent philosophy of the Head of Department, Lawrence Stenhouse, of procedural neutrality, which appeared to be interpreted in his case by simply leaving us to it. Seated beside someone who had been the most entertaining of university debaters, 'Toad' McCormick, it was wonderful knockabout fun and strengthened my belief that becoming a tutor would not be a bad way to earn a living. Teaching practice, three five-week placements in the real world of schools, was a mixed experience. The first message from the staffroom was a not particularly professional counsel – forget everything you learned at Jordanhill. There were, however, one or two teachers open to learning from what we students were being taught at College, although they frequently dismissed as the latest 'fads'. I had little opportunity to practise any of those fads in my teaching practice posting, to three of the most deprived areas of Glasgow – Castlemilk, Carnwadric and Govan, the last of these made famous by Rab C. Nesbitt, the man in the ubiquitous string vest. Carnwadric Primary proved to be the most challenging experience of my career, even more damaging to my self-esteem than the French delinquents I had tried to tame in Macon. Assigned to primary 5, I was totally overrun by forty or so ten year olds, one of whom threatened me with a 'doing' for attempting to instill some discipline. I was to arrive home one evening to find him swinging on the front gate of the drive with a gun in hand. It took a few nerve-wracked seconds to discover it was a plastic replica but the clear message was 'we know where you live'.

## Back to the future, and a new storyline

Returning to Jordanhill College ten years on from being a student, my induction into teacher education was to be totally persuaded of the power of progressive pedagogy. One of our induction sessions was led by two 'staff tutors', Fred Rendell and Steve Bell, whose place in history is assured by their invention of 'Storyline', a classroom methodology that exemplified all the tenets of progressive pedagogy and was unapologetically wedded to the greatest of all Thatcherite misdemeanors, to be 'child-centred'. I never understood how learning could conceivably be anything else. Fred and Steve's big idea was to enthuse and engage children in learning by making connections with the external world of their lived reality and the inner world of their creative imagination. It was called Storyline because all learning is a form of narrative quest for deeper meaning. Storyline has fired the imaginations of generations of teachers whose classes were transformed into inspirational places, celebrating imaginative journeys of the mind.

A typical Storyline would be to start with making a person, perhaps a child, using materials to hand such as wool, pipe cleaners, buttons, bits of cloth, wool, wire, cardboard, milk bottle tops and anything else that could be found to give life to a distinctive personality. Having given the child an identity, an age, a personality, hobbies, likes and dislikes (usually a projection of self), and pets of course, the next step would be to create a family, large or small, perhaps an extended family complete with grandparents. They too would be given names, ages, personalities and live in houses and streets all to be constructed, together with shops, cars, buses and eventually transport networks. This child and family then provide the reference point for emerging events, crises and problems to be solved. There is, for example, consternation when all that has been lovingly constructed is to be threatened by council plans to drive a motorway through the area, demolishing houses, gardens, parks and whole neighbourhoods. Time for action – letters to newspapers, neighbourhood meetings, appeals to councilors and MPs, need for expert advice from lobbyists, petitions and appeal procedures. And what to do when all these neighbourhood shops are under threat from a planned hypermarket? Or when there is a rise in crime – vandalism, stolen bicycles, shoplifting and housebreaking? Or health issues to be taken into account, needs of the elderly, or the death of cat or dog run over in the street?

Storyline is not just about social, moral or civic education, it is a vehicle for literacy and numeracy, for scientific inquiry, indeed for all subjects of the curriculum and beyond, but always embedded in real tasks, with problems to be solved and skills to be applied in meaningful situations. Over the following two decades I was to run up against Storyline in many different guises and unlikely places. In Denmark, Canada, the US and Germany I participated in Storyline sessions that have taken the basic principles and extended them into a range of new fields. To Steve Bell's delight, I came across an article in the *International Journal of School Effectiveness and Improvement*, which found that of all innovative programmes in California the one that had proven most effective in added-value attainment was Storyline.

## An andragogy – for real grown-ups

I was, as Fate's sliding doors would have it, to spend a month with Steve Bell at the University of Hamburg. It was one of those exchange programmes that did so much to expand our horizons, and reframe our thinking. Under Steve's inspiration, German teachers took to Storyline as second nature. Ulf Schwänke, a lecturer in the Education Department, demonstrated that Storyline was not simply a pedagogy for primary age children but an andragogy for real grown-ups. His teachers created miniature classrooms in shoeboxes and, to the defeat of my initial skepticism, embedded the most profound of educational discussions around issues arising in this virtual classroom. I had the privilege of travelling with Steve Bell to Denmark where Storyline was then, and still is, very much alive and, over long train journeys, we co-constructed Storyline scenarios for any occasion and any subject in the curriculum.

Then came the Dark Ages, the age of linear progression, learning dissected and measured by clearly-defined objectives, targets, quantifiable outcomes and value added. This was a world in which teachers could not be taken by surprise because what was to be learned was already known in advance. However, in the countries of the North and the East, Storyline lived on and thrived in climates more favourable to experimentation and risk, less bound by the new orthodoxy. And so, when the arc of the pendulum had eventually swung to its extremity and the Emperor's clothes began to look a little worn and shabby, Storyline returned to the place of its birth, enriched and revitalised by its sojourn in other places.

### The homecoming

An international conference in Glasgow in October 2006 saw the homecoming of Storyline. It had not merely survived but been immeasurably enriched, with a new vitality that comes from exposure to other cultures, differing conventions and lifeworlds. The Polish author Czarniawaska describes a process of seeing things anew, through different cultural lenses, which she terms 'outsidedness', denoting a form of knowing – by difference rather than by similarity: 'It aims at understanding not by identification ('they are like us') but by the recognition of differences – 'we are different from them and they are different from us'; by exploring these differences we will understand ourselves better (Narrating the Organization, p62).

Storyline has survived the vagaries of political ideology, not only because you can't keep a good idea down but perhaps because it had to go away in order to come back. Perhaps, like the wandering scholars of the Middle Ages in search of knowledge, it had to re-invent itself, be tested for its adaptability, resilience and sustainability in other climes. As the Glasgow conference demonstrated, the 2006 story is one now told with greater maturity, depth and breadth. The titles of workshop sessions testify to its enhanced scope and application – Developing metacognition and thinking skills; The multi-ethnic classroom; Storyline and ICT; Storyline in foreign language teaching; Teaching about the human body: a health-based storyline; Storyline in Science; Storyline in the Arts. Its compass is all-embracing and its applications extend from pre-school and nursery to further and higher education.

### Playing with ideas

Students at Hamburg University have been just as entranced as five year olds in Copenhagen because of one simple precept – good learning is playful. The

American scholar, Alfred North Whitehead, believed that all learning begins with Romance, and returns it in cycles in which we revisit and play with ideas, at each return visit with new levels of insight. While there is now a wide theoretical consensus that as learners we 'construct' our understanding, Storyline takes that one stage further, exemplifying the interplay of doing and knowing, showing how children are able to construct new worlds, engaging the enactive in concert with the symbolic.

'In some regards young children's intelligences are less constrained and are more competent than those of their typical adult teachers', wrote Kieran Egan, in his compelling book *The Educated Mind*. I bought the book after having been inspired by Kieran at the Storyline conference in Denmark over a decade ago. It is a text that might have been written just for Storyline as it celebrates the imagination and creativity of childhood. It takes the reader through the cycles of learning from 'Mythic' and 'Romantic' understanding to 'Philosophic' and 'Ironic' modes of thought, but unlike stage theories in which children become progressively more serious, disciplined, abstract and 'all grown up', the message is that mythic understanding remains alive and well even into our twilight years, when the child in the adult may re-emerge and be let out to play. Perhaps this explains the affinity between small children and their grandparents.

In 2007, the policy world of prescription and performativity has not gone away. What the Glasgow conference showed, with brilliant clarity, was that wherever there are inventive schools, committed teachers and a robust pedagogy, learning is able to thrive. Conference delegates came from more than thirty different countries and policy jurisdictions, from the ever-faithful Nordic countries, from Germany and the Netherlands, from countries of the Pacific Rim, and from the US and England, whose delegates testified, through practical demonstration, to the resilience and power of Storyline to survive even in 'high stakes accountability environments'.

Despite the combined onslaught of HMCI Woodhead and both Conservative and Labour governments, progressivism in the shape of Fred and Steve's 'Storyline' is still thriving half a century on. Its enduring impact is because it goes to the very heart of what Dewey and the progressives had sought to teach about the nature, and too often repressed vitality, of children's learning. It is a testament to Steve Bell and Sally Moodie/Harkness who, for nearly four decades have not only kept the movement alive but have been unwavering in their faith. They owe much, as do we all, to Fred Rendell, the grandfather of the Storyline, and to the many others around the world who have nurtured the flame and passed it on.

## Sliding doors and uninvited guests

While Dewey and progressivism were framing values, with Storyline an exemplification of theory in practice, the most significant change in my own teaching came through an entirely serendipitous sliding-door episode. It came on a rare and busy morning which found me, uncharacteristically, behind my office desk. I was slightly irritated at the interruption by two unknown and uninvited guests who asked if I could spare an hour for lunch. I was on the point of declaring myself too busy when I relented and was to spend not one but nearly three hours in the company of Phil Priestley and James Maguire. They had co-authored a book, *Social Skills and Personal Problem-solving*, and convinced me that I could spend three profitable days at one their courses, bringing the book to life.

Over the course of the three days Phil and James ran through a sequence of tasks, pausing only briefly between episodes to debrief and discuss applications and adaptations. We worked in pairs, triads, fours, snowballed, brainstormed, took part in games, quizzes, simulations, role plays, told stories, created and replayed critical incidents and came away with a repertoire of ideas and teaching strategies that continue to serve me well. One that I have now replicated in half a dozen different countries, and in the most unlikely of contexts, is television news. The basic scenario goes like this: Participants are told that they will, in forty minutes from now, be presenting the news. They will be in two teams (ITV and BBC or whatever other combination may be chosen). They will receive regular news items as they come in from Reuters (actually articles cut out from the day's newspaper). They must appoint two news readers and include two live interviews with people featuring in the news. The broadcast will be live and last for seven minutes exactly. The team (anything from seven to twelve participants) must organise themselves, allocating roles including director, camera and sound persons, presenters (these might include weather, sports, political or foreign correspondents). The biggest headlines are fed in towards the end and also when the broadcast is 'on air'.

The most unlikely of contexts for this activity was during a training session that we conducted with Strathclyde Police. Divided into two teams they entered into the spirit with competitive zeal. The Chief Constable, who dropped in, stayed to marvel at the display of energy, commenting that it captured the very essence of the police incident room, the spontaneity and simultaneity of activity and the critical nature of team work and decision making under pressure.

We ran the simulation with home helps, who had promised us at the outset that it just couldn't be done in the time and that it was beyond their capabilities, before they rose with aplomb to the occasion. We ran the simulation with social workers, health workers, educational psychologists, housing officers, welfare rights workers, staff of residential homes for the elderly, teachers, headteachers and school pupils. I was forewarned by David Alexander, headteacher of Barrhead High School, that to try this with a bottom set of third year within a forty-five-minute period would be courting mayhem and disaster. When he dropped in halfway through the period he could not believe the energy and creativity of these hitherto passive, bored and restless of young people. He, and many of the staff, were 'gobsmacked' that Adam, the least forthcoming 'special needs' young person, could both create and present the weather forecast with such panache and self-confidence.

## Sex, sexuality and sexism in the classroom

There was one issue in teacher education that was conspicuous by its omission. We never talked about sexuality in the classroom. It was not on the list of topics for seminars, booklists, papers to be read or lectures to be given. It was the elephant in the room, the ghost in the machine, the uninvited guest. Yet from my first day in a classroom the sexual energy, however repressed, had lain dangerously below the surface. One of the first classes I taught was 4S. I was five years older than the girls, young adults whose attractiveness could only be dealt with by an act of professional denial. The less sophisticated younger girls made no secret of their attraction to a young teacher and would follow me around in the playground, indulging in giggling conspiracies and making subtle, and not so subtle, overtures. It wasn't until my second year as a college lecturer that I felt secure enough to formally broach the subject with college students. I devoted a seminar session to opening up the subject and a veritable dam burst. The young women (some barely older than the pupils they were teaching) spoke about being questioned about their sex lives, about having their bottoms pinched, stage whispered exchanges clearly meant for their ears, constant innuendo and crudities to test the limits of tolerance and, its most blatant, 'How about a shag, miss?' While young men were also subject to flirtation and suggestion, they were spared the sexual intimidation experienced by some young women.

There was such a rich untapped resource in their anecdotes, and their strategies for dealing with sexual behavior, that I made a ten-minute video, *Sex and Sexism in the Classroom*, which provided stimulus material for seminar discussions and workshops with teachers in service. An ally and co-conspirator in disseminating, developing and exploiting this material was Helene Witcher, the Equal Opportunities Officer in Stirling, adding a further layer of race and racism to the mix. To be a black woman in a classroom of privileged white boys brought challenges all of its own. Helene also introduced me to issues that had previously remained invisible – the world of the travelling people whose children experienced their own special brand of discrimination.

## The politics of race, racism and anti-racism

In the late 1970s and 1980s sexism and racism were just being discovered. Although my seminar paper as a Jordanhill student in 1962 had been a treatise on images of girls and boys in comic books and children's literature (Enid Blyton a particularly rich source), this was a weak apolitical form of commentary that did nothing to affect the lives of black women and indeed, by its very insipid tackling of the issues, actually served to simply marginalise them. At least that was the critique from the anti-racism lobby, of which I became a member until its McCarthyite tendencies appropriated the agenda.

I became a member of the National Association for Multi-cultural Education (NAME) and then in its new incarnation, the National Anti-racist Movement in Education. Although at the time it was castigated for being 'against' rather than 'for' something, it proved to be a pioneering crusade against the widespread endemic and institutionalised racism of many public agencies, including the police, housing departments and the education service. Where it defeated its cause, and eventually me, was its exclusivity, its intolerance and doctrinaire opposition to everything that was not itself. Multi-culturalism was the enemy within and I sat in meetings where lifetime-committed (white) people were expelled, meetings in which I was told not to vote until I had seen how the black people voted. By virtue of being white I should not be allowed to interview, direct or edit a video on anti-racism that I had proposed. It was, in the end, better that the video never got made than it was in the hands of a white man. That much of the direction of the anti-racist movement was actually in the hands of two of my white male colleagues was deemed OK, as they were, apparently, honorary black women. The actual black women whose views differed from the official doctrine were discounted as 'bounty bars', black on the outside but white on the inside. The term 'black' was, I learned, a political reference and did not refer to the colour of one's skin. Thus not only were Indians, Pakistanis, Indonesians and Chinese encompassed by the term 'black', but also the Irish, because they too were an oppressed minority and subject to personal and insitutionalised racism. An Irish joke was a cause for immediate expulsion from the room and even the movement. Once the censor's knife had been applied to all forms of humour, nursery rhymes, films, TV programmes, comics, books, academic papers, student handouts and recommended readings, there was little left that was not tainted by the inherently racist and sexist world view. The self-appointed Solomon to whom all matters of judgment should be brought was Shahid Ashrif, whom I first met at a Glasgow University one-day seminar on racism. Shahid, in common with all designated speakers, was allotted fifteen minutes for his input. However, as a black person he was not to be tied down to an allotted time and refused to be curtailed by a white chairman who tried in vain to get him to give the floor to the next speaker. Shahid's exposition lasted the best part of an hour and caused so much resentment that, like much of the invective and sloganizing, it did little to advance the cause.

A year or two later Shahid presided over my own inquisition by the inner circle of NAME, three black people (Glasgow-born Asians) and two honorary 'black' members (English-born white men). It was a particularly bad time for me because I was on my way to visit my brother who had suffered a stroke. In attempting to excuse myself to visit him I was told that 'white pain' was of no consequence to them and I was there to learn about black pain, this line delivered by a highly successful lawyer whose Mercedes stood at the door. It was the point at which my patience ran out and, by leaving the movement, my inherent racism was finally revealed.

## On reflection

Governments, impatient to get teachers into classrooms, may bypass the irksome interlude of teacher 'training', an impatience reinforced by a deeply held suspicion of academics – too politicised, too subversive and too easily seduced by 'progressive' and child-centred 'conceits'. Such a stubborn stance willfully ignores the powerful impact of constructivist pedagogies such as Storyline or Priestley and Maguire's magic toolbox of interactive techniques. And, with a purblind antipathy to 'theory', English education ministers would deprive us of insights brought by scholars such as Kieran Egan, who inspire teachers to nurture the imagination and creativity of childhood – and show what outstanding child-centred teaching can look like.

# Part VII
# The seventh lens

# 13 Going to school

## Plus ça change?

What does it mean be a school student in 2013, compared with half a century ago? How much has changed in fifty plus years? In some respects very little. In some respects there is a world of difference, mainly because the world is a different place while the world of school has essentially changed little and, as exemplified through the first lens of policymaking, has in many respects regressed. Through this final lens two very different stories bring into sharp relief what it means to be a student, what diminishes and enhances a sense of agency, throwing into new perspective the notion of 'potential' and 'intelligence'. Both stories demand a suspension of disbelief.

## Conspiracy on the M9

John le Carré could not have provided more mystery to the opening chapter of the Learning School story, or bettered the intrigue. A phone call on a crackly line from the Shetland Islands, asking if we could meet – the venue to be a service area on the M9 motorway between Stirling and Glasgow. There would be no surreptitious exchange of a brown paper parcel but a proposition too far fetched to be credible.

The grand plan for which Stewart Hay, assistant headteacher in Anderson High School, sought my support, was to release a group of teenagers from school for a year and send them, on their own, around the world, visiting schools in South Africa, Sweden, the Czech Republic, Japan and South Korea. Each school visit would be for six weeks, allowing time for in-depth study, gathering data on approaches to learning and teaching. The visiting scholars would be a party of fourteen or so, pairs drawn from schools in each of the participating countries. As visiting researchers, they would sit alongside fellow students and teachers, researching their learning and teaching, and the coincidence (or lack of it) between these two complementary processes. The key research questions – What is the nature of learning? To what extent is it a consequence of teaching? What do we understand by leadership and what is the scope for students to exercise it?

Travel, it is said, broadens the mind. But there are those who travel without learning, reinforcing rather than challenging beliefs, confirming 'home' truths.

There are also those who travel with a mind constantly open to new insights. Nowhere is this better exemplified than in the case of the 'Learning School' – a truism or contradiction in terms? For the young people who signed up it was to prove an unsettling, and even life-changing, experience. For a year they were not only to travel beyond their own national borders, but beyond their most cherished beliefs and expectations.

In the eight successive incarnations of the Learning School, around 100 students from nine countries have been involved. They have amassed a large body of data on the schools visited, on methodology and on themselves as participants in a unique experiment. As the compass of the project has extended to embrace schools in Australia, Germany, Hong Kong and the US, so issues of voice have acquired new dimensions, and most of the Learning School researchers have been persuaded to keep diaries, documenting their experience. All have at some time told their individual stories to academics, teachers, education ministries, inspectorates and civil servants in Edinburgh, London and Cambridge, and to similar audiences in the eight other countries, as well as to the International Congress on School Effectiveness and Improvement in Copenhagen and Barcelona.

In 2003, students from Learning School cohorts 1 and 2 (LS1–2) wrote eighteen of the twenty-two chapters in the Routledge book *Self-evaluation in the Global Classroom*, and in the same year two Cambridge studies by Nishimura (2003) and Sutherland (2003) provided further in-depth accounts of the personal and institutional impact of the Learning School cohorts 1 to 4. Nishimura's MPhil thesis drew on diaries and emails kept by LS4 students over the course of nine months, followed by in-depth interviews at key points in the Shetland Islands, Malmö (Sweden) and in Cambridge, at the culmination of the project. Sutherland's study for his MEd. thesis involved interviews with teachers in Anderson High School in Shetland where the project originated and which continues to be the hub of the project.

The advantage these young people brought with them was to be of a similar age to those they mingled with and befriended, establishing a rapport that would allow candid unguarded exchanges of view. While classrooms in Japan and South Africa did appear to these young people surprisingly familiar, they were able to penetrate beneath the surface features of classroom life, and to tune into voices and in a register less easily accessible to university researchers.

In each location these young people were to live with host families, in most cases without a common first language and, in some cases, with no common linguistic ground at all. Little has been researched or written about how voice is heard across linguistic boundaries, nor how it develops in the context of the home or family. Exceptions to the rule are Weiss and Fine's edited volume on 'construction sites', Judith Harris' award winning book *The Nurture Assumption* (1998), and Per Schultz's studies in Denmark.[1]

## Homes from home

For most students involved, the Learning School was their first long-term extended disconnection from home. Many of them describe their selfhood as having been defined by parents, by school and by the peer group, all accidents of locality and propinquity. The greater the distance from the comfort zone of home the more the notion of 'home' gradually assumed new dimensions. A Swedish student, for whom home was hitherto the house in which she grew up in Malmö, now found an expanded and more ambivalent notion of home:

> This is my home, Malmö and the school is my home school and my home is my 'home-home' but now 'home' is something different. 'Home' was always where I lived with my mum and now home is also Logan's house because I stayed there, and Philippa's house, that's home as well. The Czech host sister and everything is the home, and the 'home' isn't clear now. That's the main difference. Much wider and more vague. Home can be so many different things.
>
> (Interview in Malmö, January 2003, Nishimura, p32)

Parental voice was acknowledged by many of the young people as having laid down a substratum of values that they continued to struggle with, as each new exposure to different ways of being in differing kinds of family cultures brought new challenges, most particularly in the immediacy of the peer group with whom they spent a close, and sometimes claustrophobic, nine months. The young people who wrote of their experiences with the Learning School capture some of the artistic portraiture of the novel. Their depictions of home and school speak personally and sometimes painfully of culture shock and its impact on their identity. The following is taken from a talk given in Cambridge, June 2003:

> When you have opinions and views, you realise your parents' influence. You do not notice usually how much your opinions are influenced by your parents. I did not think by myself and I used my parents' thinking. I should have my own picture.

The cross-cultural experience had helped young people to see their home culture in a new light. As Miki Nishimura, described it:

> Sophie became more critical about the home culture since she became more secure as an independent person, an active and critical player in society. This new 'persona' did not mean a change in her personality as such but allowed her to become more comfortable with herself and more able to deal with the contradictions she encountered. She did not see a serious dilemma in resolving her two separate identities.

Sophie's story, as she told it to a Cambridge University audience, was so moving in recollection that she struggled to distance herself from the experience. It was in the context of South African townships in which she had faced the most profound culture shock and re-orientation of beliefs about self and society. She had stayed with two host families, one in a 'coloured' community and the other in a 'black' township. The coloured family was poor and virulent in their dislike of black people in general. Knowing that after three weeks she would be staying with a black family it was hard to tread the line between respect for this kind family who had taken her in and trying to temper racist views that she feared might prejudice her against the black family she would shortly live with:

> I remember that I was sitting in my room with my host sister and she asked me if I wanted to hear a joke, I said yes then she began to tell me a really racist joke and expected me to find it funny, how was I supposed to react to something like that? That was something that I found difficult to understand and cope with in South Africa.

Yet, she acknowledged how much she had learned from this Muslim family, her warmth for them and how much she missed them later. After the three weeks she moved to live with the black family in the township. On the first day the daughter, who had just returned from a boarding school, expressed her dislike for white people, a 'shock' for Sophie, who had never before had to face such explicit racism. This experience was instrumental in helping Sophie reflect on her own prejudices, acknowledging her own ignorance as a root of bigotry, and coming to value harsh experiences as an important 'lesson for life':

> I have never thought of myself as a prejudiced person. I think that most people sometimes 'assume' things or think that something is a certain way in a country or in a culture, etc, and of course I am one of them. But I have learnt that I can be quite determined about some things that I actually don't know very much about. I think some things seem to me really good which are proved later on, and the other things seem not good and they are proved to be the opposite. I am really happy that I have realised how wrong I have been. It is most certainly a lesson for life which I am very happy to have experienced.
>
> (in Nishimura, pp35–6)

A Scottish student who stayed with three host families in Cape Town – Muslim, Hindu and Xhosa families – was exposed to customs such as Manhood training in the Xhosa culture, providing opportunities to visit Hindu temples and to discuss the war in Iraq from a Muslim perspective:

> You stop thinking I am Scottish, he is Japanese, she is South African, you just think they are Learning School members and my friends. Everyone is a different person and has their own qualities irrespective of where they

come from, but just because of who they are. People are the same and different all over the world, what I mean by this is that I could be more similar to a Japanese person that I have never met than I am to a Scottish person living in the same street.

(in Nishimura, p61)

The common bond of nationality or locality, which may comprise a substantive aspect of identity, may be strengthened by distance or may diminish in significance. On occasions it helped to reaffirm one's own national identity:

I became more Japanese here. My host family made me aware of 'I am Japanese'. My host mother always stresses the differences between their own culture and mine, Japanese. I showed pictures of my family and discussed about my parents and I came to understand more about my parents after discussion with her. I compared two cultures a bit and explained my opinions. I became very curious about my background – Japan, Asia and the world ... One day I went to the public library that has books about Japan written in Japanese. Now I am reading about the Second World War. When I read it, I become more aware of the fact that I am Japanese.

(in Nishimura, p44)

Their immersion in the culture through living with host families both complements and problematises studies that have focused solely on schools and classrooms, offering new insights into the persistent finding since Coleman's landmark 1966 study, and Jencks five years later, that while schools matter, families and communities matter more. It is from these young people, acolyte researchers, that we are afforded a glimpse into the nature of that home–school relationship. Through their own biographies we gain new insights into how identities are shaped and re-formed as they travel between home, classroom and community, and across cultures. For the Learning School students identity is redefined by three primary contexts – the schools in which they conduct their research; the host families they live with for a period of four to six weeks; and the peer group in whose close company they travel, work and spend their leisure time. All of these three sites are multi-lingual and multi-cultural. As they describe the impact of these new and unfamiliar contexts the impact on their learning is contrasted with their prior school experience: 'I have probably learnt as much in these ten months as I did in thirteen years of school' (Jolene, in MacBeath and Sugimine, p38[2]).

The continuous thread in the Learning School narrative is of individual lives lived in and through a kaliedoscope of sites, shifting daily from family to peer group to school classroom and back again, each new set of relationships requiring a different linguistic register and social protocol. And as the group uproots and moves every four to six weeks to new cultural contexts, mores and social boundaries have to be readjusted and relearned. In each situation self-concept and self-efficacy are confronted by the novelty of the experience. The situations perceived as 'challenges' by the three students required them to reframe their familiar self-conceptions and forced them to start a new form of negotiated identity. When they became comfortable with the new identities, there would be a quiescent period, although this proved to be a simply temporal respite, waiting for the next challenging situation to be encountered.

An Anderson High student takes a retrospective view of the impact of learning beyond school and the test it has offered to his self-awareness and academic identity:

> This year has been a massive education to us all, an almost vertical learning curve. I often worried that I was not using this opportunity to learn as much as I could, but now after having stepped back indefinitely from this particular journey I can see how by watching and feeling another culture from within you cannot help but learn infinite amounts. It is the greatest educational tool ever to have at one's disposal. Teaching things schools will never be able to teach, through first hand experience, feeding a desire to understand the world in which we live. This year has given me a real thirst to continue to test myself academically and to become more aware of different societies, cultures and people, as I am sure it has to everyone who was a part of Learning School 2.
>
> (Colin, in MacBeath and Sugimine, p36)

'Feeding a desire to understand the world' is a profound statement, a counter-point to school experience that, at best, offers a vicarious view of the world, at second hand, and always attended by the need to reproduce a condensed version for the benefit of examiners. A sixteen-year-old Korean student, speaking emotionally at a Cambridge conference at the culmination of Learning School 3, described how, for the first time, he had found his own voice after ten years of school. Preoccupation with hard work, after-hours cramming and swotting for exams, had left neither time nor incentive to think for himself, nor to question received wisdom from his teachers. The Korean researcher, Sung-Sik Kim,[3] provides confirmatory evidence for the constraining effects of Korea's school system and casts his own country's national performance (second only to Finland in the 2002 PISA study) in a more critical light.

The opportunity to accompany these young people to the Memorial Museum in Hiroshima was a profoundly moving occasion for me. German, Scottish and Swedish students were confronted together with the role of their own nations in one of history's most devastating events. Its impact was brought to bear in the remnants of everyday things – charred clothes, relics of abandoned toys, a melted tricycle to which a child's shoe still adhered. While their discussion around the exhibits had the effect of sharpening national identities, it also brought to the surface, and elucidated, values that were deeply shared.

The concept of the autobiographical self is pertinent to the process by which old identities are challenged and new identities emerge from internalisation of the medley of voices. As these young people research others' experience of school and home they become progressively more aware of the power of their own internal voices and become more self-confident in their ability to articulate the process through which self is progressively rediscovered.

The following observation from a Scottish student brings a new meaning to the concept of 'potential', which is used in such a limiting way in current school discourse: 'This year has allowed me to see things from a different angle and to realise that sometimes we place limitations on ourselves and that there is so much more that we can do' (Jolene in MacBeath and Sugimine, 2002 p38).

In Zlin, in the Czech Republic, final-year secondary students have taken over the school for the day and exchanged roles with their teachers. So the staff have to experience a day in the life of a students, moving from class to class, glancing every few minutes at their watches as the day drags out. In the debriefing session at the end of the day, they confessed to the unrelenting tedium of being on the receiving end of teaching.

Zlin is home to the Bata shoe factory where you may visit the owner's very large and sumptuous office. On the mahogany desk you may wonder at the row of buttons, numbered from one to three. One of these, when pressed, will take you to the desired floor, allowing the owner to emerge on any floor and catch his employees unawares. While the factory generously provided homes for the employees, these had to be built on the shady side of the mountain, so as to avoid the temptation for the luckless inhabitants to enjoy themselves too much.

## A £25,000 menu

Gregor Sutherland, one of the original architects of the Learning School, is the subject of conversation over lunch in the summer of 2012, as his seminal contribution to HCD, Highest Common Denominator, the Charity founded by Richard Timberlake over a decade ago, is recalled. The venue is the Athenaeum gentleman's club, sited on the corner of Pall Mall and Regent Street, so that during the Olympics you could just about see the 'beach' volleyball below. It is Clive Barham-Carter's club and the occasion for lunch – Dressed Crab, Gressingham Duck, Strawberries and Cream – is to discuss how to spend £25,000 of HCD's money over the next year. Since Gregor's departure the charity has continued to finance projects in which the voice and leadership of young people is centre stage, a valuable source of support for numerous ground-breaking projects, pre-dating my move to Cambridge. However, the business will have to wait until after lunch, with coffee and cakes in the library. Clive is the former headmaster of Charterhouse and Richard a notable in the 'city'. Lunchtime conversation about the state of education requires some studied diplomacy, although Richard, provocatively, suggests the abolition of private education. This would have the effect of spreading the talent more evenly, he contends, both in respect of the gifted students and the excellent teachers. For Clive though, Eton is the benchmark for both sides of that equation.

Previous disquisitions have taken place in other prestigious London venues such as the Savoy and Richard's club, and Boodle's, as Google tells us:

> Boodle's is a London gentlemen's club, founded in 1762, at 49–51 Pall Mall, London by Lord Shelburne the future Marquess of Lansdowne and Prime Minister of the United Kingdom, and the club came to be known after the name of its head waiter Edward Boodle.

Boodle's, Richard tells us over lunch, does not admit women to the inner sanctum, but does allow them their own separate dining room to which they may invite their spouses. Currently there is a three-year waiting list for membership but it does require seven testimonials from members which someone, or some committee, will peruse at their leisure over the coming year.

The world of the London clubs is so far removed from the townships of South Africa, the communities still living with the Hiroshima fallout and the Soviet legacy in Zlin in the Czech Republic that it is difficult to override the sense of guilt at the opulence and exclusivity, the province of gentlemen. HCD's sponsorship has, however, helped us to see school and society, living and learning, through a new lens and, for young people themselves, to discover new ways of seeing and understanding the world.

## On reflection

Travel can broaden the mind. It can challenge long-held beliefs and 'home' truths, nurtured in the precious sanctuary of the gentleman's club or the exclusive public school. But, as the Learning School taught us, with each new iteration, to travel with a mind constantly open to new insights can be a deeply disturbing educational experience. On every journey from school to school, from home to home and from one community to the next, these young people found themselves confronted with dilemma, heresy and paradox. Disconfirming rather than confirming their vicarious classroom learning, each new experience 'fed a desire to understand the world', an objective, we might have imagined, of a school education.

## Notes

1   Harris, J.R. (1998) *The Nurture Assumption*, London, Bloomsbury.
2   MacBeath, J. and Sugimine, H. with Gregor Sutherland, Miki Nishimura and Students of the Learning School (2003) *Self-Evaluation in the Global Classroom*, London, RoutledgeFalmer
3   Sung-Sik Kim (2002) 'The influence of private education on schooling in Korea: High academic achievement and "school collapse"'. Paper presented at the ICSEI 2002 Conference, Copenhagen, Denmark, 3–7 January.

# 14 Testing classroom learning – connect, extend and challenge

The experience of the Learning School students showed how travel can broaden the mind, often in dramatic ways. The traveller often sees things his or her hosts fail to see, what the Icelanders call 'the visitor's eye view'. As a teenager, coming from Toronto, Canada in the new world, to Glasgow, Scotland in the very old world, it was 'a time traveller's worst nightmare'. It raises the question – How much have we, collectively, travelled since then in our understanding of learning, school, education, curriculum and sanctions? This final, highly personal, account, returns us to the opening chapter of the book and to a government that would, apparently, like to turn the clock back to those less than golden days.

## A travel through space and time

In the summer of 1954, a boy walked down the gangplank of the SS Ryndam into the Southampton docks and the beginning of a new life. He was fourteen. He left behind his best friends Gordon Rostoker and Derek Coates. He left behind the girl he loved, although she was never to know it and she had scarcely met him. He left behind the Toronto Maple Leafs (baseball and ice hockey), hot summers and crisp snowy winters – summer camp, covered wagon expeditions, summer cottage by Lake Magnetawan, winter skating and Pee Wee hockey in Leaside Park. Hello to policemen with helmets, double-decker buses, black taxis, terrace houses with chimneys, smoke, rain and a new addition to his vocabulary – smog. Goodbye to North Toronto Collegiate College, proms, cheerleaders and football played with your hands, and girls! And hello to the High School of Glasgow for boys – jeans and T shirts exchanged for brown shorts, brown blazers and brown- and orange-striped ties. It was a time traveller's worst nightmare.

Glasgow High School's four grey buildings – Blocks A to D – struck him as an apt nomenclature for an institution designed more for punishment than rehabilitation. Connected by underground tunnels with escape hatches in the floor of some classrooms, for the adventurous it offered a breakout route from the tedium of History and the oppression of Latin. Such behaviour was punishable by six of the best, but great escapes also came with heroic status among one's peers.

I was, in my third year of school, to record 260 beltings by Christmas, five more than my nearest competitor Caldwell (whose Christian name I have forgotten or never knew). Being a 'Yank', although I didn't know until long after I arrived what that term meant, was an awesome accolade that had to be justified by daring acts of subversive leadership. The crowning moment was, with a little help from my friends, the hoisting of Mr Runciman's little Renault Quatre on to the roof of one of the lavatory blocks in the playground. Six of the best was a totally inadequate reward for such an act of defiance. Poor Mr Runciman (age 102), he was one of the more humane of teachers.

## Failing to measure up

The journey from Southampton to London and on to Glasgow by steam train took over twelve hours and left you covered in grime and in need of a shower, although such a thing had not yet been invented and a bath was a once-weekly event. From Central Station to my new home was only three city blocks. The Bible Training Institute (now demolished to be replaced by a glass and concrete office block) was a seven-storey Victorian pile topped by an impressive tower, which an intrepid fourteen year old could climb on to through a hatch in the ceiling of the table tennis room on floor seven. It gave a view of a smoke-blackened city, the underlying elegance of red sandstone Georgian buildings still to be revealed, many of which would be knocked down to make way for the age of brutalist architecture and the highest residential tower blocks in Europe.

My father wanted me to go to the High School but I had first to undergo an inquisition with the Rector to see if I, and my little brother Murray, measured up to the high standards of one of Glasgow's elite schools. The interview was the first indication that the Rector and I were never going to hit it off – a relationship, as it proved, that was going to go from bad to worse. It was made clear to me, apparently to the Rector's considerable satisfaction, that my inferior Canadian education would prevent me going into Year 3 where the rest of my age group were. My rudimentary French, insufficient Algebra and Geometry and no Latin at all, meant that I would have to join the twelve year olds in IA. Although I was to drop Latin after year two and, in retrospect, could easily have made up the ground in Maths and languages, such is the slow pace of the intermittent learning that a timetable affords, this was not an option on offer.

In my new school, attired in my brown shorts and matching blazer, each day began with prayers in the hall and a grand entrance by the begowned Rector. His distinctive gait, walking on the balls of his feet, we were sure was an effort at compensation for his diminutive stature. We decided, even at that tender age, that our leader suffered, like many small men, from an inferiority complex and that was why he would, in future, take such pleasure in belting me at regular intervals. I was, in the view of my classmates, seen by him as a threat, confirmed by a famous aside one day as we crossed paths in the playground, 'MacBeath, I'm gunning for you'. Perhaps the result of watching too many Westerns, I decided, which were, in the mid 1950s, a staple cinematic diet. We did have one thing in common at least. For years I would take Tuesday afternoons off to go to one of the dozens of cinemas within easy reach of the school. My favourite cinema was the Western in Partick, which usually ran a double feature. You could guarantee that somewhere Alan Ladd, Rory Calhoun, James Stewart, Glenn Ford, John Wayne, Rod Steiger or Lee Van Cleef would figure, and if I was never to be a Latin scholar, I was the undisputed Mastermind on Westerns specifically, and cinema in general. However, since cinematic knowledge was not a recognised academic subject, and was a cardinal sin in my father's book, his discovery of my duplicity was a greater source of worry to me than a potential exposure by the Rector, who did not count at all as an authority figure in my scheme of things. I was already developing a deep scepticism about school, softening me up emotionally for the advent of deschooling in the 1970s, which I embraced fervently and perhaps a little too uncritically.

My two best friends at school were Ian Lindsay and James MacBrayne whom I was seated between at assembly in order of alphabet. I was in my thirties before I discovered propinquity theory, providing me with a useful party trick in which I would test out the hypothesis that many people have friends whose names are closest to them alphabetically. At least it worked pretty consistently for that generation. And for me.

## Lessons on authority

My lack of reverence for authority was not in my genes. It was the most important lesson learned in school. In my first year, in 1A, I got ninety-eight in Latin, an accomplishment driven at that time by fear of the belt that accompanied every mistake made in class. I didn't want to end up like poor Freddy Greenlees, at the receiving end of the Rector's belt almost every day for grave sins such as stressing the wrong syllable in amamus (The Rector: 'I'll am-a-moose you'), as Freddy tried to staunch the flow of tears. 'It really hurt, you know'. I got ninety-eight in the exam because I didn't know that the proper name Victoria took an accusative case – Victoriam. It seemed to give the Rector great pleasure to let me know I had fallen short of the perfect mark, perhaps a compensation for not having had an excuse to belt me for the whole year. A cherished moment for all of us who had suffered at his hand was his appearance on the television programme Mastermind, in which he managed to achieve one of the lowest scores on record. Every wrong answer, 'don't know' and 'pass' was greeted by silent cheers around Scotland.

More meaningful than Latin, which I was to drop after two years in favour of German, was my initiation into the culture of the school. On the first day of term, on the first period of the day in Norman Macaulay's register class, the door opened and I was peremptorily summoned by two prefects to appear before them. Such was their authority, I was then subjected to a humiliating ritual so profound that it was to stay with me as burning resentment of years to come – even to the point of hatching a plot to follow the two prefects after school and exact retribution. The brown and yellow regulation tie, which one had to buy at Pettigrew and Stephens, or Copeland and Lye, was no longer in stock and I had worn the next best thing, a brown tie with a yellow *horizontal* stripe that my father had brought as a gift from Philadelphia. It had sentimental value. So to see it ripped from my neck, thrown to the ground and spat on did nothing to endear me to my persecutors who, after a verbal tirade in which I was accused, among other things, of being a 'Ted' (a new concept to add to my growing vocabulary) I was commanded to write out the rule book five times and present myself for further humiliation the following morning in the prefect's room. In fact, my institutional attire could hardly have been further from the Teddy Boy drainpipes, knee-length jacket and velvet collar to which 'Ted' was a shorthand form of abuse. I have since discovered, in researching seminal moments in people's lifetimes, the extent to which a burning sense of injustice can remain. At a conference in Denmark a woman spoke of continuing, forty years later, to visit the grave of a teacher who had badly wronged her, reminding the long-dead pedagogue of her past misdeeds in the most choice of language.

My second initiation was to fight Ritchie, Lyndsey and Macniven in turn, in ascending order of challenge. Having been badly beaten up and nearly choked to death in a school fight in Canada, I was able to apply the headlock that had nearly finished me off then and, on this occasion, to emerge victorious. Macniven was to become a lifetime friend. At seventy-plus years of age he is still Skyping and emailing me almost daily from Canberra in Australia where he went after his expulsion from school at the age of fifteen. His heinous crime was to be in possession of a Health and Efficiency mag, a 'dirty' magazine which featured naturists playing volleyball and disporting naked with naughty bits on display. Perhaps it was less the possession of such an offensive item than Macniven's refusal to surrender it to Pluto, the Maths 'master' – who deemed attention to quadratic equations to be of more consequence than sex education. Macniven was never to return to school but as a highly-educated man now in his eightieth decade he has, by his own admission, benefited singularly from his lack of schooling. His education came from hitchhiking around the world, from Glasgow to Sydney by way of the Middle East, India, the Far East and working his passage or stowing away on tramp steamers and cargo ships.

Old boys have given up phoning me to contribute to the High School funds (although the present school in a different location bears no resemblance to the Do-the-boys Hall of the Fifties) and have expressed surprise when I reminded them of the awfulness of our school days. Then I ask them to recall some of the arcane rituals which were perhaps only bizarre to someone who had come from another planet, or from somewhere that felt like another universe.

## The cast of characters: stranger than fiction

There was Doc Low, whom we believed was at least 100, a caricature of the mad scientist, oblivious to the diversionary ploys going around him, while getting every experiment wrong and enjoining us to write up in our books what should have happened, and certainly not what *had* happened.

Hector, who taught English, also had his blind spots as he took up a position a third of the way down the class so, with his back to the two front rows, he failed to spot that the strategically-placed bad boys were playing games, passing notes and generally having their own form of education behind his back. We only joined in spiritedly when it came to Chaucer's *Wife of Bath's Tale*, Hector reading all the salacious bits deadpan and unmoved by the titters of delight. If only all English lessons could always be like this. Hector did from time to time bring out the tea towel to admonish those caught in flagrante. This was laid over your wrists so as to avoid breaking them, as only with careful and practiced aim could the scarring, and even breaking, of the wrist be avoided.

The formidable Campbell (too formidable for a nickname) had his own method of torture, which was a black ebony stick that descended on the knuckles of the unwary, especially anyone named Macdonald as old battles were re-enacted – 'If there's any massacre in here it will be by the Campbells'.

I cannot recall Captain Cowper ever using the belt. Perhaps because of his formidable presence or his frequent absence. Due to his duties with the school corps he only made an intermittent appearance in the class. Days would pass without a sight of him, leaving us to devise the most obscene and unprintable forms of laddish competitions, secure in the knowledge that the bold Captain was unlikely to enter at an inopportune moment.

Then there was Jake and Mono, a comic pair who taught us Physics. They were an impressive double act, finishing each other's sentences as in: 'In this experiment (Jake) you will receive (Mono) a metal ring and (Jake) a ball.' 'On your table you will find a bunsen (Mono) burner (Jake).' On day one we were introduced to the 'Stool (Mono) of Repentance (Jake)'. This was a laboratory stool on which the miscreant balanced, to be administered the belt to the exposed posterior. According to Macniven, not prone to wild invention, once sent on an errand to deliver a message to Mono, he witnessed a compromising situation with our favourite lady Maths teacher in the lab's back room. Although we cast doubt on the tall schoolboy tale at the time, to this day Macniven confirms its authenticity.

She, whom we all lusted after, was known to us as Ivy. In 1A Maths, dropping of rubbers and pencils on the floor became a contagious activity whenever she was in the vicinity. Crawling under the desk to retrieve the lost object gave a view that was not available from the desk seat. This was not, though, entirely necessary as Ivy also had a habit of perching on the broad windowsill, which gave an unobstructed view of her comely figure. On one occasion I was volunteered by my cowardly classmates to inquire as the meaning of a problem on the board, the problem couched as 12 FLs@ 1/9. For us this could only mean French letters and Ivy was clearly teasing. 'Why MacBeath, Firelighters', she said, in her response to my impudent inquiry. To this day I don't know if she was simply naïve, or teasing little boys who were, one and all, in love with her. I never really understood anything I was taught in Ivy's class. There are three possible hypotheses. One, I was stupid. Two, Ivy wasn't a great teacher. Three, I was permanently distracted. As the first explanation has little appeal I have to have recourse to the other two.

## Teaching without learning

At fourteen I was entering my second person. Apparently, every cell in our body changes every seven years, so as I entered my fifteenth year I was a completely new being and in the throes of puberty. The now-well-established learning loss between primary and secondary has to be explained by coming of age – from innocent childhood to troubled (and sex-obsessed) adolescence. This was compounded by what I believed then, and am convinced of now, was simply bad teaching. That I squeezed a pass in Maths at O grade was achieved without an inkling of what I was doing. I never understood, for example, why in Algebra when alpha or beta cross over the equal sign the negative becomes a plus, or vice versa. It was simply a piece of magic that had to be learned and was needed to solve arcane problems. It was not until many years later in a primary school where I saw six year olds playing with a balance beam that the light went on. If only Ivy had given us balance beams to play with all would have come clear. Or if she had read Jerome Bruner.

I passed my Geometry paper because if you could reproduce a theorem or two it accounted for 50 per cent of the mark. So, I laboriously memorised theorem after theorem, line by painful line. It was only much later I understood that a theorem was actually an argument and that I didn't have to memorise by heart on which line the 'but', 'then', 'if' and 'and' occurred. Perhaps the first of the three hypotheses as to bad teaching versus native intelligence doesn't look so bad after all. One has to ask how a relatively intelligent fourteen year old, who would one day be a Cambridge professor, could be so stupid. Little wonder I found solace and much to identify with in John Holt's *Schools are Bad Places for Children* and Paul Goodman's treatise on schooled incompetence, *Growing Up Absurd*.[1]

History and Geography, which in adulthood are two realms of knowing that absorb me most, although never thought of in those discrete terms, were a complete anathema to me at school. How I ever passed an exam in either I cannot recall, but again was a feat of memorisation completely devoid of understanding. Drawing rivers and mountains on a blank map was a bafflingly futile exercise. Crops, imports and exports I cared even less about. In 2012 I was to marvel at a Coalition Government that wanted to bring back the naming of rivers and mountains. To this day I still cannot name rivers and mountains, and cannot for the life of me see why it should be of any importance.

The fictional Serena (described in the second lens), bored to death by her school experience, was only woken up to learning by a teacher who stirred her imagination, her story inspired in part by my own experience of trying to make sense out of nonsense. I perhaps had in mind at that time on two occasions in my Scottish schooling where I looked at my watch and hoped the bell wouldn't ring. One was in Bulldog Drummond's History class, the only period in which he taught us before mysteriously disappearing. We relived in our imaginations life in a Stone Age village so completely that time passed far too quickly. The second experience that still remains with me vividly was Daddy Orr reading to us the epic poem, *Sorhab and Rustum*, which left us spellbound and impatient for the next English lesson to finish the story. When interviewed in 1962 for my MA. Honours year placement in France, and asked to give an example of what I would teach these little French weans, I suggested, to the panel's complete bewilderment, *Sorhab and Rustum*. Well it had been one of the only things in my school experience to have moved me!

Later in my work with teachers I often used an excerpt from a classic fly-on-the-wall Channel 4 series *Space Between Words*, in which a teacher, the Head of the English Department, struggles in vain to engage a class of disinterested and rebellious fifteen year olds. There is one brief interlude in a depressing catalogue of mayhem when the class is suddenly totally emotionally engaged as she reads them a poem.

## Zombie, Paddy and Big Joe

Why I ended up as a Modern Languages teacher is owed very largely to the serendipity of having teachers whom I actually liked and even respected. Top of the list was Zombie, who entertained us royally with his idiosyncratic approach to teaching and his surrealistic and deadpan humour. We never saw him even crack a smile but he had the wickedest putdowns that we generally took in good part.

Paddy O'Neill never smiled either but he commanded respect by his no-nonsense approach and with rare recourse to the tawse, his only concession to that instrument of torture was for the cardinal sin of a mistake in an ink exercise. This strange idiosyncratic ritual was for all homework to be done in your 'jotter', with mistakes then corrected and copied in the finest script into an ink exercise book – with old-fashioned pen and nib, no blots and certainly no new-fangled implements such as biros permitted.

Paddy's best pal was big Joe Simmie. Big Joe smiled constantly. Big Joe taught us, perched on the desk in front of the six of us elite pupils who were allowed to take German, and engaged us in conversation and anecdote, enjoying hugely our embarrassment as he teased us pubertal boys guessing why a certain Swiss mountain was called the Jungfrau. Strange the things that stay vividly in memory fifty-five years on! Paddy and Big Joe would accompany each other on the short walk to Central Station after school. Their path took them along Bothwell Street where I lived at number 64 in the Bible Training Institute, only a block away from where my exiled pal Macniven had secured his first job, packing condoms (FLs) for two pounds fifty a week. It was an obligatory stop on my way back from school to hang out at the front door, recount the madness of the day and remind Macniven of what he was missing. As my bad luck would have it, he chose on this particular day to shout abuse at the passing Joe and Paddy. They glided on majestically without a sideways or backward glance, and not only ignored my presence at Macniven's side but continued studiously to ignore me the following day. In Joe's German class I experienced what it was like to be invisible. For the whole of a miserable double period he never called on me for an answer or made eye contact. Paddy also gave me the silent treatment. Sent to Coventry! This was possibly the worst punishment of all as it came from two of the teachers in school whom I actually held in respect. My respect for them was increased by their later forgiveness without punishment. Had it been the Rector, or some of the crazy belting fraternity, I would probably have been flayed alive.

## My part in my downfall

Among memorable events was the ceremonial belting in the playground of most of the fifth year. It followed an event in the lecture theatre where the fifth year was allowed to eat their packed lunch. Someone, yet to be identified, had thrown half a sandwich across the room, which had happened to connect with the supervising teacher, a bit of a wimp in fact and strangely lacking in a sense of humour, immediately calling for the Rector. In a period of intense cross-questioning, the front row claimed that the missile had come from behind them while the back row insisted that its trajectory was before them. Suspicion fell heavily on one, MacBeath, whose declaration of innocence and expression of profound shock was taken as evidence of guilt, but without proof the solution lay in punishing everyone seated between the front and back row. David Grant, good boy, most obedient of students and innocent of all misdoings, ran home to his parents for protection. They ceremoniously returned him to school to take his punishment like a man.

The event that led to my ultimate downfall happened in the very same room where a probationer teacher was trying vainly to conduct a music lesson in which I was not being a lot of help. The reason for my belting I have since forgotten but it was seminal as I got six of the best, protesting in not the most polite of languages at the seventh stroke which, as I saw it, and indeed was commonly agreed, was an infringement of the rule of six. I was summarily dispatched to the office of the Rector, accompanied by the music teacher who solemnly testified that 'this boy said F'. No greater crime could have been committed and on top of the six there was a measure of value-added. In the Rector's office along one wall was a massive filing cabinet, each drawer containing a different weight of belt, from light through medium to heavy and extra heavy. As the Rector lovingly opened each drawer, prolonging the suspense until at last deciding, 'this one I think is best for you MacBeath', at which point I bent over the table and proferred my backside to the chastisement designed to make me a better person.

As if this, a second beating, were not enough I was to read out an apology to the whole school the following morning at assembly. My facility with English prose and my addiction to the movies stood me in good stead (in fact condemned me irretrievably) as the apology I read out the following morning was both in content and delivery a masterly satire. So good was the delivery that the Rector was moved to comment 'We'll have less of your Marlon Brando impressions, MacBeath' to which, recognizing the common ground of a fellow moveiegoer, I retorted, 'So you got it!'. The further sanction was to bar me from the end of year school prizegiving. The French and German prizes were given to me in absentia. The last word as I left school behind forever came from the man whose life I had made a misery, Mr Pitkeathly, who wished me well. I felt like a heel.

## Making the most of a university education?

Whatever the failings in my school experience, none was as catastrophic as its failure to prepare us for higher education. Well before the end of our first year at university most of my classmates had dropped out. Best pal 'Jess' Stewart was gone by Christmas. Al, Norrie, Monty, Donny, Ewing, quickly followed suit and by the end of term one I was a virtually lone survivor, although my own academic future hung precariously in the balance. School had done nothing to prepare us for a 'higher' education. Left to our own devices, we became not expert scholars but accomplished snooker and basketball players, committed beer drinkers, loyal frequenters of the local bookies and, in sum, 'corporate lifers' (well, we were told by no less an eminence grise than Donald Dewar, one day to be Scotland's First Minister, to make the most of university life). On the top floor of the Men's Union was a long dark hall in which could be found at any time of day the unchallenged maestro of the green velvet, one Tommy Gilligan who, as urban myth had it, would take forty-nine years to complete an MA. at the present rate of one degree pass every seven years. Also culpable was the basement beer bar, the local betting shop, university debates which started at lunchtime and would run late into the night, the training ground for MPs, party leaders and prime ministers, John Smith, Donald Dewar, Menzies Campbell, Ian and Neil McCormick and many others.

Little surprise then that the remnants of Glasgow High School's elite class of fifty-nine plowed their end-of-year exams, including myself, having to spend a tedious summer swotting up on my three failed subjects – French, German and Zoology (my compulsory Science subject). I am still haunted by the practical Zoology exam in which I had to dissect and label the parts of a snail. All I could remember was its extremely impressive penis that I uncoiled and pinned out in its totally enviable length. Another lesson in what sticks so indelibly in memory! 'Shell' did not get me any marks.

When I returned to university in October hardly one of my schoolmates remained – a tribute to their 'schooling', a not inappropriate term to describe the ritual compliance and absence of independent thought. The case study of Seven Kings School in London (described in the second lens) concludes with the testimony of young people who returned from university to remonstrate with their headteacher, bitter at their schooled intelligence that left them floundering when required to think for themselves.

In Glasgow the honey trap for the unwary was a haven called Pierce Lodge, home to the Students' Representative Council (SRC), rectorial election campaigns and the *University Guardian* newspaper. Despite my early failure I had managed to pass all subsequent exams at first go, if not gloriously, but by virtue of what I have since learned as 'tactical' and 'strategic' rather than 'deep' learning. In Peirce Lodge many hours and many days were whiled away in the congenial company of SRC members, many outstandingly bright people who, as a consequence of corporate living, earned third class honours and subsequently became local and national politicians and leaders in their respective fields. One SRC President, an outstanding, and largely wasted, intellect whom I accompanied on one or two occasions to the Starlight Lounge, where five card stud was the name of the game, would spend an entire night in the company of high rollers, losing spectacular amounts of money, not always his own. Playing a hand for him while he visited the toilet was not my most therapeutic experience. We did exciting things in those heady days when corporate life included riots, stopping traffic with missiles such as flour bombs and eggs in University Avenue and getting headlines on the television news. I wrote the campaign newsheets for Billy Butlin for Rector and later for Chief Albert Luthuli, and earned the dubious privilege of becoming editor of the *University Guardian*, which involved not only interviewing, writing and trying to commission stories, but staying up all night at the printing works laying out the pages line by line. We failed to win the Observer Award for the best university newspaper but were highly commended. Nor did I win the award for the most outstanding student and I was not highly commended.

If I hoped that University teaching would inspire me in ways that school had failed to do I was to be sadly disllusioned. While the teaching was scarcely any better – and often considerably worse – than school, the attitude of lecturers to their students could not have been more different. Essentially, whether you learned or didn't was of little concern and lecturers carried on in sublime indifference to the mayhem going on around them. Paper planes sailed across the lecture theatre, ripples of laughter at witty remarks, e.g. Professor Chambers: 'Young Werther stood half aloof'; Ian Thorburn: 'Half aloof is better than no bread'. General laughter. A favourite ploy in the steeped lecture theatre was to fill an Ovaltine can with nails and set it in motion on the top tier and allow it to roll slowly and with acoustic impact from top to bottom tier. The lecturer would continue reading from his notes or the chapter in the book as if this was simply an endemic feature of classroom life that he or she had witnessed many times before. It was not unknown for a lecturer to simply read his (the appropriate pronoun for an exclusive male club) latest book, each lecture opening a new chapter in the book. Although everyone had a copy of the prescribed work and simply followed line by line, most of us got wise and stopped attending lectures. I'm not sure the lecturer ever noticed. A psychology class that began with a few hundred students contained, by week four, only seven.

That such ineptitude was tolerated for two further decades led me to visit the Psychology department to complain that my daughter was reliving my own history. This clearly did not endear me to her as 'daddies' did not intervene on behalf of their grown-up charges.

Paradoxically perhaps, one of our favorite lecturers was Professor Saunders, an amiable man who spoke very slowly at dictation speed so we got very good notes. Why he couldn't have simply printed them and given them out we never thought of at the time, perhaps because he would stop the dictation from time to time for an anecdote or joke, perhaps because the notes provided the script for the exam answers which the good professor would hint at, not too broadly, in advance.

## Back to the future

In 1970 I was once again sitting exam papers, once again a student but this time round determined to repair the ruins of my miseducation and wasted years, and to restore the esteem of my deeply disappointed father for whom anything less than a first class honours brought shame on the good MacBeath name. My sister and younger brother did not disappoint in that department and my older brother, Len, excelled in his chosen field of medicine, becoming a leading-edge eye surgeon.

Perhaps the most life-changing of sliding doors was a seminal moment at dinner with Ron Cassidy, an accidental acquaintance at Jordanhill College who was to become a lifelong friend. A passing comment, that could have easily slipped through the general chat unremarked, caught my interest. Ron had been up to the University to enroll for the MEd. It was by now October and university courses were about to start. The last day for enrolment was imminent. Admitted at the eleventh hour to the course, I was to commit myself wholeheartedly for the next five years to gaining a first, if only for my father! Once more I was to find myself sitting in lectures at Glasgow University, often no more inspirational than those I had long since left behind. Kenneth Richmond, profligate author, would initiate us into his latest work, a stream of consciousness discourse that defined note taking and left us little wiser at the end of the hour. Professor Nisbet was a total counterpoint. Stanley (as he was known affectionately to us) would start his lecture with one idea. He would revisit this over the next hour, a one-man Socratic dialogue, so carefully constructed and deliberately expounded that it would have been impossible by the end of the hour not to have got the message.

Saturday mornings were Psychology labs led by the entirely archetypical eccentric Professor Pickford, in which we were inducted into Rorschach methodology and the arcane interpretation of inkblots that we had to administer to unsuspecting subjects, if we could locate at least eight children willing to share with us the deeper mysteries laying beneath the incoherent shapes. In addition to the four years of Psychology and Education lectures, seminars and labs we had to take two elective subjects, in my case History of Educational Thought and Comparative Education. To graduate one had to endure two three-hour exams on Education, two three-hour exams on Psychology and two three-hour papers on our respective electives followed by a thesis, in my case on the implementation of the Langevin-Wallon reforms in France, intensive research undertaken over the course of year, in Provence, following the final exams.

In the end I got my first. My father came to my graduation.

## On reflection

It has been said that the most powerful lessons we learn at school are not through what is taught but through the 'hidden' curriculum – the lessons we learn about conformity, the nature of authority – of knowledge and of human relationships. Trying to make sense out of nonsense is, for many young people, an apt description for their classroom experience. To paraphrase Jean Jacques Rousseau, 'how can I learn something when I know nothing about it?' Good teaching not only models relationships and honours the authority of children but also makes connections with, and builds on, prior experience. This is encapsulated in one of David Perkins' key pedagogic principles: connect, extend and challenge – in what ways does our new learning connect with, challenge and extend what we thought we knew? When we grow up, move on to 'higher' education and put away childish things, the Perkins' principle assumes even greater weight. And, of course, any novel, any text, any book, any autobiographical account is tested by the degree to which it exemplifies that cardinal principle!

## Note

1    Holt's essay can be found at http://holtgws.com/underachievingsc.html
Goodman, P. (1962) *Growing Up Absurd*, New York, Vintage Books.

# Epilogue
## In hindsight and retrospect

In seventy years of educating and being educated, the most critical years evade recall. I remember nothing of the first nine months swimming in an amniotic bath, constructing my own intelligence with a little help from my mother and no one else. There was no Luis Machado, the Venezuelan Minister, to persuade 'pregnant fathers' to talk to their unborn offspring. So I did it largely by myself, and soon after birth, so I am told, I fought off malaria in infantile determination to stay alive after everyone else had given up hope. A sliding door opened at the eleventh hour and the blood of a Congolese woman saved my life.

I remember virtually nothing of those vital first five war years that shaped my capabilities, dispositions and beliefs, so the most important chapters are missing and the story that is told is through an insitutionalised life, learning in captivity. Even the hours spent at home have been given over to dancing on a keyboard, from an ancient Olivetti and unforgiving carbon paper, to an IBM golf ball typewriter with built-in eraser, to a BBC tape-driven computer, a portable Macintosh, and ultimately to the a featherlight Airbook on which this book came to fruition. On a balcony in the Canary Islands.

What, in those seven decades have I/we, learned about learning and about the indulgences, conceits and efforts of successive generations of policymakers, researchers, teachers and world travellers to reshape our thinking and redirect our lives?

## Plus ça change?

Nearly six decades on from my introduction to school life in Scotland, how much has changed? No longer is there licence to humiliate and degrade children, physically or verbally. Autonomy and idiosyncrasy are now bounded by monitoring and accountability. There is a deeper and more explicit understanding of sexism, racism and disability. Teachers have at their disposal a wider and richer repertoire of tools and strategies, and research has challenged inert ideas about 'potential' and the critical nature of linkages between learning in and out of school. Yet, in many respects, classrooms look very similar to those I inhabited in the 1950s and, in the UK, it seems that politicians are determined to push back the clock to the good old days when teachers taught and children learned. 'How can children learn if they are not facing the front?' asks the one-time government Education 'Tsar'. While this was probably not even true fifty years ago it is considerably less credible in the information age. The curriculum is stuck in a time warp and continues, impervious to a world in which shades of the medieval trivium and quadrivium continue to influence what teachers teach and what children are expected to learn. Nor is there much evidence to show that assessment of how children learn, and what they take with them from tests and exams, has any lasting value. And, despite research, raised awareness and legal injunction, discrimination is endemic and more subtly expressed than in the past. Bullying, no longer crudely institutionalised, continues to thrive in the 'underlife' of schools and classrooms. And, despite a burgeoning literature and policy rhetoric of 'distributed leadership', bullying of teachers is exacerbated by hierarchical pressures to conform and meet impatient targets.

For university academics, targets, conformity and bullying come in more subtle forms. As financial resourcing depends heavily on the four-yearly research assessment exercise (the REF), research is what they are expected to prioritise and, for the quality of their work to be validated, the less practical, accessible and policy-related it is, the greater the credit in a bizarre world where 'popularity' is a mark of an inferior mind. In consequence a more refined form of academic 'bullying' takes place – publish or be damned. For those whose commitment is to teaching, to professional development and to making arcane theory accessible to teachers, relegation to the lower divisions is their reward. So, as the dreaded cycle of the REF comes round, students must learn to forgive their tutors because the Faculty's survival depends on it.

Meanwhile, politicians and policymakers can afford to ignore the esoteric indulgences of academics, and where research has something vital and challenging to say to policy it is rarely likely to be congruent with simple (or simplistic) common sense. As, in the political world, 'common sense' is the currency, personal experience is the warrant and pragmatism trumps integrity. Why fund research when there are good practice examplars to be cherry-picked from successful countries? So the constant quest for the holy grail continues, from Taiwan, to Singapore, to Hong Kong, and most recently to Finland, where the elixir is, apparently, to be found in the classroom, not in the values, culture, history or economy, nor in the social and ethnic composition of the population.

Yet, it is through international experience that we learn most about our own practice and about ourselves, travelling with insight – the perception of things to come rather than the extension of things gone by. Through the seventh lens and the experience of the Learning School students travelling to other countries, we gain a new understanding of release from captivity of the familiar, and the challenges of coming to terms with the unfamiliar. Learning to know what we see rather than seeing what we already know.

## A chain of voices

My own journey of knowing is owed to the many who were keepers of the sliding doors, each in turn opening to unforeseen opportunities. I would like to record my thanks to those who changed the course of my academic life, in almost chronological order: Walter Gardner, Head of Department at Paisley Grammar, always willing to take my side in my (many) contretemps with the Rector. Ron Cassidy who, over dinner and at the eleventh hour, alerted me to the last opportunity to register for the MEd. at Glasgow University. It opened many doors, through Professor Stanley Nisbet, a scholarship to France, an invitation to Jordanhill College from Tom Bone, a recruiting agent for Glasgow MEd. 'Firsts', and, after only one term there, through the offices of Don Myers, I was to spend a hugely formative year at the State University of New York where one Bruce Leslie was to become a lifelong friend and unending source of wisdom.

I owe a debt to James Priestly and Phil Maguire who opened my office door and then a portal to interactive pedagogy, which forever changed my teaching, with the support and encouragement of two colleagues, Dave Mearns and Bill Thomson, the latter persuading me that interactive pedagogy (or andragogy) can travel to community work, home helps, welfare rights and many other unforeseen agents and agencies. And, of the many University of Strathclyde colleagues, a particular thanks to the entirely idiosyncratic and loyal colleague, Ian Smith. Alexis Jay, now Director of Social Work in Glasgow, was to open the doors of social work training and to collaborative work on Strathclyde Region's major initiatives *Social Strategy for the Eighties*, and later *Nineties*.

While I have no fond memories of HMCIs in England (David Bell the rule-proving exception), in Scotland, Walter Beveridge, Bill Clark, Graham Donaldson and Frank Crawford have been good friends as well as major gatekeepers of my future. To Archie McGlynn I owe more than the nomination for an OBE, setting in train adventurous rule breaking and the embedding of self-evaluation in policy in Scotland. It opened the door to international initiatives in self-evaluation in many other countries, not least the European Commission twenty-one country project with Lars Bo Jakobsen, EU Policy Officer in Brussels.

A 'LinkedIn' website tells me I am connected to Lars Bo through Norberto Bottani and Alain Michel, which is not, in fact, the source of my connection, but it was Norberto who brought me first to Washington in 1971 and then to the OECD where I was to work with Alain Michel of the French Ministry, greeting me after a decade and a half later in Barcelona in November 2012 – a conference to which I had been invited by the visionary David Istance, author of the famous OECD six scenarios and sponsor of ongoing work with that international agency.

It was Jock Barr who opened the door to five hugely significant years with the Prince's Trust, putting me in touch with the incredible and unsinkable Molly Lowell, and with Tom Shebaare and Arwyn Thomas. The EU and collaboration on the self-evaluation was also my introduction to fellow traveller and ideas man, Michael Schratz. In England and Wales John Bangs, Mr NUT extraordinaire himself, championed school self-evaluation and persuaded Routledge to publish *Schools Speak for Themselves*, and so to Anna Clarkson, Routledge editor, who launched my publishing career and is responsible for this book among many others, including the unsolicited *Selected Works*. It was John who took me to the Fish and Chip Plaice to meet Guntar Catlaks, who commissioned a book that remains one of my most cherished, and the only volume for which I have been paid a princely sum!

A different sliding door might have taken me to the Institute in London, but I got there by proxy, thanks to the invaluable relationship with Peter Mortimore, and with Louise Stoll and Kate Myers. For nearly fifteen years we have benefited from the HCD Trust, the Timberlake family of Trustees and the entrepreneurial Clive Barham-Carter. They, in turn, owe a debt to Gregor Sutherland and to Matthew Boyle who kept pupil voice alive and took it into new unforeseen territories. It was Matthew who opened the door to the Improving School Project and helped 'the worst school in Scotland' to become one of the most improved.

That self-evaluation has become such a major plank of policy and practice in Hong Kong is owed to Andrew Poon, See Ming Tsui (S.M.), Anita Mo and many others, and not least my long-standing collaboration with Stephen Yip. The journey of self-evaluation to Shanghai is owed to Mark Upton and Mr Bao and the continuing Commonwealth initiatives in Kuala Lumpur are courtesy of Suseela Malakalunthu and Judy Curry.

In Denmark Lejf Moos, in Norway Jorunn Moller, in Italy Francesca Brotto and Giovanna Barzano, in Switzerland Emmanuele Berger, in Poland Gzregorz Mazurkiewicz, in Slovenia Andrej Koren, John Collins in Dubai, Brad Portin in Seattle, David Green in Princeton, and the two wonderful Georges, Oduro in Ghana, and Bagakis in Athens, all of whom opened doors to unexpected and rich sources of learning. And what a huge gap would exist in my education were it not for two incredible Aussies, Neil Dempster and Tony Townsend with whom I have travelled, over two decades, virtually and literally, between Glasgow, Brissy and Melbourne. To Tony I owe particular gratitude not only correcting my many mistakes in the manuscript but counseling on unnecessary, and perhaps invidious, indiscretions.

I got to Japan through the initiative of one of education's most unforgettable characters, Stewart Hay, for whom the unthinkable was never impracticable, as evidence from eight successive incarnations of the Learning School demonstrate.

Thank you to Andy Hargreaves for opening the door to ILERN and travels with some exceptional people who have remained inspired, and inspirational friends, with special mention for Ann Lieberman and Jonathan Jansen. In the lexicon of exceptional people there is Tim Brighouse (Sir), his promise to take up golf and grandchildren, not enough to stop him from acceding to pleas to come and speak to the unconverted one more time. Founder of the Children's

University he passed the baton to his golfing chum David Winkley (Sir) and to Ger Graus who, with a little help from a few friends, has built that organisation into an international phenomenon.

It was another Hargreaves, David, who took me to Cambridge, and to an education from colleagues, allies and friends, too numerous to mention, but without the support and unlimited generosity of Sue Swaffield I might not be where I am today, nor without the friendship and advocacy of David Frost, and the kindness to strangers of Joanne Waterhouse and Mike Younger who, as Head of Faculty, knew a thing or two about rule breaking. And of course, my roommate, fellow traveller and infinite source of wisdom, Maurice Galton. And despite his footballing allegiance, my Glasgow inspiration, Jim O'Brien. Finally, but by no means least, the Commonwealth stalwart Sally Roach, and my long-suffering secretary and wonderwoman, Katie O'Donovan.

# Index